Lloyd Shaw and the Cheyenne Mountain Dancers

by
Lloyd and Dorothy Shaw
edited and completed by
Enid Obee Cocke

Published by the Lloyd Shaw Foundation, 2014

ISBN:0692335560
ISBN-13: 9780692335567

Table of Contents

INTRODUCTION *(Enid)*

In the summer of 1950, the citizens of Santa Monica, California, staged the world's largest square dance in celebration of the 75th anniversary of their city's founding. Governor Earl Warren issued a general invitation to square dancers everywhere in the country to join the event. Four blocks of a city street were coated with powdered soapstone to make a danceable surface, speakers were strung the length of the street, and a stand was erected to accommodate the callers and musicians. Thirty seven of the country's best callers filled the 3½-hour event with square and round dances. It was estimated that 15,200 people were dancing and that an additional 35,000 spectators came to watch the celebration. Governor Warren arrived in a limousine, was greeted by the dancers, took his place on the reviewing stand, and stayed the entire evening. The highlight of the evening was the arrival down Wilshire Boulevard of Lloyd "Pappy" Shaw who had given these people the dances that they were enjoying. Grateful dancers swarmed around the convertible to greet him and his wife Dorothy and to thank him before he assumed his duties as master of ceremonies.

How did he make this particular folk art the passion of millions of people? How could he not? He was a born teacher and he was also a born showman. There was a passion in him to share whatever he found that was beautiful and unique.

He was only a 25-year-old high school teacher in 1916 when he was recruited to apply for the position as superintendent of Cheyenne Mountain School, a small K-12 suburban school on

INTRODUCTION

the southwestern outskirts of Colorado Springs. For the first few years he coached the football team with marked success but decided that it wasn't good for either the boys or the girls. The boys risked injury since sophomores and freshmen were needed to field a team, and the girls had no adequate role in the activity. He happened upon international folk dancing when researcher and teacher Elizabeth Burchenal came through Colorado and he invited her to come to Cheyenne School to conduct a workshop. He and his students loved the activity, and soon the entire school population was folk dancing. With his passion for performance and for sharing whatever was interesting and beautiful, he soon had his students putting on exhibitions around the city and then farther afield around the state.

Square dancing did exist at this time, but only in little pockets where the traditions of the pioneers had endured. It was in December of 1935 that Guy Parker, a local square dance caller, came to Lloyd and asked if he could provide a few students to fill out two squares that Guy wanted to enter in a square dance competition at the local seed show. Lloyd provided the dancers and became fascinated with this genuine American folk art. Determined to learn as much as he could, he attended square dances all over the state recording dances and interviewing callers and musicians.

Soon his Cheyenne students were presenting performances of the traditional American dances that he had researched. In 1937 a group of recent alumni made the first out-of-state trip to southern California. Two years later the Cheyenne Mountain Dancers performed at the National Folk Festival in Washington, D.C. Thereafter they made spring and fall tours, traveling to the east one semester and to the west the other. Lloyd published *Cowboy Dances* in 1939. It included some history, but largely it was designed as a manual for an aspiring caller to learn the dances and how to teach and call them. *The Round Dance Book* would follow in 1948, rich with the history of each form of couple dance and with detailed instructions for dancing them. Soon teachers and recreation leaders began asking Lloyd to conduct classes where they could learn the dances and how to teach and call them. His summer institutes, held in Colorado Springs at Cheyenne Mountain School, taught a generation of callers and dance leaders from across the nation.

But Lloyd Shaw was much more than the man who got the country dancing. He was an extraordinary educator who conducted a 36-year experiment in public education. One of his strategies was to keep his students at Cheyenne School so busy that they wouldn't have time to go astray. He also wanted them to experience the extended world around them. There were camping trips around the state for the older students, ski outings before there were any ski resorts, a nature preserve as part of the school campus, a student-owned school cabin up above Seven Falls, and performances of every sort. A lover of the theater, Lloyd wrote plays that ultimately drew attendance from neighboring states. There was of course good teaching. As the school's reputation grew, Lloyd was swamped with applications by teachers who wanted to be a part of his extraordinary program.

The impetus for this book came from a former Cheyenne School student who became a newspaper editor in a western Nebraska town. He wrote Lloyd in 1952 urging him to write his autobiography, saying, "The things you gave your students, and which they so often discuss when together, should be projected for more to know. They are fine intangibles. Many of us who learned the bulk of our moral judgments of the world from you would love it if you would set them in print. You know you gave a terrific amount to your students. In my case, for instance, thoughts that you gave and attitudes you offered stuck to be thought out a lot of nights on the Pacific and in Europe: your feelings about the absurdity of sophistication, your emphasis on the only stable things in our lives—things that the mind and heart can hold—and your love of the world."

INTRODUCTION

Lloyd set about the task. He and his wife Dorothy worked to recreate a timeline of events, and he wrote some drafts about the trips taken by the Cheyenne Mountain Dancers. He was at the same time extremely busy, traveling around the country attending dance festivals, conducting clinics, continuing his summer dance institutes, and managing a recording company to provide music for dancers who lacked musicians.

The writing project was cut short on July 18, 1958 when Lloyd died suddenly of a stroke. Dorothy took on the task of completing the book. She wrote with lyricism and insight about his early childhood as well as some exquisite chapters, telling as no one else could, what it was like to be a student at Cheyenne Mountain School. But there were many demands on her time as she had picked up Lloyd's banner and was carrying on with his commitments. She indeed became the spiritual head and executive secretary of the Lloyd Shaw Foundation, which was established in 1964, six years after Lloyd passed away.

The task has now come to me, their granddaughter, writing over a half century since Lloyd died and over a quarter of a century since Dorothy passed from the scene. To the extent possible, I use their words, but much more needed to be told than they had chronicled.

IN DULCI JUBILO (Lloyd)

A little after seven o'clock the boys would be out at the hotel entrance with the baggage trunks piled between them, and the bus would come curling up the driveway and stop at the entrance. The boys would set to work with amazing speed. A couple would be on top of the bus immediately and strip the canvas cover off the carrying rack, and other boys would be tossing the costume trunks up to them. The girls and a few of the boys not assigned to this loading of the bus would begin stringing out of the hotel and climbing into the open door of the bus, everybody kidding and chatting with one another as they quickly filled the bus.

The trunks would be loaded on the top by now, and the canvas cover would be spread over them and instantly strapped down to place. Howard, our driver, would give his approval to the job that was done and would enter the bus again. The boys would all be inside by now. And at the last minute some late-comer would come rushing from the door of the hotel and make the bus just in time.

Everybody kidding and excited! A lot of changing of seats and getting settled down. Questions as to how we were going, comments on the last experiences in the hotel, laughter, and joyous talk filled the bus for a while. Then gradually as we neared the auditorium at which we were to perform that evening, the bus would become strangely quiet. Perhaps someone who had not caught the mood of the crowd would have to be silenced, but it was always done inconspicuously.

Then in the dead silence, the low voices of the singers would come to me. "In Dulci Jubilo," they always sang. It had unconsciously become their own song. In four rich parts, it gradually grew in volume, the sopranos sometimes taking the lead for a few bars, then the tenors leading into the next part, then the basses taking their turn. The song would swell in volume, all of them putting their whole hearts into the part they had chosen to sing.

In this beautiful arrangement it is a difficult song with tricky parts and strange balances. We had sung it for years at our annual Christmas service, and somehow they had chosen it instinctively as their song of approach for a coming show. It is an old 12th or 13th century carol, and it carries the longing and the faith of that period. It is a beautiful thing. It was a form of prayer with them, a reaching for that beauty and that harmony that lies beyond the use of words.

"In dulci jubilo let us our homage show!" "In dulci jubilo" and some of them couldn't have translated it, but they knew that it meant something beyond words; it meant something beyond the stars for them. "In dulci jubilo" might, for instance, be translated "in sweet joy," but it would miss entirely the meaning, and the meaning as well of the creators of the song. The word "dulci" can be translated merely as "sweet," but it means so much more than that. Sweetness, loving tenderness, all that is beautiful is included in the ancient meaning, and joy means more than mere joy, wonderful as that word is. There is a sense of jubilation, of overflowing joy. In this untranslatable phrase let us show our tender homage to all that is most beautiful and worthwhile in the world. And homage is a word that we use but little today. We might call it allegiance touched with reverence, but it goes back to old medieval times, when a man expressed homage to his lord, with an allegiance that was more than loyalty and a reverence that

2

showed more than respect or honor. It is a beautiful word by which we can express our loyalty and our faith to the great powers that lie beyond this world.

And our dancers simply did that! They knew that they had a beauty to express for which there were no words. They simply appealed, in this simple and beautiful old song, to that great power that lies beyond us all, for help, for preparation for the job they had to do that evening. They dedicated themselves without knowing what the word dedication meant. But they knew instinctively if their mood became imbued with this seeking that they might find a little of the beauty that they sought. That this subtle beauty might seize their audience!

We never talked about it. We just sang our school song as any school might do. But deep in our hearts we knew that our song was different, and we knew that if we sang it sincerely enough, doors opened up above us, and we could wander out into the very light of the stars.

Many of the students, I am sure, didn't understand what it was all about. But since everyone else was quiet, they became quiet too, and since everyone else sang, they sang too. And, unconsciously feeling something intangible happening to the group, they felt it too and took a special and unspoken delight in it. To a few of them it became a real need; to the others it became a pleasant and very moving custom. And I was never able to tell exactly which was which. I knew only that the hunger existed, and I thanked God that it did.

Sometimes they would misjudge the distance and then have time to sing other school songs. But these were different. They were pleasant but didn't especially count. Sometimes they would time it exactly so they finished their special song just as the bus pulled up to the auditorium. And sometimes they would be a little late in their calculation, and we would sit in the bus until the song was finished.

Then quietly they would leave the bus, and as soon as they were outside, they would be happy and talkative as though nothing at all had happened. We would rush the costume trunks into the auditorium and assign the dressing rooms, and soon everything was in the noisy commotion of getting ready for a show.

But as we approached the theater or the auditorium, I soon learned to judge the excellence of the show that night by the sincerity with which they sang their prayer of transformation. When the hunger was great, and their spirits were deeply moved, they would go on beyond themselves, and touch heights of beauty that they had never touched before. And when they took an engagement more or less for granted and merely sang their song without much feeling, the whole evening's entertainment was on this lower plane.

Now and then they would reach for a beauty that was beyond all understanding. They would simply thrill me with their dancing. They would venture far up on their way to the stars. And the beauty of their striving would make my pulse beat faster and my heart open with an unknown joy.

LLOYD'S EARLY YEARS (Dorothy)

The little boy stood at the edge of the dusty road, carefully appraising a great magnolia tree. The clean, soft California sunshine enfolded him; the talcum-fine dust worked up pleasantly between his bare toes; somewhere an indolent mockingbird was practicing. It was a beautiful magnolia tree, more symmetrical than most, and quite tall. And nesting among its shining green leaves he had discovered an occasional great ivory-white bud just breaking into bloom. He had sharp eyes, but his nose had been far ahead of them. Halfway down the block the lovely fragrance had shouted to him – the magnolia's in bloom! He thought he knew the tree; it stood in a big yard that had myrtle for a lawn and was close to the road. He came straight to it, like a bee.

Having decided that the tree was readily climbable, he embraced the grey trunk with his skinny arms, laid his bare feet alongside the smooth bark, and went up like an awkward but competent monkey. How sweet, how sweet it was! He paused for a moment on a low branch, sniffing. Then he scrambled on to his prize – the biggest, the whitest, the first, the best magnolia blossom. He had had no experience with words like "innocent," immaculate," or "chaste." He stared into the opening heart of the wonderful flower, and there was a tiny moment of communion between it and him. You had to pick them because they were so entirely beautiful and desirable; but you must be very careful never to touch them, for, whatever you did, the waxen petals turned brown and ugly and the magic was gone. He broke off the blossoming twig as close as possible to the branch, maneuvered it cautiously, and, holding the stem between his teeth, descended slowly and triumphantly to the ground.

A little whisper of dust trailed his heels as he swished his feet on the road. A small soundless song went on somewhere in the back of his head. He cradled his white miracle tenderly, like some flowering Holy Grail, protected by its own green leaves from his hot, grimy little hands.

In a yard on his own street a lady that he knew was pottering about among her rose geraniums. "You like to buy a magnolia blossom, Mrs. Eaton?" he called, marching briskly through the hedge.

"Oh, Lloyd! I didn't know they were out. How beautiful! How much are you selling them for?"

"A nickel, I guess. They're pretty hard to get."

The kitchen smelled of Swiss steak and apple cobbler. He burst in and banged the screen door. "The magnolias are out, Mama. I sold four on the way home from school." He detached three coins from the grubby miscellany in the depths of a pants pocket and laid them on the table – two five-cent pieces and a dime.

She gathered them up thoughtfully. "You know, Lloyd," she said, "you must have almost enough to buy a suit. The next time we go into town with your father, we'll shop for one."

Flowers could be converted into nickels, and nickels, endlessly accumulated, could be converted into suits and shoes. The suits and shoes wore out, but the flowers you kept forever – the white ones, the pure, pure ones. "I can sell lots of magnolias in L.A." he said. "It's easy to sell them in town; people aren't used to them."

He was a nice little boy. He was going on seven and tall for that. He had ordinary colored hair and wide-set green-gray eyes, a straight slightly tilted nose bridged with freckles, and a most remarkable mouth – wide, mobile, and eloquent. The nose was to change completely as noses do, but the eyes and the mouth were to remain steadfast. They could sparkle with mischief or excitement or curiosity; or they could be stern and brooding. When they were brooding, he was a long way off; after you got to know him well, you could tell by looking at him. And how it could laugh! Even at going on seven he was beginning to learn what a light and durable armor laughter is. He had good hands too, sensitive and eloquent like the mouth. Long hands, slender without being narrow, with square-tipped fingers.

He was a happy little boy. The great confused tumultuous twentieth century was just around the corner, but the lazy sun-drenched village of Glendale did not yet dream what was in store for it. It still lay in countryside, and the countryside was a small boy's paradise. In spring after the rains, it was fragrant with eucalyptus, and with all the small pungent growing things that cushion the desert. There were creatures in the brush and birds and numberless kinds of astonishing insects. You never needed to come back empty-handed from any expedition, however trifling. The sun shone through clean air, and even when there was fog, it came in untainted and smelling faintly of the sea. There was nothing for children to do, aside from their household tasks, but improvise their own play, plan their own wayfarings, and dream. He went to school of course, having passed unscathed through something known as "chart class." School offered endless opportunities for experiments with human relationships. Teachers were excellent subjects for such experiments. The swift, inquisitive mind never tired of devising situations that might test the resources of the teacher. It was fun to learn things, but it was more fun to teach – "Look, I can show you how to do that an easier way. You just do this – and this – and this – and there you are!" He wondered why teachers made things so hard for themselves, but he dutifully helped them to make it as hard as possible.

His family lived in a quite fine and large house in a spacious yard. It was supposed to be haunted and no one else would live in it, so it was made available to them upon terms that common sense must accept while pride writhed in humiliation. For they lived on the edge of poverty. To the little boy this was a matter of almost no consequence except upon the occasions when he saw his mother weep or his oldest brother come home from high school, tight-lipped and alone. There was one puzzling time when there was a wonderful surprise party that went somehow bitterly awry. His father was a deacon and the superintendent of the Sunday school and was much loved too, so it seemed quite natural when a great crowd of the good church folk arrived, shouting "Surprise!" and bringing with them great loads and boxes of food of all kinds and useful gifts of other sorts. His mother was a gay and pleasant hostess, but after all the guests had left and the gifts were put away, he lay in bed listening in bewilderment to her long and bitter weeping. Since he had been six, he had quietly undertaken earning the money to pay for his own clothes. But he cherished a long, long dream that someday someone would give him a gift, a lovely and wonderful and incredible gift. He felt quite sure he would not weep. Like a great wall behind him stood his mother's courage and her self-respect. He would put his back against it and then hold out his hands and say "Thank you."

There was one desolate, giftless Christmas that shook him soul-deep. Even after the sunny winter days had filled again with games and plannings, and joy had returned to him, the scar of it lay across his life – always. Why were gifts so important? For they were. And if they were important, they shouldn't have to be bought with money! What sort of gift did one not buy with money? He was off on a long and great adventure. He was beginning, without ever being aware of it, to seek for Something Else.

His mother was not given to tears, but there was another occasion upon which he was deeply shaken by her weeping,

8

finding it somehow more akin to his own, although the reason for it struck him as utterly unreasonable. She had bought a new hat for early spring, using funds slowly and legitimately hoarded, small coin after small coin, in some obscure domestic hiding place. It was a pretty hat; the child found himself secretly enchanted by it. It had clusters of delicately wrought flowers set around little bunches of some fragile net-like stuff that would probably have been called *tulle* or *maline*. There were feathers too, an elegant little tuft of ostrich tips, lightly tinted with creamy yellow to match the centers of the flowers. How long it had been since she had had a new hat she alone knew; she alone cared, perhaps. But now that she had it, he found himself feeling quite proud of her as they set out for an evening meeting at the church in the soft spring twilight. The little carriage rolled lightly in the soft roadway; the horse's hoofs scarcely troubled the dust. His father drove, and his mother sat very straight in the front seat, and he sat pleasantly crushed between them, sniffing in the falling darkness the breaking flowers, the remembered sea.

What transpired at the meeting could not possibly have been of any consequence, but as they drove home again, the fog rolled in – thick, wet, dripping into rain. There was no escaping it. In no time at all the crisp tulle melted, the flowers dissolved into gelatinous blobs, the little ostrich tips drooped like soaked chicks. His mother took off the once pretty hat and held it; she tried to comfort it under her light coat; she looked at it as a child looks at what was once a buoyant balloon and is now a little scrap of rubber. And then she cried. She cried like a child, quietly and then with long breath-catching sobs. Why was she crying? It was just a hat. He felt for the first time the terrible need to comfort someone without knowing how to go about it. He wished with almost unbearable anguish that he could buy her another hat. He searched painfully through his own modest social equipment for something that might distract or reassure her. And then he pressed closer to her and, shyly at first and then more valiantly, he sang to her. He didn't consider himself much of a singer, but he sang with all his heart hymns and songs he had learned in school, and "Row, row, row your boat" all by himself, and finally in a burst of enthusiasm

> *Mary an' Martha's just gone along,*
> *Mary an' Martha's just gone along,*
> *Mary an' Martha's just gone along*
> *To ring those charming bells.*
> *Singing free grace and a dyin' love*
> *Free grace and a dyin' love*
> *Free grace and a dyin' love*
> *To ring those charming bells.*

He looked at her, cautiously and sidewise, judging that she did look a tiny bit comforted. He would have to give her a jolt and sing that daring second verse:

> *The Methodists an' Baptists just gone along,*
> *Methodists an' Baptists just gone along,*
> *Methodists an' Baptists just gone along—*

Why there was a shiver of wickedness connected with singing that verse he could never have told. Perhaps because they were Baptists and should not be going along like that, apparently hand in hand with Methodists. He looked at her again, sidewise, almost frantically, for she was still crying, and then she smiled at him and gave him a little pat.

All his life he remembered this as if it were yesterday. All his life it never occurred to him to wonder what his father was thinking.

Julia Banker Shaw had not had much training in scrimping and saving. She had been the only daughter of a prosperous and progressive farmer with large holdings of land in the lush Miami

10

Valley of Ohio. There had always been more than enough of everything, including suitors, for she was a handsome girl, tall, slender, and animated, full of animal vigor, high-spirited, warm-hearted, quick to make friends, and strong to hold them. She was loved and spoiled, squired and admired into a self-reliant young womanhood.

But it was while visiting elsewhere that she was introduced to a romantic and appealing stranger, a handsome, gifted, charming young man, lately and touchingly widowed. "He has buried his young bride," they whispered to her. Her gaiety comforted him; her quality delighted him, for he himself had quality. He could do almost anything—sing, write poetry, tell stories—and his character was unimpeachable. She was willing to spend the rest of her life with William Goodman Shaw, not foreseeing that she was to miss in him the kind of driving strength that her own character demanded while he might miss in her a certain tenderness, a particular kind of compassion.

She made a wonderful mother of sons. Their father was frankly proud of them; he took delight in each of them; he related all their exploits. Julia Shaw was more contained; she recognized them as great responsibilities; she actually believed that she was obliged to make men of them. After the first son died in infancy, she may have felt an added obligation to the three who came along at four-year intervals, brimming with eager life, bubbling with ideas, everlastingly beset with enthusiasms, each in his turn, and for the moment world-shaking. She was a rock. Headlong desires collided with her—and crumpled. "But, Mother, all the other boys—" "I don't care what the other boys do. *My* Boy doesn't do that!" She was not inclined to soften her technique toward her last-born, her baby. He was, after three sons, to have been a daughter named Lois. Confronted with his belligerent masculinity and with what must have been an awareness that this one looked capable of a dozen new ideas within the space of half an hour, she took him

11

quietly into her arms and into her heart. "Well, Lloyd," she might have said, "now we'll have to make a man out of *you*."

Making a man out of a little boy was a thing you started right away. You couldn't wait until he was ten or fourteen or even six. From the very beginning there were "yes" and "no," each definite. The spirit went free; the imagination soared unquestioned; the bright being within the flesh had time to dream. But the small citizen had obligations to society and to his own self-respect, and she saw that they were met. The feet often went quite free also. They scurried afield, stirring up new fragrances to remember long afterward: the bruised drying leaves of laurel and eucalyptus. But there were rules about returning, and the wayfarer turned homeward.

The three brothers raced, they shrieked, they plotted. The broke their arms and legs. They flayed their knees and elbows. The bumped their heads and raised great welts. Julia Shaw said "Oh sugar," and handled everything but broken bones herself, making light of the hurts, offering just the right minimum of sympathy. "Lloyd," she would cry, "don't you tear your pants!" Skins healed.

There were some fine things in that big back yard, finer than the playhouse left behind by the small daughter of the original owners to make a perfect club house. There was courage. . . Lloyd learned not to cry. Looking with fear and admiration at big brother Glenn and bigger brother Ray, he pinched his lips tight, winked his eyes fast, and went ahead. There was honesty . . . "You really did win that game. You couldn't see it but my ball was just over the line." "Don't blame him, Papa. I was the one who did it." There was beautiful cleanness of mind and speech . . . "Don't ever use that word again, kid, or I'll wash your mouth out with soap myself . . . No, I won't tell your mother . . . just get it that we don't talk like that around here." There was tenderness, always unspoken, but never failing, and loyalty . . . once in a while the Shaw boys back to back against the world. Above all, there was enthusiasm, that gift of gifts—*entheos*—inspired by God. The divine excitement in the human creature, the never-failing, always-repeated new idea and the welling delight that met it, accepted it, transmitted it. It was all articulate, joyous, and furiously busy.

If this could possibly have been called "supervised play," the supervision was kept a complete secret by the woman in the house, going about her tasks with only the fraction of a corner of an eye on what went on outside. But she was always there. She was a rock.

The edge of poverty had not been the only way station for this family. Before they had moved to Denver the first time, there had been an interval of great prosperity. The successful real estate firm of Wilcox and Shaw had done its part in the development of what was to become the phenomenon of Los Angeles. Ray and Glen could remember when their father and Mr. Wilcox had acquired control of an old ranch and were planning to subdivide it. The family had sat around the table discussing a suitable name for the new development. "Why not call it by the name of the old ranch, Hollywood?" someone finally said. And Hollywood it was. But Father could not hang on to Hollywood. The small fortune he had accumulated was swept away. It was strange that a man so intelligent, personable, and honest should be so incapable of any sustained degree of financial success. There are still streets in Glendale that were named for the two older Shaw brothers, but not a scrap of the property that lined the streets remained long in their father's hands. After a brief interlude in Denver, where Lloyd was born, they were back in Glendale and the wonderful, hospitable haunted house.

Father worked in a store in the middle of town, and Lloyd at going-on-seven sold newspapers on the teeming streets of Los Angeles in the rather hazy security of knowing where to find him in an emergency. He scooted about the busy intersections, lifting a bright convincing smile to tall businessmen and hurrying workers. "Paper, mister? Paper? All about the big wreck! Paper, mister?" Amazingly, he sold them. Amazingly, he turned up unscathed at his father's store at closing time, empty-handed, with a pocket full of nickels. Once he ran a huge splinter, half the thickness of a pencil, deep into the sole of his foot. Shivering with pain and shock, he limped to Father, papers under his arm, forlorn and smudged of countenance.

Father was the compassionate one. He swiftly appraised the injury as requiring professional equipment, gathered the child into his arms, and carried him to the dispensary of the police station nearby. In an immaculate room, lined with shining bottles, a very clean and pleasant young man in a white uniform took over, dispensing along with his deft and gentle service the most incredible information. Yes, they had received the casualties from this morning's terrible fire on Figueroa Street here in the dispensary. Yes, a man had died on the very table on which the wide-eyed child lay. It had taken them hours to clean the place up. Yes, he was a trustee from the county jail—used to be a pharmacist before the law caught up with him. "Sorry, son"—he was using some tweezers as big as pliers and a tiny sharp knife with a long handle—"we'll have it in a minute now." The little boy clenched his fists and shut his eyes tight to hold in the welling tears. "There you are! We've got it!" There was the clean smell of carbolic acid and the comforting softness of gauze and a big white bandage. His father carried him back, and he did not sell all of his papers that day, but there were ideas to be thought through that took away the pain.

"Papa, was that man a *criminal*?"

"Well, he certainly broke some kind of law."

"D'you think he murdered somebody?"

"No, no, he's not the violent type. I'd say he filched from the till in the drugstore or perhaps he forged a check."

"He sure was nice, wasn't he?"

14

"Yes, yes, he *was* nice," said Father.

So people could be nice and just like everybody else and still get put in jail! He had seemed to be quite cheerful about it too, as if he thought he deserved it. What if you didn't? What if you got put in jail by mistake for something you *didn't* do? He was sound asleep in his father's lap long before they got home.

There was a boy his own age who sold a rival paper on his beat. They were great friends; he liked Wally. Sometimes they would scamper along together working the same block in cheerful contest. "Paper, mister?" Wally would shout at the tall man with the gray fedora. "Read all about it in the *News*." "Paper, mister?" Lloyd would urge his stout companion in the brown derby. "Read all about it in the *Times*." They would look perfectly solemn and business-like, and the men would buy both papers. They used to make small wagers about the chance of selling two papers to the same man. Sometimes they could.

It was an absolutely right afternoon, partly brisk, partly dreamy. It was one of those days when the sky is higher than usual, and there is something heavenly in the light, and somebody inside of you stands up and shouts, "I'm here!" The flags on the country buildings snapped in a fresh wind; the pepper trees in the square were in bloom: pigeons preened by the fountain. Papers were selling slowly.

"I'm goin' up Main," Lloyd said, "see if I have any luck."

"See you later, kid," called Wally. "I'm going around on Seventh."

A half hour later Lloyd turned onto the streetcar line, rounding a block back to Main. A growing crowd of people was milling in the street. There were sharply raised voices and the hoof beats of hurrying horses. He made out the grim outline of an ambulance. "Accident," he thought. He and Wally always went to accidents. They squirmed and wiggled between the legs of

15

bystanders and policemen to get a good view. Sometimes they wished they hadn't.

He ran now. Wally would be there already. This was a bad one—so many people and an ambulance. Somebody had been struck by a street car. He wiggled expertly beneath the coat-tails of the men, through the hushed, packed crowd, clear to the streetcar track and the little cleared space in the center just beyond where the streetcar stood still, its white-faced passengers sitting numbly in their places. A little moan escaped him. His bright world reeled. (Never, never, never again would it turn quite so steadily on its spindle!) He felt terribly, impossibly, unbearably ill. This unbelievable thing lying here—half an hour ago, it had been Wally.

The policeman had drawn off the cloak that had been thrown over the pitiful remnant so everyone could see. He had to ask a question.

"Does anybody know him? Anybody know who he is?"

The child heard his own voice, small and strange and far away, whisper, "I do."

The big policeman squatted down beside him, put an arm around him, and drew him gently against his knee. "Who is he, son? What's his name?"

"Wally." He could not believe that he said it. How could anyone have said it?

"Wally who? What's his last name, son?"

"Wilson. Wally Wilson."

"D'you know where he lives?" The child nodded blindly. He could no longer speak.

"Where?" He only shook his head. He knew where Wally lived. He had gone there with him several times. It wasn't far. But he did not know the name of all the streets even if he could have spoken.

The policeman understood. "Is it far? Can you take me there?"

(Must I? Oh, must I tell him that I can?) Blindly, he nodded.

The tall policeman stood up and took the small hand in his big one. "Come with me," he said. "Come and show me."

Oh, no—oh, no! They were going to tell Wally's mother! He was not yet eight years old, and suddenly compassion—vast, adult, and terrible—was bent on occupying a mind and heart and body not nearly big enough to hold it. It was pure anguish. He found a voice, not his own but audible.

"Oh, no! I can't, I *can't*!"

"You have to, son. I need you."

The big hand held the little one firmly. They walked along. The child sobbed and stumbled, but he went. He recognized acertain rightness in the policeman. You had to do what you alone could do. It would be years before he would begin to see the policeman as another suffering creature like himself. It would be many years before he would come up against the conviction that compassion becomes more terrible, the bigger you are to hold it.

They came to Wally's house. They went up the walk and onto the porch.

"Is this his mother coming to the door?" the big man asked.

"Yes. Yes, sir," the child whispered.

"Thanks, kid." The big hand relaxed.

He didn't have to stay! He didn't have to hear it! He didn't have to know, not now, not yet, what it was like—what she would say, what she would do. He ran. He ran as he had never run before, in purest escape.

The Pacific Ocean was as flat and as still and as shining as a piece of gold foil. The outbound sun had just gone over the horizon, leaving behind a wake of vermillion. Only at the surf line was there motion, where the in-whispering and out-sighing sea rocked back and forth on a tilting world; and where sandpipers made little sallies against the languid waves, and pelicans beat

17

great wings close above them, looking like quaint wrought-iron devices in slow motion against an apricot-colored sky.

The child sat very still, for a creature usually so incessantly in motion, on the salt-hard sand of the clean, wide beach below the Palisades of Santa Monica. He had worked two little hollows into the packed sand with his round bare heels and, thus braced, sat hugging his knees dreaming himself out into the endlessness and the shining. Beside him was a little bucket full of clams. He didn't care about eating them, but he loved finding them, running like the sandpipers in the wash of a receding wave, watching for air bubbles in the sand, digging down quickly until his fingers found their shells hard underneath and brought them forth, all sandy, to drop into the bucket. He had filled his bucket quickly and long since; he had washed the clams in the surf; the other children had all gone to supper. Briefly it was his world, his sky, his ocean.

This was the very best of all. Most times were good, but these days in midsummer, when the family camped in tents on the beach at Santa Monica—lived there for days on end—this was good beyond all reckoning. The camping families were a world alone, almost unaware of the easy-going little town behind the palisades, tuned in rather to the fishing vessels endlessly passing, the occasional liner far out to sea, the everlasting squabbling of the gulls—so beautiful in flight. A child was continually wet, sandy, sun-burned, and happy. His mother tried to keep the sand out of the beds, the skillets, the clean clothes—in vain. There was a little coal-oil stove for cooking, water in buckets, and great bonfires at night.

He learned to swim. He learned to go out beyond the surf line and come in, belly-flopping with the shattering wave. He learned where there were low-tide rocks to explore for sea anemones and sand dollars. He could spend hours watching the fishermen on the wharf or a sea-going fisherman scrubbing out his boat. He was perfectly happy.

Just now he felt himself drifting into a sort of communion with his surroundings, something of which he was sometimes capable in times of crisis. Was this, perhaps, to be his last experience with this world of wonder? Would he never again in any other summer sit on hard sand and watch the sun go down? But of course he would! No child ever shuts a door behind him; he lets it swing wildly open, ready for his returning. Nevertheless, at the close of the summer the family was moving to Denver to live. He viewed the prospect with a suitable mixture of regret and anticipation. Father was to have a store in Denver, a grocery store of his own, partially financed by an interested relative. He would probably make great quantities of money. Even skeptical Ray admitted that there was merit in this sort of business. "At least we can get our food at wholesale prices," he said. Denver was a good town, they said, bustling, crowded with opportunities, growing like a healthy urchin. Father could hardly fail in Denver, not with the store all set up and operating. And Denver was in the Rocky Mountains.

Something inside him, loving and loyal, was crying a little . . .oh, ocean, my beautiful ocean, never, never let me go! Go with me, ocean, forever and ever—in the blood of my heart, in the blood of my brain. Beat on the rock of my memory; wash it clean with salt! "Probably I'll like mountains," he thought, more matter-of-factly. "I've always thought I would. But not as much as I like you, beautiful Pacific Ocean. I won't let you go. I'll come back. I'll make a great deal of money, and I'll come back and take a great ship and go clear to China. It won't be the least bit like going to Catalina Island in the glass-bottomed boat. It will be so wide and wonderful! Maybe I could run away and be a cabin boy, but probably I'll have to go to school first and make a lot of money." How would he make money in Denver, he wondered, never doubting that he would.

A campfire blazed up into splendor nearby. Somebody was having a clam bake. He caught bits of conversation, trickles of

19

laughter, the strummed music of a banjo, singing "Just a song at twilight." He shivered a little, stretched his legs, got up and went with his bucket into the circle of firelight. "You like to buy a bucket of clams?" he said. "Nobody ever has enough, you know." They laughed. "Guess you're right at that, fella," said the banjo player. "How much?" "A nickel. They're kind of hard to get."

Back near the tents, his brother whistled through two fingers, shrilly, "Hey, Lloyd! Come on in." He went slowly, trailing each free foot behind him, toes bent under, making a queer little pattern of alternating five-lined parentheses, with footprints down the middle. His mother made him wash. His father told a funny story and sang a little while. Beyond the palisade a great yellow moon slowly disentangled itself from palm fronds and cluttered eucalyptus branches and stood in heaven.

The child slept. He slept to the sighing song of the sea, the sea that held him and would never let him go. He slept under the moon that would go with him to all places and the stars whose names he would come to know and which he was to seek out as the friends of his loneliest hours. He slept in the sense of fragrances— laurel and eucalyptus, viburnum and magnolia. He was the eternal Odysseus, the wayfaring child, and from his first remember-able hours he had begun to be a part of all that he had met. Do not believe that places, any more than persons, stay put where they appear to be on the map. This place went with this child. This stretch of sunny orchard land, glistening coast, elfin forest and sprawling city went with him when he went; he kept and held it long after the map knew it no longer. It made a clean core around which to build a life. And he never forgot that his mountains, which he came to love as he loved no other created things, had once been sea.

TWO SHORT PENCILS: The Denver Years (Dorothy)

It was cold in Denver in the winter of 1900. Wind from the mountains howled down 17th Street, stirring up little funnels of dry sharp snow. West-bound walkers went with heads bowed against the wind, chins in mufflers. Street cars had windows opaque with steam, and scarcely anyone loitered to look at the Christmas displays in the store windows. Lloyd loitered a moment. He shifted his sack of *Saturday Evening Posts* to the other shoulder, pulled his stocking cap down around his ears, curled the fingers in one mitten, and paused to study the lovely little fur pieces in the great window at Daniels and Fisher. They were bright-eyed little skins, two fastened together, heads to tails. He could feel how silky they were just by looking. They were very discreet, very elegant; they gave the imitation ladies who were wearing them an air of great quality. "Genuine Mink," the little signs said, but the prices were not noted. They couldn't cost so terribly much, he thought, little things like that. One of them would look exactly right on Mother. It was mink or nothing, he supposed, with a weary little shrug. He was beginning to find that out about himself.

He rounded the corner onto Arapahoe Street and hugged the great building for comfort as he trudged to 17th and the lawyers' offices. The elevator girl smiled at him. "Here's you

Post," he said and pocketed her nickel. The first office was finished in red plush and was very warm. "Here's your *Post*," Mr. Ames."

"Thank you, Lloyd. Cold out, isn't it? Keep the change," and he handed him a dime.

"Thank you, sir!"

The next office was oak, plain and substantial. "Here's your *Post*, Mr. McLean."

"Oh, thanks, my boy, and how's business?"

"Pretty good, sir. Thank you very much." It was another dime. Sometimes they felt that way—Christmas probably.

All along 17th Street, clear to the railway station, building after building, office after office. The sack grew lighter over the thin shoulders; the street lights came on; the wind died down. Nickels and dimes! All over the country in those years, boys selling the *Saturday Evening Post*, saving money for college or to buy a good bicycle or to help pay for the groceries. This boy was ten years old, buying his own clothes and his own shoes, and dreaming of buying for his mother something in "genuine mink."

Just now he turned into Hamilton—Kendrick's book store. "Good afternoon, Mr. Kendrick, here's your *Post*. It's got a real good article about Mr. Bryan." Then he went into the stationery department and methodically spent ten cents—five for a small notebook, vertically tabulated, and five for two pencils, long, bright, and beautiful. He passed the new book section and looked longingly at a beautifully bound copy of a new one by Mr. James Whitcomb Riley. Mr. Riley was wonderful for reciting out loud. Lloyd had just learned one called "When the Frost Is on the Punkin" for his fourth grade teacher at Emerson Grade School.

At home he took one of the beautiful new pencils, measured carefully, allowing for the extra length of the eraser, and cut it cleanly in two with his amazingly sharp penknife. He smoothed the end of the eraserless half neatly and then sharpened each half pencil to a needle-fine point. He did this all his life. It

22

was not that there was any real economy in thus producing two pencils for the price of one. It was a matter of the closeness to the receptive paper, as if the thought had less distance to travel from the boy's fingers to the white sheet, as if the clutching fingers had less pencil to hold and more idea.

He wrote the necessary notes about the day's business, added the total, and deducted his commission. The short pencil ground into the pulpy paper. The profit was good for ten years old, but it wasn't enough. The next year he won the contest. He sold the most *Posts* of anyone in Colorado. But it was never enough for a little mink fur piece with the silky skins of two bright-eyed little creatures fastened head to tail.

The second short pencil—he needed the eraser for this one—he filed with another book, a big notebook with horizontal lines, in which he was writing a play. Perhaps this was the pencil that would finally buy the mink fur piece, for he had definitely decided to be an author. Several pages were already written. The title looked fine:

The Brave Defenders

A Play by Lloyd L. Shaw

Sir Harold: Squire, bring me my long bow and some arrows, for yonder I see my wicked kinsman come riding over the flowery mead.

They would undoubtedly be willing for him to play the part of Sir Harold; no one else would want to learn so many lines. But he was planning good parts for all of them, parts custom-built to suit them. They were building a theater in the loft of the Rogers' barn, and when it was done, the play would be presented.

Denver had turned out to be all right. The mountains were farther away than he had been led to believe, but they were tall and blue at sunset, and in the summer there were excursions—church picnics, school picnics—on the trains that ran into the inviting canyons that cut into that great wall. The kids were all right. They had a club and a club house and a constant stream of projects. Their interest in girls disturbed him, but you had to be on good terms with a few in order to cast a play. School was all right, and the teacher liked him. But Father was failing in the grocery business in spite of everything. They began eating half-spoiled fruit, the stale bakery goods, the dubious cuts of meat. Mother took in roomers. Father lost the store and went into the insurance business. Times were hard.

It was time for Ray to go to college, and only their mother's determination would ever make it possible. Then Father took to selling advertising for the Colorado Business directories. He was a friendly man and a good talker, and he did this well. Many years later Lloyd wrote, "I keep thinking of Father and realizing what a remarkable man he was, after all. I can see him with his rather distinguished mustache, which he wore all his life, his fine head with its heavy crown of snow-white hair, his genial manner. I can hear him telling his grandchildren the same appealingly ridiculous little stories he used to tell me. And I can still see, when he was overcome by anxiety, how the light within him, which was his great charm, would go completely out. I was his baby, the child of his middle age. It can take a man a long time to catch up with his father."

Ray had enrolled in Colorado College in Colorado Springs. It was an outstanding college with a nationwide reputation and a truly great faculty. "Since you are out of town most of the time anyway, Will," Mother said, "you can just as well come home to one place as another. I am going to move to Colorado Springs. It will be simpler for all three of the boys to get through college." She did not intend to let *their* lights go out.

Mountains, like women, have their good days. It was one of Pikes Peak's magnificent days when the Shaw family left the Rio Grande train at the Colorado Springs station on a clear

September afternoon. Lloyd scampered at once around the end of the train to look at this mountain squarely and unencumbered. Blue-lavender, it lifted high and higher into the columbine-blue sky, almost close enough to touch, its summit powdered with the first fall snow. It was love at first sight. Something in the child sang wordlessly, "My mountain—mine —mine," and, because mountains do communicate, who knows how, the mountain answered what it was to answer forever—"Come." "I'll try to make it next Saturday," answered the child, almost aloud.

When they had got settled and had found a place to stay and to unpack their personal belongings, he laid out his notebooks and his fresh pads of paper for school and his two short pencils. From now on there were going to be things to tell about every day. And he knew how, now. First he would tell about the mountain.

THE TRAIL LEADS FORTH (Lloyd)

It was in the fall of the year 1902 that I first came to Colorado Springs. And I have lived here ever since! I was twelve years old that autumn, still young enough for the peculiar joy of children, but old enough to hide it from my fellows. I can recall being very much impressed with the beauty of the city that was to be my home. In early October autumn seemed to be painting the town especially for my coming. Gorgeous reds and gorgeous golds were everywhere.

Almost a hundred years earlier Zebulon Pike had sighted at a great distance the peak that would bear his name. He would propose to climb it and fail, having underestimated the distance and the bitter winter cold. Here in the clear air as an impressionable little boy of 12, I also entered into a lifelong love affair with a great peak and a little town at its foot, and I started a lifelong friendship with a man who had been dead for almost a century.

In the same block as our first home was the large residence of Winfield Scott Stratton, the man who became a millionaire in the gold mines of Cripple Creek and became an eccentric benefactor to our city. Across the street was the home of William S. Jackson, who used to speak to me, or should I say, let me speak to him? His children grew up friends of mine. And although the children rarely spoke of her, built into the very structure of the stately old house was the precious memory of Helen Hunt Jackson, poet and novelist, the first wife of William S. Jackson. There was no paving in this city. After a heavy rain we had to watch our steps in crossing the puddle-filled streets. And everything was real, and gorgeous, and just right for a boy of twelve.

I still remember how eagerly I waited for a nearby pond to freeze in the late fall. And since it was shallow enough to risk, how a few of us put our skates on too early each year, just to try it out and often got a complete dunking through the "rubber ice" that rose and fell in waves as we attempted to skate on it. I especially remember one very cold morning in late fall when I went down to skate before breakfast. It was the first ice, and I put on my skates and darted across the finest rubber I had ever been on. It was really cold that morning! I skimmed around the island on the far side of the lake, and the rubber got worse, and I finally broke through. O, how cold! I fought my way to the island, breaking ice as I went, and finally crawled up on the grass. Almost too frozen to move, I finally got my skates off and ran across the bridge and back up my hill, getting more and more brittle with every step. I made it into the house and changed my clothes while my mother was scolding me vigorously for being so wet and for being so foolish.

My school master self never forgot the three years that I was in Garfield School. My mind turns back to the great moments, such as the debates with Steele School, debates over such profound questions as "Resolved that President Lincoln was a greater man than President Washington." Or was it the other way around? I remember only the intensity with which I spoke my little piece. In a way, that is a great shame, for we settled a good many questions for all time. If this intensity of experience can sometimes spring into flame within, in the curriculum, in the physics lab, at the eyepiece of a telescope, in an English class ("Absent thee from felicity a while"), then blessed be the school in which it happens. But it needs to happen somewhere. It even needs to happen physically.

But other incidents of a different and less happy kind stand out even more boldly in my mind When I was a year or so older, a couple of stern police officers came to visit me and to ask me about the theft of some of some fountain pens at a downtown store. I was completely astounded and said that I knew nothing about it. They held firmly to the point, and I held just as naturally to the denial since I knew nothing of what they were talking about. I was completely crushed. They had been missing fountain pens at this store for some time and had set up a watch to catch the thief. At last they found a young boy about my age in the very act of theft. He readily told them his name: it was "Lloyd Shaw, 3 Beverly Place." That was my name and address, and they apparently let him go with a promise to appear at court. When he didn't show up, they came to my house to investigate. They must have recognized that I was not the boy who had talked to them. In any case no more was said.

But someone told the story to the principal of Garfield School and he called me to his office and accused me of the theft. He was a sort of a friend of mine, I had thought, and I answered him, breaking into tears in the telling, for by this time it was occurring to me that someone was evidently using my name. Within the next few days the principal called me in again saying that they had definite evidence that I had stolen the pens, and he wanted a full confession. I still had nothing to confess and was terribly confused and broke into tears again. Nonetheless he called me in a third time and was more menacing than ever. He wanted my confession; nothing would do but my confession. And I still had nothing to confess. I kept telling him the innocent story that I first told him. But he was sure I was guilty and bore down on me cruelly. I cried and cried. That only made him madder.

I went home, desperate, and repeated my story again to my parents. I refused to go back to school—ever. That of course was no answer. I begged my father, who was traveling at the time and chanced to be at home, to go and tell the principal that I wasn't the thief.

I have sometimes wished, in some of the darker hours of a school administrator, that I could have had my mother as a parent in the community. She had such a fine sense of "hands off and let them work it out together." But she also had a clean, uncluttered sense of justice. She convinced my father that it was his duty to go, and he went. He told the principal, I believe, that he didn't think I was guilty, but that if it could be proven that I had any connection with it, he would cooperate in the most thorough punishment. But he insisted that the prying and talking should stop. The persecution did stop, and in after years this principal always went out of his way to be kind to me. But I never truly trusted him again.

A few years later when I was in high school and lived on North Weber Street, our postman stopped by one day to tell me of an incident that had happened at the post office the day before. Someone had obtained keys to some of the lock boxes and some valuable mail had been lost, so a couple of detectives had been set to watch the boxes. They had found a boy, a boy of about my age, in the process of opening one of the boxes. He gave the name of Lloyd Shaw, 1338 North Weber, and said that the owner of the box had asked him to pick up the mail. They were on the point of turning him loose, planning to pick him up at my address, when my postman stepped up and said, "That's not Lloyd Shaw. I deliver mail at the Shaw home and I know Lloyd." So they took the boy to jail, and I have always felt that he also stole the fountain pens. I followed the case in the papers and I believe he was sent to the reformatory. It does not seem at all strange to me that the experience of this kind can almost ruin a small boy's life.

Out of these miserable days came a fundamental principle of my teaching. If a boy looked me in the eye and steadfastly denied a charge, and if I could not positively prove his guilt, I learned to say, "All right. I'll believe you. And we shall let it drop."

I used to go to town by skirting up the alley between the last of the houses and the Westover because it was the shortest way. There was a cook working in the kitchen of the Westover who soon became very friendly with me. He was always out to greet me when I went by. I didn't quite like him but I tried to be pleasant to him.

One day as I came by, he was down on the bottom of the long stairs that led to his kitchen, and he engaged me in conversation. And, smiling, he invited me to look at some large reproductions of art that he had acquired. I didn't quite trust him, but I went in. He led me through the kitchen and down a long flight of stairs to his rooms. And there he got out a large folder measuring some 18 by 20 inches of finished reproduction of pieces of "Art." I turned back the tissue paper covering the first one and found myself looking at such a startling picture as I had never seen before, beautifully drawn. He smiled and told me to go on. So I turned the page and found myself looking at an equally beautiful and even more suggestive picture. I swallowed hard and said I didn't care for that sort of Art.

"Go on," he laughed, "in a minute they'll get real good!"

The blood rushed to my face. I was dreadfully frightened, but I decided that I had had enough. And I said, "No, thank you! I'm going outdoors!"

"You like 'em," he said. Everybody likes 'em. And you're going to look at them."

He started for me.

"Maybe so, but I don't think so!" I exclaimed and dashed for the stairs. He was close after me, and I was scared to death. But I ran like mad and made it to the top of his staircase and was outside in a minute and was off toward my yard. All I heard was his voice crying after me menacingly, "If you tell anybody, I'll kill you!"

The next morning I told my big brother who was in college. It left him in a tough spot. He thought a long while and then said, "Don't worry, kid! The world is full of a good many men of that kind. And you've got to learn to avoid them. They're cowards; they're all cowards. Don't worry! Go by every day! Look him in the eye fearlessly and be ready to run. And come to me immediately if anything turns up!"

At one of the hotels where I worked later on I had my second experience with such a man. He was an assistant chef. He saved the best of every dish for me and was objectionably kind to me about everything. I didn't like him, but I didn't know what to do. At last one day when I came to him for something for a guest in the mid-afternoon, when no one else was around, he made his proposition.

He started for me and said, "You know what I mean! Don't look so innocent. Don't try to stall me off!" All of a sudden it was perfectly evident what he meant. I took a great breath and cried a great "NO!" I ducked and ran for the staircase. He was clattering after me, like the giant in Jack and the Beanstalk, but he had to run around the long kitchen table before he could really start.

I felt something whizz by my ear and saw a big kitchen knife, some 18 inches long, shoot past me and stick in the wall above my head. Terror-stricken, I tore down the steps and headed for my room. I got into my room and frantically barricaded the door with all of the furniture in the place. I was distraught! And not knowing what else to do, I knelt down by my bed and prayed and prayed.

It was not the last such experience that I had but it was the most memorable. I think it was my mother who forged my invisible armament. Mothers have to bring up their lads so that when they move out into the world, they can take it. And they have to move out! Give them strength! I have always felt dreadfully sorry for the boy whose mother thought he had enough character without her having to bother!

I must have been in the eighth grade when a friend of mine took me down to Hardy's where he worked and introduced me for special Christmas delivery work. I loved it because the Hardys were friendly and charming people, and the shop was delightful—half book store, half gift shop. But the stock was chiefly very beautiful items such as the fine Van Briggle vases that were so precious at that time, for Artus Van Briggle was still living and winning international prizes for his pottery, and his own bench-mark was on the bottom of the pieces. One of my jobs was to deliver these costly Christmas purchases to the elegant houses up on Cascade and Wood Avenues at the north end of town. But I didn't like it! I was scared! To ride up into the strange end of town with expensive packages in the dark night was a little too much for a boy of my tender years. Big houses, big yards, deep shadows, and mystery—mystery tugging at me and all but scaring the pants off of me. And under my arm a package of great value. It was truly terrifying.

I remember vividly one night when I couldn't find the house. I thought I would ride on to the arc light on the corner and try to read the address written on the package again. By some chance I looked down at the package and was aghast to find that I could read it there, where I stood. It was perfectly plain. I could read it easily. I recall then looking up and seeing the full moon and seeing the moonlight all around me wherever I looked—and the beautiful feeling of deliverance that came over my whole being. To be sure, I had taken happy note of the full moon many times before, but this was the first time that I, my real self, really looked, all by myself, upon the magic of its light. All about me it was shining like silver, and something changed within me. I increased in stature all of a moment, and I was never so afraid in the night again.

With a feeling of ecstasy of having established something of rarest value, I moved on. I went to the house and delivered the package. To be sure, there were mysterious trees in the yard along the winding walk, but how beautiful they had suddenly become. The whole world had become beautiful and inviting. And I entered in. I still remember with an indescribable exultation that moment and that night. I suddenly grew up to the night and found it beautiful and trustworthy and even protective. I was exalted! It was soul-shaking and important; it was an unfolding experience that I chanced upon. The night, the terrible night, dropped all its terror and suddenly became my friend.

Don't misunderstand me. There were nights to come when I was, quite literally, to quake in my boots. But I had found the way into the peace and beauty of a calm moonlit night. And I felt that I had grown a thousand years older. I had really grown up. When one stops to think of all the little animals and birds and other living things that come out only at night, the night becomes natural and inviting. When children at last throw the old wives' tales away and enter into the full beauty and peace of the night, they have taken one of the most important steps of their entire lives.

One by one, like a small unconvincing knights errant, growing children must fight their way through the dragons that are the natural fears and uncertainties of childhood. If the child is to deal with other children in later years, this is particularly necessary. The dragons must not only be met with, they must be recognized by the subconscious being for what they are—the fear of the darkness, the fear of evil, the fear of the crowd.

Danger! Why did I court it so? Surely the need to meet it is a part of the normal growing up, something that must be dropped at last and channeled into a kind of daring less concrete and more important. Imagination widens out into adventure, and adventure narrows down into danger. There was the matter of the canoes.

From a magazine article Joe Sinton and I got the idea of building a couple of canoes. They consisted of a light framework about ten feet long, covered with canvas which was stretched tight over the frame and sealed with many coats of paint. When they were completed, we took them over to the Mesa and rowed around in the big irrigation ditch clear to the north end of town, dragging them out and portaging at a few street crossings where the ditch went underground. We finally became so expert that we thought nothing could spill us again.

One summer day Monument Creek reared up into a real flood, running six to ten feet deep and filling the whole channel with its angry water. This was a beautiful flood, and I ran into the house and telephoned Joe to bring down his canoe. Joe said he would come right away. I suspect that his parents had too much sense to let him come. I waited around for a long time, and then little boys around me were getting mighty impatient for me to start. So I let a few of them hold the canoe tightly while I got in and settled down with my paddle for a real experience. The little boys had trouble holding the canoe—flood waters run so smoothly and so fast—and I was off almost before I gave the word that I was ready.

It took only a second for me to realize that I was up against a speed and a force that I had never known before. I could not control the boat, and the flood took it. All I could do was hold it straight downstream and pray for luck. In about a city block there was a little dam running straight across the stream bed. The flood water swirled over it and then dipped a little in a smooth trough and then piled up in a mad crest that swirled back in a vertical and menacing eddy and then ducked under and continued downstream. I hit this little dam squarely, feeling thoroughly alarmed. I hesitated for a moment on the crest of water beyond it, which was curling wildly back upstream, and then I began to slip with it upstream too until that end of my beautiful canoe was under the smooth line of the fall and I was sinking. I realized that I would never see my canoe again, and somehow I didn't care.

Thoroughly frightened, I had only myself to think of then, and with a few quick strokes I made it to the east shore. I snatched at some willows that had been planted there. The force of the water was so great that the bark and the branches that were washed parallel with the stream stripped off in my hands. I grabbed again, bending the willows with all my strength. They held for a minute, whipping my body against the bank, and then they broke off in my hands while I was turned head over heels in the wild stream.

It took me a minute to right myself. I was filled with water and with the filth that the stream had picked up. Desperate and confused, I struggled with the rushing water, afraid to grab the willows again. In a quick second I had visions of swimming on until I was south of town. There, I thought, the stream widened and spread out, and perhaps I could with a mighty effort lodge myself in a cottonwood tree as the water raced through its branches. Perhaps I could hang on there until the flood subsided.

Before heading downstream, I decided to make one last attempt to cling to the willows on this bank. I swam to the shore and made a grab at a huge willow washing in the water. I clung to it with desperation, and it held. My body was swept against the bank, but it held! I didn't realize that this was the inside of a long curve and the current's course was far less fierce.

With a soiled sort of triumph I managed to reach the next willow growing above the first one on the bank, and I worked my way inch by inch up the shore. A few more desperate grabs and I made it. I crawled out and sat on solid ground, far too exhausted to move.

I didn't care about the canoe any longer. I felt that I had miraculously crawled back from the portals of death. With a little prayer I thanked God, too tired to more than whisper.

It was not the last time I put myself in danger exploring my extended environment, but I mellowed with time and the responsibilities of a husband and father in my adult years. Nonetheless, as a school superintendent I believed in the need for young people to face challenges in their environment and, through facing them, to learn more about themselves.

AN EDUCATION IN WORK (Enid)

Lloyd worked throughout his childhood and youth, from the time he sold newspapers on the streets of Los Angeles at the age of six. After coming to Colorado Springs, he worked first as a delivery boy for a department store. He lived near a YMCA and earned his membership by setting pins in the bowling alley. Ten cents an hour times 60 hours, and he had a junior membership. An expert bowler showed him how to set the pins just a bit to the right or left of the spot where the pin should be placed, making it easier to get a strike. For the likeable men Lloyd set the pins in those advantageous places, and for the men he came to dislike he set the pins on the other side of the spots.

When Lloyd was in junior high school, he got a job as a bell hop at the small Plaza Hotel and then moved on to the more elegant Broadmoor Hotel. Just before he began high school he worked in a dressmaker's shop. As he proved himself at various tasks, he was charged with ordering all the fabrics and other materials for the stylish dresses that would clothe the wealthier ladies in Colorado Springs. One day he was asked if he could wire the long work room for electricity. When he hesitantly said he could do the job, Miss Patton, his employer, sent him off to get prices for the job. Knowing nothing, he went to the first hardware store where he learned what type of wire was needed for the job. As his ignorance began to be apparent, he was challenged and quickly left the store. He went to the next store where he now knew to ask for #14 black covered wire. He also learned the names for the wall fixtures before he was found out as an amateur. At the next shop with his increased vocabulary he learned the prices of more items that he needed. At the next store he was furnished with the names "fuse boxes" and "fuse plugs." Finally at the last hardware store he was equipped with the vocabulary to request a bid for the entire project, which he took back to Miss Patton. She approved it, and he bought the materials and wired the workroom for her.

Early in his high school career Lloyd worked for half the summer at a hotel restaurant beyond Manitou Springs in Cascade. He and a few friends lived in tents nearby and became adept waiters. But the chef seemed to have taken a dislike to Lloyd and made his life as difficult as possible. Whereas the other waiters could call out their orders in an oral shorthand, the chef demanded that he write down every order. On Lloyd's last day at work he had to deliver a message to the chef from the office. He found him outside peeling a big pan of potatoes. To his surprise, the chef smiled and said, "Lloyd, I have tried to make you hate me," to which Lloyd answered, "Well, you've almost succeeded." The chef replied pleasantly that he had tried to make waiting table a punishment just so Lloyd would learn to hate the job. He said that he hadn't made much of his own life, but he saw promise in Lloyd: "I haven't cared about the other kids on the job this summer, but you struck me as someone who had something that was worth saving, and I have tried to save it. Go on and hate me plenty. Perhaps I have done one thing well at last."

A job that came sporadically that Lloyd loved was "suping"—serving as a supernumerary on the stage of the opera house in Colorado Springs. He earned 50 cents a performance, but he felt well paid to witness some of the great actors of the day so close at hand. He served as a member of armies, crowds, and even riots. He became "so stage struck as a young boy that Shakespeare became a passion with me. I bought a full set of his plays with my summer's earnings when I attended a real book store auction." Another experience on the stage was serving as the subject of a hypnotist. "We were promised good money if we did a good job. We did a very good job, and we never got a cent," he reported. In his college years he learned the tricks of hypnotists and some relevant facts of human physiology and staged his own shows, but he soon discontinued them. He didn't like the deception and was disturbed by people's readiness to be fooled.

When Lloyd was 15, he took a job as a news butch on the Short Line Railroad to Cripple Creek. His task was to serve as the "spieler," to call out the sights as they went by. His pay came from the items that he could sell along the way from his trunk of oranges, postcards, and other curios. But the owner of the line cheated him by taking items from his trunk and then blaming Lloyd for the loss. Fortunately a better job turned up calling out the scenery on the Midland Railway on a longer outing to Cripple Creek. Lloyd used a megaphone and called out the sights at each end of each car on the train. "I got the job and a perfectly honest boss who let me set up my own trunk and make for myself on some days what seemed to me to be a considerable amount."

He continued to develop his skills as a spieler and conductor, the next summer finding work on the Manitou Incline, a cable car that ran up a track on the very steep mountain on the west side of Manitou Springs. It gained 2000 vertical feet in ¾ of a mile, offering tourists panoramic views and access to miles of trails in Mount Manitou Park. He wrote, "My summers on Mt. Manitou were a joy! The crowds of tourists were wonderful and appreciative, everyone who worked on the incline was pleasant and friendly, and in the evenings and early mornings we had a lot of beautiful country to run over as we pleased. It was a sort of idyllic time." Lloyd and the other young spielers camped for the summer in a tent halfway up Manitou Mountain. He worked there for several summers. On his last summer there, he was joined by his older brother Ray, who had the summer off. They hiked all around the area, and after hours they could go dancing or ride the donkeys that carried tourists up Pikes Peak.

During the first summer after he started college, Lloyd was hired to serve as a "passenger agent" for the Crystal Park Auto Highway, which went up into the mountains above Manitou Springs. It involved making the rounds of the hotels and inducing the tourists there to sign up for "the incomparable experience" of a ride to Crystal Park in the company's big Packard touring cars. He soon discovered that other agents were offering tour guides some illegal "benefits" on the side to sign up their group, so he resigned in disgust. The manager, learning of Lloyd's reason for quitting, was impressed enough to offer him a job as a chief conductor on the tours. So he rode in the big open-sided 20-passenger touring cars, telling of all the sights and visiting with the tourists. He had never driven a car, so he peppered the driver with questions about its workings. Finally one day as they were returning from a tour, the driver stepped out on the running board and instructed Lloyd to take the wheel. Terrified but with the driver coaching him, he got his first driving experience.

For the following two summers of his college career, Lloyd worked as the photographer for the Crystal Park Auto Highway. He wrote, "About a quarter mile below the park we had our tent, and we stopped each bus as it came up, unloaded the passengers, draped them around the bus, and took their picture. Then we would stop the next bus and do the same. After the last bus of the series had passed, we would rush down to our tent cottage, develop the plates, and fix them for a few minutes and make a quick wet print to show the tourists. We would be ready to catch the buses when they came down again. We would show the people their own picture and take orders on the bus. It was surprising how many would order. It was almost a rule that either the man or the woman would say, 'It's just terrible of me, but I do like the picture of my husband (or wife), so I think we'll take one.' We would drop off the running board and catch the next bus, until we had seen them all and had all our orders taken. Then we would ride on to the nearest trail crossing and climb up to the photography camp again. Sometimes with all the buses running, and everyone taking a long time to admire their picture, we'd be carried clear down to Manitou and would have to hit the trail back up from there."

During the summer after he graduated from college, Lloyd worked as an independent photographer as well as the spieler on the Colorado Midland Railway, which took passengers all the way from Colorado Springs to South Park, the great treeless basin that lies about 50 miles to the west. For this new job he would have to buy expensive equipment, so he "took a deep breath and bought a big Goerz-Dagor lens on credit, a big 8x10 beauty with a brand new shutter, and a big camera to hold it all and to take my 8x10 plates." He converted a toilet on the train into his darkroom to do his preliminary work to provide proofs to his customers. At various points along the itinerary, the train would stop, and the tourists were encouraged to gather wild flowers and pose around the train engine.

What a wealth of experiences he had, what a diverse cross section of humanity he met, and what a varied skill set he acquired. He learned a great deal about human nature, both its sterling and less admirable qualities. He had amassed hundreds of hours of public speaking experience. He had lived in and explored the glorious mountain landscape around Colorado Springs, climbing every mountain in sight, most of them many times. He knew every wild flower that grew there. He developed a passion for star gazing, acquiring a collection of astronomy books and spending hours watching the night sky. He learned the names of the first and second magnitude stars and even the third that had names. He and his friend would get up early in the morning, hike to a lookout point, and with star maps and a flash light puzzle out the stars as they rose in the east.

THE FORMAL EDUCATION (Enid)

Lloyd's formal education of course paralleled his summers of work. In 1905 he enrolled in Colorado Springs High School . He was one of those boys who excelled in classes for which he had a passion. Then there were the classes in which he scraped by, one of which was Latin. Since it was part of the college preparatory curriculum, he dutifully enrolled in it, but an accident his first year, falling out of a tree and rupturing a lung, kept him out of school for several weeks. When he returned to school, he was hopelessly behind, and he never caught up. When he became a biology major in college, he had no problem learning and remembering the Latin names of plants and animals, but Julius Caesar was beyond him.

He was also a joker, something that did not endear him to his principal. As Lloyd told the story, "We had a good-natured and completely ineffective teacher who was often put in charge of our study periods in the large auditorium. He was a fall guy for the whole auditorium. He trusted me so much that I couldn't help falling a little too—and letting him fall with me. I would get excused to go to the basement and going down the back stairs, I would make the greatest racket of which I was capable, sliding down the steps, clattering and making all the noise I could. And I would raise my voice in protest against my tormentors, who weren't there, of course, except in my imagination.

"By the time this study-hall teacher had made it to the isolated staircase, I would be shouting down the steps in high

42

indignation, 'You dirty cowards, come on back up here if you want to fight! You are below my contempt! A dirty bunch of sneaks, trying to disturb the auditorium!' It made no difference how absurd I made my demands, he fell for it.

"One day, after a football victory, or something of the kind, two gangs began marching around the auditorium, each boy with his hands on the shoulders of the boy in front of him. We were intense in our school spirit, and the poor teacher didn't know what to do. Just as my line came down the aisle nearest the office of J. R. Richards, the principal, he suddenly appeared. He grabbed me under each arm and raised me up bodily toward him and then, with a terrible thrust, he threw me backward and into the line of marchers. The line of boys fell, incurring more than one bloody nose. He stood glaring contemptuously at us and then cried, 'Get to your seats!' "

Although Lloyd was light in weight, he went out for the high school football team. Realizing that he probably couldn't make the team, he turned to making wise cracks that amused his teammates. It was at that moment that J. R. Richards, who was coach as well as principal, shouted at him, "Shaw, turn in your suit! You're through with football!" Lloyd later reminisced about the incident, "While I pretended not to understand, I understood fully! I tried to make light out of what he took seriously. There was no room for anyone of my kind on his team. My wheels were turning slowly. I was beginning to understand."

In his junior year he entered the school's oratorical contest and won it. He was then headed for the state contest to be held at the University of Colorado in Boulder. At the request of J. R. Richards, Lloyd went to him daily for coaching on his speech. Richards would go through the speech with him, paragraph by paragraph, suggesting changes until it was no longer Lloyd's speech, not even his chosen topic. Richards "would suggest new thoughts for me to put in, and I would put them in, and finally when they were worded just right to suit him, he would accept them. And I thought I was writing the oration!" Then they worked on delivery. Lloyd was coached to start each paragraph softly and build to a crescendo. "In this quiet mood, I worked up to quite a climax. Then I attacked on a little higher scale and worked up into a mightier climax. And then, waiting a moment, I would start in on the next paragraph with my voice as low as I could get it, and would say, 'We have been following false gods.' He never told me to put it in, but he said it so often after reading my climactic paragraph that at last I got the idea and included it. And he thought it was a splendid suggestion 'on my part.'"

The next morning Lloyd had a few hours to spend at school before taking the train to Boulder. "I didn't have to go to classes that day. In the library we chanced to have a substitute who was ridiculously incompetent. So I found myself in there amusing the students no end with my clever turns and innocent tricks on her. It eased my situation tremendously! But at last, just before my train time, she blew up and asked me in no uncertain terms to leave the room for good. 'Get out!' she said, 'and never come back!' I was standing by an open window, so, very obligingly, I climbed out of it and down a drain pipe to the ground beneath. I heard the roar of laughter that greeted my exit. I had won that one. I felt very good, very clever, as I went to the train to start for Boulder."

In Boulder he got settled in his hotel. In the evening he proceeded to the auditorium, where J. R. Richards was waiting for him. Noting Lloyd's bright red tie, Richards took off his own black tie and suggested that they trade. Of his speech, Lloyd reminisced, "I got a tremendous hand on my first climax and then built up to second one and got an even greater hand on that one. A red-haired boy from Golden was pretty good, but he got nowhere near the applause I did."

The judging, he was told, would take a minute, but it was over half an hour before the judges returned with confusion and consternation on their faces. Then the winner of the contest was announced—the boy from Golden! "Everyone was really surprised, and they looked at each other a moment and then gave a sort of half-hearted applause. The room went black for me! I was completely overwhelmed. As soon as the meeting was dismissed, I rushed out and started for the hills. I didn't want to see anybody!" He was followed by some boys from his school who were competing in a track meet the next day. They persuaded him to return to the hotel.

"Mr. Richards explained to me that it had been a steal, just a plain steal—as anyone could see by watching the audience. He told me I had two firsts, and the young brewer from Golden had given me a seventh. The Golden boy had two seconds, and the brewer had given him a first, and they could not move the brewer. He had made up his mind before the contest, and nothing could change him.

"Soon after we got back to Colorado Springs, Mr. Richards heard about my conduct in the library. He called me in and gave me thunder! He ruled that I could not represent the school in the Colorado College Oratorical Contest, which was to be held in a couple of weeks and was offering a cash prize of $50. He was simply robbing me of $50! But I gave up; one did to all of Mr. Richards' ideas. Imagine my surprise then the day of the contest when Mr. Richards called me into his office and told me he had done his best to keep me out of the contest, but the organizers had insisted that since my name had been submitted, I should represent the school. 'So go home, Lloyd, and wash your face. And,' slapping me on the back and winking at me, he added, 'win that $50!' I didn't know he had planned it all the time. I had believed him. I rushed home and rushed through my oration a couple of times. I dressed carefully, with a black tie, and hurried down to Perkins Hall.

"It was raining cats and dogs as I ran down, and the ditches were running over. I miscalculated on a jump and landed square in a ditch at the corner, filling my shoes with water. My toes squishing with water in the half-full shoes, I won the contest. I got the $50!"

Lloyd fancied himself a writer from an early age. In high school he submitted articles to *The Lever*, the school's monthly publication, and was gratified to see them in print. By the end of his junior year there was general agreement among the student staff that he should be the editor the next year. The day the new editor was to be elected, Lloyd went to the meeting feeling confident even though, as he later wrote, "I had had a little trouble with our principal, from acting what he considered to be a little too 'cocky.' When I entered, I became suddenly aware that something catastrophic had happened. The whole board, including my closest friends, was in terrible confusion, and my entrance seemed to make them worse. I was startled, deeply puzzled, and sat down. Nothing happened. Everyone seemed stunned.

"Then the editor said that the nominations were open for the next year's editor. They just sat there, and my heart dropped. No one said a word. Then he cleared his voice, and said, 'Nominations are in order!' They sat still again. I could hardly breathe! Something had happened. Then Joe Sinton, one of my friends, suddenly blurted out, 'I don't care what he says. I nominate Lloyd Shaw!' They all sat still again.

"Then Dwight, another of my close friends said, so low that you could hardly hear him, 'I nominate Cora Kampf!' Good night! They had never had a girl edit *The Lever*, and Cora was the girl I was going with! It was Dwight Sisco, my best friend, who had nominated her. I was crushed! There were no more nominations. The editor put it to a vote, and they were unanimous in voting for Cora. They didn't look at me. And when my name was put up, I think that even Joe, the rebel, failed to vote for me. It was just too hopeless.

"None of them had the courage to tell me what had happened. Some time later I found out that J.R. Richards had called the board into his office and had announced that he had decided that I could not edit *The Lever*. If they elected me, *The Lever* would be dropped for a year. And he urged, in a manner all his own, that no one was to tell me that he had had a thing to do with it. It was for my own good.

"Oh, that man! What he did to me that year! I am afraid that I had murderous thoughts to the extent of wishing that he might step in front of a fast-moving street car. I was baffled, frustrated, undone. It was the first of a series of carefully planned regulations that he put upon me. I could have screamed and fought, but it would have done no good. He had decided to make something out of me. But oh, that making was hard!

"I gave up being The World's Greatest Author. I got busy on the load he had put upon me, the load that I figured would make or break me. And he didn't seem to care which. This was his first blow. And this touched me to the very quick! But I think that it was the first thing that really put steel into my soul. He may have been a very wise educator."

At the end of his junior year Lloyd received another blow. His English teacher called him in and told him "that he had received orders from the office to flunk me in English. He had gone down to the office and told J. R. Richards that he couldn't do it—that I was one of the best students in the class. They evidently had quite a talk, and J.R. finally agreed that I would probably be satisfactory in English. But surely I didn't hand in all my work! The teacher told him that I liked it well enough that I had handed in almost everything he had asked for. Finally J. R. said, 'Give him the lowest passing grade, and let him go on.' So the teacher apologized for the grade he had given me. That is why he had called me in, to tell me about it—nothing personal!

"Other teachers called me in and told me that they too had been requested to flunk me. And after all, I was somewhat irregular, and I knew it well enough. I knew that there was no use in arguing with them, so I kept my mouth shut. Mrs. Reinhardt, my Spanish teacher, was very sweet about it. But she was inflexible, and I knew that she would obey the orders and flunk me. So I held my peace, but inside my small self I got madder and madder.

"At last, I went to Mr. Richards and told him what the teachers had told me. 'Yes,' he said, he 'had heard of it.' 'Yes,' I said, 'and they told me it was on orders from you.' I saw his jaw harden. I knew trouble was in store. So I said, 'I just wanted to thank you!' in my most accusing tones, which were a little green at that time, and I added, 'Very much!' His smile became harder, as he said, 'You're quite welcome!' And I walked out. It was purely hopeless to start a fight with that man. I knew that much anyway.

"Word had got around by now. My friends had heard of the ruling and were talking too much about it. A few helpful souls wanted to bet with me that I couldn't make it, that I wouldn't graduate. I took them up and set my jaw. Seven subjects I would have to take next year, and there were only six periods in the day.

"So I went to Mrs. Reinhardt and asked her if I could tutor Spanish in the summer, and she said she would be glad to have me. I had passed the first semester of Spanish, but it wouldn't count until I passed the second. So we arranged for me to go to her home for 20 lessons, and if I passed a good examination, she would give me credit for the work. A lot of trouble! I had to get those 20 lessons in spite of my summer job! I believe I did them in the first 20 days of the summer. The tourist crowd didn't really show up in any numbers until the Fourth of July, so I had finished my Spanish and was ready for the heavy tourist load in time. I surprised myself and did well in it. With nothing to do but get each assignment of lessons, I did a good job. I wasn't taking any chances. Spanish is the only foreign language I ever really studied and therefore ever really loved."

When Lloyd came back to high school in the fall, he was eligible for graduation only if he passed all six courses, and he made sure that his classwork came first. Nonetheless he managed to win the state oratorical contest in Boulder that year, he wrote articles for *The Lever,* and he had a leading role in the senior class play. He even managed to make the football team. Lloyd reminisced, "In spite of myself, I had grown to admire J. R. Richards. He was right!"

Lloyd reluctantly entered Colorado College in the fall of 1909. What he really wanted to do was to follow his oldest brother Ray to New York. Ray had earned a degree in engineering from CC, but he had wearied of his job and headed to New York where he finally landed a small part in a production of Franz Lehar's *Merry Widow.* Lloyd wrote, "I wanted with all my heart to go to New York and take my try at it. College didn't seem to make any difference. If anything, it was a handicap. I had proved I could handle a big schedule in my last year at high school. I proved it to everyone but my mother. She was determined that I should go to college, and when she was determined, one usually did what she wanted." In his reluctance to enter Colorado College, Lloyd did win one point: he got a dispensation from the Latin requirement from CC President Slocum.

Lloyd continued to be the sort of student who excelled in the classes he loved and performed less well in classes or with faculty that didn't excite him. For example, there was a course in medieval history where the professor, as Lloyd recounts, "had the reputation of letting the pupils get away with murder, but he always picked one or two of the class whom he knew and heckled them relentlessly. It soon became evident that he knew me quite well!" Irked by the continual teasing, Lloyd finally challenged the professor and then walked out of the class. He continued to attend but didn't open a book after that encounter. When exam time came, he saw his girlfriend Dorothy to the door of the classroom but didn't enter. She urged him to try at least, so he decided he would stay outside long enough to memorize the table of contents of the textbook and then go in and take a chance at the exam. He reported "I got quite inspired as I wrote. I put every question in relation with the big dates and the big events of the course. Mine was a somewhat sweeping view. I imagined I had flunked and would have to drop the course. A few days later when the professor came to class, he said that one of the exam papers had delighted him. It completely ignored all the petty dates that filled the usual student's mind. It had a sweep and an understanding that was completely unexpected. He had given this, the best exam paper he had ever received in this class, the highest grade in the course. I was astounded—and very grateful. For I realized that the professor, who was always after that a close friend of mine, had taken advantage of the fact that I had done a wise thing for a wrong reason. He had leaned a little way when he found that he could praise me a bit. With a less discerning professor, I would have flunked."

Another course that he passed in an unorthodox fashion was trigonometry, which was a freshman year requirement for his pre-med major. Goaded by his fraternity brothers who assured him that he would fail the class, he bet them that he could pass the course without ever opening the book. He agreed that he would not look at the text outside of class with the exception of two hours before each of the two final exam periods. He wrote, "I played the game straight, and I never paid such attention in any class in my life. I learned trigonometry in class! If I was lucky enough to hear a couple of other students recite first, I would actually get the idea and rush up to the board when I was asked to recite. If I was the first one to recite on a new method, I flunked of course for that day.

"It got to be fascinating! I'd study and think intently all through the class. I'd listen carefully and recite my best. And I would bone up at a terrible rate when we had the exams. I really studied those two times in the semester! And there was always someone there to take the book away from me when my two hours were done. It was an exciting process! I passed the course with a famous, mean, low-grading professor. He took pity on my apparent blind spots and my lack of his kind of easy intelligence.

And I was so cooperative and eager every minute of his classes that he took quite a fancy to me. After he had passed me and the story went around that I had passed his course without a book on a bet, he was a little ruffled. Then he decided to make the best of it and told it far and wide. If Lloyd Shaw could pass his course without a text book, then surely anyone could pass it if they showed the least bit of interest. And he was right! The more I thought about it, the truer it seemed to me. Most people flunked courses simply because they were inattentive in the classroom. Complete application will take the place of many hours of study."

Colorado College qualified even in those early days for a Phi Beta Kappa chapter. Some students had supplemented this honor with their own organization: Kappa Beta Phi. It consisted of people who didn't necessarily get good grades but were considered likely to go far in the world. Its members wore raw wieners for pledge pins at the college chapel where the real Phi Beta Kappa students were being inducted. Lloyd, who became president of Kappa Beta Phi, qualified with his indifferent academic record and his ultimate success in life.

One who easily qualified for Phi Beta Kappa was his girlfriend, Dorothy Stott, a coed from Denver. The daughter of a printer, Jerome Stott, she was a poet from the time she could read and write. Her father printed little volumes of her poetry to give as Christmas gifts to the aunts and uncles. The publisher's note on the first extant volume in 1900 reads: "Dorothy Cory Stott was born November 26, 1891. She was a very attractive baby and, when she commenced to walk, was the observed of all observers. She began talking at nine months; at seven months she said her first word." Dorothy and Lloyd bonded over their shared loves: the written and spoken word and the magnificence of the natural world. They both majored in biology, not because they foresaw a career path but because a biology professor, Dr. Schneider, won their admiration and loyalty. They majored in the man. By the spring of 1913, Lloyd and Dorothy were engaged, and they were married at her family home in Denver at the end of that summer.

AS CLOSE TO EARTH AS A FOX'S TAIL (Dorothy)

While Lloyd wrote about his escapades and irregularities in college, Dorothy presents a different picture. Here, written half a century later, is Dorothy's intimate view of Lloyd as a student.

> *And holding me, till earth shall fail,*
> *As close to earth as a fox's tail. . .*

Witter Bynner wrote that. It is the end of the first stanza of a remarkable longish poem that starts

> *You have never seen rain, unless you see*
> *Them dance for rain at Cochiti...*

Witter Bynner was one of our favorite poets in Senior English, modern poets, that is. We knew him, after a fashion. He had even invited the dance team to his wonderful house one time when they were dancing at the fall festival in Santa Fe, and he had shown them his priceless collection of Chinese jade and had been very docile, if uncomprehending, about giving them Coca Cola to drink instead of highballs. What we loved about him was that closeness to the southwestern earth, that understanding of the poet in the Indian, that awareness of the fact that we live on a small planet.

I want to tell about the sort of man that the boy of the earlier chapters had grown into. This is an asking of the question that a great many residents of the district were beginning to ask, "What is this Lloyd Shaw anyway?" Was he something of a charlatan when it came to education? Was he a kind of Peter Pan who had refused to grow up himself? Was he just a dreamer? He was certainly an idealist, with all the undesirable attributes that that term suggested. A very wise man once said to me, "Your husband was the only practical idealist I ever knew. I have known a few real idealists whom I admired greatly, but he was the only one who made it work."

I am glad the wise man was so sure, for I am not. I am not sure that I think Lloyd was an idealist, practical or otherwise. I think he was a realist, in the simplest sense of the word: he was interested in what was real, as opposed to what was false. That was where being close to earth came in, "as close to earth as a fox's tail." Here it was, this lovely and lonely and dreadful and desirable earth, this hospitable planet. And we lived on it. It was a perfectly straightforward, diagramable sentence: We live on the earth. We—kind of being, quite obviously made in the spiritual image of *something* and sharing with that *something* differences from all other creatures, sharing the capacity to create, deliberately. *Live*—the act of living, of being alive, whether we liked it or not. *Earth*—a small, life-inviting hospitable planet, third out from a small sun. It is a situation and we are stuck with it—I believe this is what he thought— so why not make the very best of it? It is an absolutely beautiful jam to be in!

He really had an excellent education for the task. He took a pre-med degree with a major in biology and a minor in psychology. (He promptly categorized psychology as phony but fascinating.) He was really majoring in greatness, and earnest students do this or tear themselves to pieces. The greatness lay in the head of the Biology Department, and when you cross the path of a great man, you lay aside your other plans and follow him. It does not mean that you have to become a doctor of medicine; it only means that you will try to go your own little way toward greatness, following his example. It was the simple goodness and learned-ness and common sense and stability of Dr. Edwin C. Schneider that sent such numbers of good physicians out into the world. The material was in the textbooks and on the growing earth. It was his respect for it that mattered.

There was a professor of Spanish whose usefulness lay only secondarily in the writing of standard texts that endured for years; what he was gave the student respect for what he taught. That was Dr. Elijah C. Hills. There was Homer Woodbridge of the English Department, salty and sound, who always wrote the front-page reviews for the *Saturday Review of Literature* when a new Galsworthy novel came out. There was the great Dr. Florian Cajori, one of the mighty mathematicians of his time. There was Dr. Gile of the Greek Department, an eloquent proof of the fact that nothing is dead unless you let it die. Above all, there was Dr. Slocum himself, Prexy, bumbling and forgetful and real. Lloyd wrote to him long afterward, "I have charted my own course and gone my own voyage toward my own port, but you were the old cartographer who gave me a map."

And yet, it was to some who were not there at all that he owed some of the richest credits in that credit-packed degree, and chief among these was a great man who had once taught astronomy in the little college of the first days of the town, Dr. Frank Loud. He was long since gone, and it was many years since there had been a course in astronomy, but the small observatory that his enthusiasm had brought into being and the very good telescope that inhabited it were still there, halfway down the hill toward the park, waiting in the dust.

Anyone who lives in Colorado and does not fall in love with the stars is only half alive. Lloyd had been in love with the stars for years, and suddenly the opportunity struck him as being no less real for lack of a course and a professor. He would set up his own course. I cannot quite remember how he wheedled the key to the observatory out of the administration and Dr. Loud's old textbooks out of the librarian, and persuaded a charming young French teacher to be chaperone to the three or four of us who joined his "class," I cannot quite remember. I can only remember how he kept ahead of us, drawing his "lectures" out of the assorted books and putting us in turn on the tall, revolving stool behind that telescope, breathlessly watching while he told us, just as breathlessly, what we were seeing. We, stuck on the little planet, were looking at the majesties of suns.

Lloyd's older brother Ray, who was living at home at the time, and who was an engineer by profession and a mathematician by the grace of God—one of those inspired spirits, maintained his dignity while he followed his little brother on his chase across the sky by taking a bold personal leap into the field of astrology. He became the mathematician and Lloyd the writer for a team that turned out horoscopes of their closest friends with exuberant relish. Piles of celestial logbooks took their place beside the astronomy texts, and we looked out upon the stars that our ancient kinsmen saw, mysterious shining things that perhaps controlled human destinies. We knew their names, but only Lloyd called out to literal hundreds of them, as if they were battalions of great mounted riders charging across space.

As I think of it now, I am suddenly amazed at the hours he found for his extra-curricular curriculum. Dr. Edward R. Warren, who was curator of the college museum, was one of the notable mammalogists of the country and the outstanding one of the Rocky Mountain West, and his colleague, Charles Aiken, was the greatest avian specialist of his era. Dr. Warren set Lloyd up in a private course, helping him with his personal research into the nesting habits of our local birds and into the ecology of the mammals of the high mountains, and he was off, week after week, Sunday after Sunday, doing what he loved best, trudging the red disintegrated granite of his timberline slopes, listening for the call of a pica to lead him to its nest.

"Already," he wrote in his notebook, "it has stopped snowing, the wall of gray is beginning to break, and in a half hour the cloud has blown past and we are in bright sunshine. We are still wet and very cold, but there, hopping about in the slushy snow is a cheerful feathered sunbeam. It is a pipit, or tit-lark. All the rocks seem alive with them. They are out laughing at the welcome sunshine, and it is a sweet little note they utter as they run over the rocks. They wear a grayish-olive suit that is buffy-white underneath. The outer tail feathers show a flash of white. They can't stand still, but rhythmically squat or teeter. This is their home. They rear their babies in grass-lined cups under the cold boulders, and add a touch of cheer to these cold heights."

In addition, Lloyd and I worked together on a special course in which we completed the research project for a master's degree in psychology, which we had no intention of working out to the end. The eight hours of credit for each of us was goal enough. But, like all good research projects, this thing was fun for its own sake. We were analyzing the psychology of humor. Lloyd set up a program, after selecting four very good funny stories, representing a graded approach to humor which he classified as "low-type physical, high-type physical, low-type mental and high-type mental."

Dr. Schneider made him laboratory assistant the year that spring came on the 9th of March instead of the middle of May as is its custom in this state. The flowers came into the botany lab, ten, twelve, twenty new species in a day. Lloyd met them all at the door, inquired their names, loved them, and made them his own. I was a student in the course, and he made them my own, too, with his enthusiasm transmitter wide open. Even now, walking a lonely trail, I will meet a mutual friend, and I will speak its name, "Good morning, Linnea, linnea," and the twin flower and my teacher and I are all there together. "As close to earth as a fox's tail."

Lloyd described their college graduation: "1913! It was a wonderful commencement! We did our very best to honor President Slocum in his 25th anniversary as president of Colorado College. We all met at Palmer Hall, we plain-gowned 'bachelors' mingling with the gorgeous academic regalia of the great scholars who had been invited to participate, and formed our academic procession. We marched across the campus and down the east sidewalk of Cascade Avenue with crowds of women and children leaving their houses to watch us pass. How superbly we marched! Our tall starched and recurved collars choking our necks, and the women with their ankle-length dresses covered by ankle-length black gowns and their high collars held well up by the little erect whale-bone strips. We were marching into a new world that we utterly failed to comprehend. The few automobiles were being accepted about town without laughter. While the streets were utterly unpaved, they were usually in pretty good condition except when a couple of days of rain poured on them and roughed them up a bit. Some people, dare-devils in spirit, even rode all the way to Denver on the country roads, taking four or five hours for the trip.

"We had a Marconi telegraph located on the campus, receiving wireless messages in code from all over the world. We used to point to it with pride although it would be several years before human speech took to the airwaves, and real radio was known. We knew that we faced an expanding and perfectly wonderful world. Some of us already had jobs arranged. Mine was to pay $1000 a year! That seemed ample to face a world that would soon become complicated beyond our wildest imaginings. We faced the future eagerly."

From his spotty career as a student, Lloyd would go the next fall into a lifetime as an educator. He was indeed a born teacher. He felt compelled to share whatever he found that was beautiful and exciting. He would inspire and cajole his own students, and he would bring out the best in them. He would soon attract national attention for the extraordinary school that he directed. Only 15 years after he graduated from Colorado College with his mixed academic record, the same institution awarded him an honorary Doctor of Law degree. This would be followed nine years later, in 1937, by an honorary doctorate in Education from the University of Colorado. To those who said they weren't *real* doctorates, that he hadn't done the extensive work involved in earning a doctorate, he would serenely suggest that they get themselves an honorary doctorate too.

NATURE NOTES OF THE PIKES PEAK REGION (Lloyd)

When we finished at the Springs High School, our daughter was a year old, so we decided to spend that summer on the summit of Manitou in a little cabin the management offered us. In return for the cabin, I was to be nature guide for the Mt. Manitou Incline and take parties on long hikes into the nearby mountains. I was going to have a much better salary for my teaching the next year, so I decided to take the offer.

It was a very pleasant summer, and, while the crowds weren't large, we took long trips all over the back country, and I had a very happy time. The chief thing that made the summer possible for me was the fact that the *Colorado Springs Gazette,* then the morning paper, employed me to write a daily column during the summer called "Nature Notes." They paid me for it, not much, but enough to take a chance on living, so I took the job.

It was a lot of fun. The first articles were sort of slaved out of a stiff and frightened brain. But I soon found myself and started to go to town with them. I had the time of my life. And, I must admit that some of the articles I wrote toward the end of the summer impressed even me a little as being rather good. Maybe I had the touch, and people kept telling me how much the articles meant to them.

Biology was my line, and nature study was my hobby, and the whole Pikes Peak region was my field. I could write one day about the dim trails that were seldom followed and another about the spring glory of the anemones, another about the ubiquitous magpies flying so noisily all about us, another day about the glorious yucca and the little dolls that can be made from its blossoms and the use of the plant by the Indians for food, for moccasins, and for a hundred other uses. The prairie dog was good for an article and then the blossoms of our fragrant primrose that makes our summer nights so lovely, and then the next day it might be the white-throated swifts flying high above the gateway rocks of the Garden of the Gods.

There was a whole series of articles on the pines and spruces and firs and cedars of the region. And I told how each might be identified. Then I would give an article on the beauty of our shooting stars growing along the mountain stream; then I would slip up Pikes Peak and describe the cony (or pika), that little furred inhabitant who lives above timberline. With shrubs and lilies, and all the animals from badger to buffalo, and the loveliest of our fair flowers and all our mammals from the lowly skunk to the wapiti [elk], the antelope, the deer, and our big game, I pretty well covered the field.

While I gave the scientific name of each species and worked in a careful description of the bird or animal or flower I discussed, so no one could miss identifying it, I kept my spirit easy and my descriptions would include my own personal experience on the trails and in the cabins of the region. For instance, in my description of the mountain rat, I first described his great clutter of sticks and piles in a crevice of the rocks for a nest, with his ill-smelling brown stains running all over the rocks. I described the terrible noise a rat or two can make running around in a deserted cabin in which you try to sleep, his tendency, like a human being, to gather in one place everything that could possibly have any value to him, or that he thinks could ever have any value. And I ended by discussing his habit of leaving something in place of whatever he steals from your cabin, giving him the name of Trade

Rat. My conclusion was that he always had something in his mouth and, seeing something that he thought he wanted, he would drop the stick he was carrying and grab up your spoon.

My silly articles won a host of friends, and many people clamored for me to publish them. To my own surprise, I found that I had written a book. So the Dentan Printing Co. arranged for a printing of a thousand copies. I had my high school pal, Charley Butner, do a cover design and make little drawings and do the initial letters with which each article began. He was an artist, and we had often kidded each other about doing a book together some day. But some of my beautiful photographs with which I decided to illustrate the volume and some of Kenneth Hartley's marvelous flower photographs turned out to be quite dull in the printing. And Dentan's binder had a little trouble with the covers, which somehow didn't have an authentic look.

Several folks in Broadmoor who had ordered quite a few copies for friends cancelled their orders when they saw the finished product. But in spite of this, the little book sold and the edition was soon exhausted. Years afterwards my friend Mr. Dentan phoned me one day and told me that he had several dozen books down in his basement that had been very slightly damaged by water. Did I want them? So I brought them out to the house, and folks who wanted a copy turned up now and then. Then I realized that there were so very few left that I would be compelled to raise the price in order to hold on to a few copies for my grandchildren. Still they sold, until it is almost impossible to find a copy today. And I found that I was not only the author of a "book," but that I was also the possessor of a "collector's item."

[Here is Lloyd's article about one of his granddaughter's favorite places and one of her favorite alpine creatures, the pika.]

THE CONY OR PIKA

Someday, when you are on top of Pikes Peak, make your way down toward the Seven Lakes. Leave the roads and trails and railroad tracks to take care of themselves and start down across the huge boulder fields. As you jump from one boulder to the next, you find some of them are loose and teeter, and you have to dance for your balance. You will start some boulders rolling down the slope and break the silence of those high places with their rattling. Under the rocks is the gurgle of water, which seems to flow from the summit on all sides of the peak. Here and there you will cross over tiny meadows, soggy under foot, dark green with alpine grasses and starred with brilliant though tiny flowers.

The summit house and all the roads to it are now out of sight. You are alone on this vast field of boulders. Above you a few cumulus clouds sail in the blue sky, and now and then a huge black raven flies over, craning his head to one side and the other. Way down below, the glassy surfaces of the Seven Lakes mirror the opposite hills in their clear waters. Old Baldy is streaked and patched with black masses of timber. To the right of Baldy, barren and timbered hills are piled in great confusion. On beyond them can be seen parts of the Cripple Creek district with its unsightly dumps and slides, and on farther and farther are the snow-capped peaks of the Continental Divide. It is all so large, so infinite that your soul fairly shrinks into itself. As you look upon the immensity of it, the silence bears in upon you. Speak, and your voice sounds queer, and you wonder why you did it. The silence is broken only by the gurgle of the water under the rocks.

What was that? You jump and turn around as you hear a sharp, staccato squeak in the boulders above you. In a moment it is repeated, a sort of squeaky little bark ejected from a tiny pair of lungs with an explosive suddenness. It seems to be within a few feet of you, and still you cannot see it.

A little streak suddenly darts into a crevice. That was he. Watch now, keep quiet, quiet—there he is again. Well, I don't blame you for not seeing him before. He looks like a patch of

63

discolored lichen on the boulder on which he sits. My! What a pudgy, funny-looking little fellow. He looks a good deal like a guinea pig. He is rather fat and round and without a tail. His head is very large with neat little rounded ears on it, and he jerks it forward suddenly as he ejects each squeak. His back is a salt-and-pepper color, with a suggestion of cinnamon about the collar and a grayer head. His legs seem very short as he scurries over the boulders and then rolls up into an erect ball on top of one of them, takes in a view that almost terrifies you, and utters his squeaky defiance to the world.

Farther down the slope several others can now be seen scurrying about. What sort of beasts are they? Cony or pika is the name they go by. They are structurally related to the rabbits although they look more like rats. They live on these rock slides usually above the timberline, where they are probably active the year around. They feed on the arctic vegetation, and in the late summer and fall they work like little demons piling up their winter's supply of plants in little haycocks. "Making hay" is the most noteworthy thing they do.

But they haven't started on this interesting occupation yet, and it is time we were moving on. So let's travel on down toward the lake and leave these little lovers of the high places to scurry around in their boulders unmolested until another human chances to come by this way.

I REALLY WANTED TO TEACH (Lloyd)

After three years of high school teaching, I knew quite well that this was where I belonged. Never, alas, would I tread the ancient boards in Hamlet's black velvet doublet, in spite of all my dreaming. Never, I felt quite sure, would I stand in the Senate and, turning on my ultimate eloquence, rescue my country from some headlong plunge into stupidity. I was to be neither actor nor orator. But I could direct plays, perhaps even write them. And I could send shivers up the spines of 18-year-olds with Hamlet's brave and forlorn and heart-aching speeches. I could make young people into patriots, a few. I didn't need a stage or a Senate chamber; I just needed a classroom. And freedom! Freedom to do it my way, to use what gift I had in my own spontaneous fashion.

There were some things I needed to work out about education—some nebulous certitudes about the joys of the life of the mind. And they weren't in the textbooks on education. They had to do with enthusiasm, and carrying a fire around under one's cloak, a fire that you might permit to consume you gladly if you could just ignite somebody else.

This probably meant that that I would have to make some arrangements about being a big frog in a little puddle until I could find a bigger puddle that would have me. For I was determined to make some of my own decisions when it came to teaching. I was 25. I had a wife and a small daughter. And I was making $1120 a year! When I had gone to Colorado Springs High School from the academy at the college, I was so anxious to head up their new biology department that it hadn't occurred to me to dicker over the salary. They, of course, gave me a generous raise over my Cutler Academy salary and paid me a munificent $1060 for my first year's teaching. And then they paid me $1120 for my second year.

$1120 for a year's hard work! Hours and hours a week outside the classroom, including coaching all the plays and an astronomy club that I worked up myself that went orbiting off into Colorado's clear and chilly heavens one night a week. And still my monthly paycheck was in two figures! This was in 1916, remember. The maximum at the high school was $1800.

I had replaced two people when I went to Colorado Springs High School—an athletic manager who was paid a salary for managing football alone, a more or less full-time job; and a part-time dramatic coach. This was in addition to my own job of carrying the biology department alone. Occasionally some school official would remark that I was doing the best job in the science department; and then someone interested in football would commend me for handling the managerial job "better than it had been handled in years." Then another of my superiors would tell me what a good job I was doing for dramatics in the high school, that they had not had anyone for years who had done that particular job as well. I would gently remind these people that the last dramatic director had been paid more for that job alone than I was being paid for handling a full teaching load and doing her job besides, and he would admit that it seemed unfair. But they had learned that it was best for the dramatic director to be a member of the regular teaching staff. I must be patient, they would say.

I went to Superintendent Hill. He assured me that I was doing a good job in all departments, that he was most pleased with me. "But I can't pay my bills!" I said. "I am always running behind, regardless of how careful I am." Yes, he would admit that; it was unfortunate that I had started too low. I reminded him specifically concerning the amount of my salary and that of others in the science department. He was embarrassed, but said," That's right, Lloyd, you started too low, but you will soon be working up to the maximum." I thought of the eight or ten years it would take me to reach it, and I thought, of course, that perhaps I could start at the higher figure someplace else. Mr. Hill looked alarmed, but he assured me that I didn't know what the future held for me. "Just go on, you are doing fine!"

The "system" loomed above me, a mountain that I would not be permitted to go around. I must climb laboriously over the top, a step at a time. And during that time, if I wished to keep from going deeper into debt, I must escape all illnesses, I must not have another child. I must not buy books or music for my phonograph. Any financial emergency, such as a big doctor or hospital bill simply had to be absorbed by my pitiful little budget—five dollars a month to the doctor, five dollars a month to the hospital, for there was no hospitalization insurance in those days, no group insurance of any kind for a number of years to come. I was not thinking very many years into the future, or I would have been appalled at the lack of any sort of retirement provision in most of Colorado. I just wanted to pay my current bills.

At last I made up my mind. I would have to go. I turned in my resignation to the superintendent, and I started writing letters yet again, scattering applications all over the west.

One day Mr. O. E. Hemenway, the leading grocer in Colorado Springs and a very fine man, phoned and asked me to come down and see him. I appeared very promptly. He sat back and looked me over and then said that he had heard that I was leaving the high school. I admitted that I had reached that decision. "You are right," he said. "They should pay you more." Then with the quizzical smile that was so endearing and so characteristic, he said, "How would you like to be superintendent of Cheyenne School?"

"Cheyenne School, out by the canyon?" I asked.

"Yes. It's a small school now, but it has a certain future." He smiled. "You would be superintendent and principal and teacher, all in one!"

A monstrous big frog in a very tiny puddle, I thought.

"What would it pay?" I asked, and I explained that it was salary alone that was causing me to leave Colorado Springs High School. I told him that I had all but decided to accept the superintendency at Silverton, Colorado at a salary of at least $1800. But my mind was beginning to spin. Silverton—caught to be sure in a bowl of peaks, and just below timberline in a situation of great majesty; but such a Siberian sort of a valley even in summertime, and such Arctic peaks and so closed away from the world. Cheyenne Canyon: the school stood just across the road from where the creek was blanketed in English buttercups in June, and the woods were flowering with thimbleberry and New Jersey tea and Colorado ninebark and simply alive with birds, and the eye would lift from the school yard to the gracious rising of Cheyenne Mountain, and then to the triangular summit of St. Peter's Dome, and beautiful Rosa that Charles Kingsley named, and my own beloved Baldy. "You would be superintendent and principal and teacher all in one!" Freedom! Freedom to do it my way. (Alas, I didn't know much about parents yet or school boards.) I suppose I must have been laying out my program right then and there while Mr. Hemenway was talking, for what could one not do with bird-wild woods in the school yard and mountains within walking distance.

Mr. Hemenway was saying that it might take a year to get up to $1800. Miss Sheridan, he was pretty sure, was getting $1600, and they were not likely to pay her successor more than that, for she was greatly loved and was leaving to take a position in the Department of Agriculture. I think I had already made up my mind. I told Mr. Hemenway that I would leave the details to him. "There is one thing, Lloyd," he said, "say nothing about this and do absolutely nothing about it until you hear from me. In that case, I think I can promise you the job."

So that is the way things are done, I thought. I had had confidence in Mr. Hemenway ever since I was a boy, so I told him that I would trust him and that I would much rather be in the Pikes Peak region than anywhere else in the world. "Perhaps," I said, "after a couple of years, I could re-apply at Colorado Springs High School at a proper salary."

I stopped sending out applications, and when Mr. Hemenway sent for me again, I went eagerly. "Lloyd!" he said, "things are going fine. There have been a lot of applications, and now it is time for you to go into a very subdued bit of action. I want you to phone each of the board members and make a date to meet them and their wives in their homes, just for a short visit. I want them to know who you are. But I don't want them to have the least chance to get tired of you." (How well he knew me and my talkative ways!) "Make it as short as possible, and I think you had better start on Mr. and Mrs. Perkins."

Immediately, I called Mr. Perkins and arranged to call upon him and his wife that evening. I appeared at exactly the hour agreed upon. I behaved my very best for that wonderful couple, and after a few minutes I took my leave. They begged me to stay, but I had carefully arranged a previous engagement. As I left, Mr. Perkins squeezed my arm and said, "Good work! Exactly right!"

The next evening I arrived promptly to meet Mr. C. D. Weimer, owner and manager of Seven Falls, and his charming wife. I hit the door at exactly the time agreed upon. I stayed, and I scattered all the charm I knew how to scatter for a few minutes. And then, in spite of the fact that I was having a very good time and was enjoying these delightful people very much, I hurried away. Dear Cal and Elsie Weimer, I was hoping they would think it wise to offer me the job. I could not possibly dream what stores of love and loyalty and understanding they were to offer me—what stimulating excitement as the experiments developed later on.

The next evening belonged to the third and last member of the board, Mr. John Hinch, a local contractor. Here was a double hazard, for Mrs. Hinch had also once been a member of the School Board and was a former teacher and a lady of great gifts and abilities. I was a little terrified, but I went promptly as before, turned on all the charm I could generate, and feared I had offended them by leaving so soon.

Then I went down to see Mr. Hemenway the next day, feeling that I should report, but he had heard all about it. "Good work!" was all he said. "Now lie low, and I mean low. It may be rather late in August before you hear from them again. But you will hear, and you will be offered the job." It took faith, but I believed him and went about my other activities. It was all surprising and rather strange, we thought, Dorothy and I. Why this honest friend and good businessman had undertaken to become my voluntary agent I could not guess. He didn't even live in the Cheyenne School district! And what was important about it anyway? My friends would be horrified when they heard about the size of the puddle in which I was deciding to become a big frog.

About the middle of August when my faith was really faltering, Mr. Perkins called me up, on the summit of Mt. Manitou where I was living, and said "We elected you last night to be the new superintendent of Cheyenne School, but I'm awfully sorry that, do what I would, I couldn't quite bring them up to $1800. They refuse to go a cent beyond Miss Sheridan's salary. I hope very much that you can find it possible to accept." Thinking fast for a moment, I said yes. And my life took a right-angle turn up a tall and different mountain.

.

THE BEGINNINGS AT CHEYENNE
(Enid and Lloyd)

Lying outside the city, Cheyenne Mountain School was its own school district, thus giving its principal the elevated title of superintendent. The school lay between Cheyenne Boulevard and Cheyenne Road, south and west of Colorado Springs. No roads anywhere in Colorado Springs were yet paved, but there was a streetcar line that ran along Cheyenne Boulevard on the north side of the school.

Even for a rural school, Cheyenne was startlingly small. The entire student body, first grade through high school, numbered only 98 children in the fall of 1916. Two grades of students shared a room, with the four classrooms on the ground floor housing grades one through eight. There were two more classrooms upstairs for the high school students, plus a small auditorium, the principal's office, and a study area with two large tables. Despite its modest size, the previous spring the school had been designated a "Superior School," one of only two third-class district schools in the state to win that honor. Lloyd had the plaque proclaiming the honor installed on an outer wall of the building and held a festive unveiling to the cheers of the school community.

Of the opening of this, his first year at Cheyenne, Lloyd wrote, "At last school opened in the fall of 1916. A horde of parents to meet, a horde of new kids to meet, a horde of everything all thrown at you at once. It was an exciting and gorgeous day!"

71

Having emerged only three years previously from college himself, and having taught at only the high school level, Lloyd was unprepared for the little ones. He wrote, "I was completely shattered by the first grade. When I dropped in and saw their great eyes shining, I was undone. Tears welled up and I wanted to cry. Out of sheer love for them, for their eagerness, I wanted to cry! They are the loveliest things in all the world. Eager and unafraid. Breathless with an eagerness that reaches out toward you with a wistful happiness. All their little lives they have waited for this day. At last it is here now! They present themselves to you all quivering with excitement for you to perform the miracles of life on them. They throw themselves at you with all their tiny mights. Let's start. Let's immediately make them into the wonderful beings that they long to be. Look into their eyes on the first day of school, and you'll never be the same again!" Returning Lloyd's affection, the first graders took to waiting for him to arrive each morning. They would throng around him, each trying to lay claim to one of his fingers, to conduct him into the school building.

He quickly learned that the students at Cheyenne School had little experience with parties. He wrote, "I taught them to play. I really had to teach them, slowly and deliberately, how to let their hair down and have a good time. And, oh, what good times they soon learned to have! Even some of the parents, hearing so much about it, wanted to come down. We'd let them come, provided they would agree to enter in and play with us. We had only one inviolable rule—no mere onlookers.

"I was surprised to see how the small grounds of Cheyenne School were covered with rocks, small rocks, big rocks, a multitude of rocks. So we arranged to have a contest, a rock-picking-up contest, to clear our grounds. We put the girls on one side and the boys on the other. We let them bring baskets, small wagons, anything they could think of to carry the rocks. We let them build up a true competitive spirit for a few days until it got quite intense. Then on a Friday afternoon we turned them loose for a couple of hours. How they worked! How the stones piled up! They worked like fury, and the two piles of stones grew and grew incredibly. We almost had them digging for stones at the end of the two hours. They laughed and hollered as they worked. Everybody was happy, and the playground was completely changed. It was fit for human beings at last, and ready for children to run and scramble and have a wonderful time. It was lovely.

"Immediately afterward, we had a big barbecue, or we called it that, even if it was only a wienie roast, and we sang and sang. It is the spirit you bring to a party that makes it wonderful or that makes it just another bore. It doesn't matter what you do so long as you laugh heartily. The finest party in the world, given by the finest party director with the finest decorations, is a complete failure if it lacks wholesome laughter and joyous enthusiasm. What parties we would have! We really learned to play. Every Friday night, it seems to me, we had another party, each one a bigger success than the one before it. I discovered sources whose existence I had never suspected as I tracked down old American games to play. The spirit was beautiful."

Lloyd was fascinated by the area of native woodland that lay beyond Cheyenne Road south of the school. Aside from a trail that led up to Broadmoor, he described it as "exactly as nature had left it, with stream bank flowers and bushes and all the birds that could be expected at that elevation. There were even a half dozen gnarled and twisted apple trees that had crept in from somewhere and were a pink and white joy of blossom each spring. The stream bank of early spring was simply golden with buttercups, an English species that I learned an English woman had brought as seed from England and planted along the tiny creek. They were very beautiful with their rich, golden petals shining over a bed of lush, green feather leaves.

"One of my worries a little later was a 'chili parlor and eating joint' that had been built right opposite the school on the creek side of Cheyenne Road. It became the headquarters of the always dissatisfied and their talk against the school and the way it was being run. When the county was ready to rebuild the road, I talked them into putting it a little to the south of this store. We thereby straightened out several things including the road. I went to the Stratton estate [the entity entrusted with managing the wealth and land of Winfield Scott Stratton, an early settler in Colorado Springs, who, after many years of prospecting, struck it rich in the gold fields of Cripple Creek] who owned the property across from the school. They generously agreed to give it to the school for little or nothing if we would agree that it would never be used for any other purpose than for the school.

"We held a small bond election to cover the purchase of the little store building and other incidental expenses. We changed the store into a little much-needed kindergarten. It was just before the summer vacation, so we had a few months to get it ready. We studied the little square, flat-roofed building, and I wondered and wondered how to adapt it into an acceptable kindergarten. Then the inspiration came to me: make it into a little New Mexican building. It would be very attractive (and also very cheap to do so.) I got to figuring: we could build a little porch on the front of it, the side facing the school, and we could cover this porch with sod and plant flowers on top. We could build it of cedar logs for the uprights, and give it a pueblo flare.

"Then if we covered the whole building in concrete in an adobe color and put a little coping around the top, we would have it. So I set an architect friend of mine on the job, and we had a perfect little pueblo building in no time at all. We decided to paint the woodwork of the doors and windows a pale blue like the buildings we had seen in Santa Fe. As they finished, the little structure was a dream of loveliness.

"Then the interior began to worry me. We had all the little chairs finished in Spanish light blue paint. We put linoleum tile on the floor. Then we talked the painter Lloyd Moylan into doing a mural for the little building, a picture that would be decorative and

74

yet an integral part of the building, a picture of little Indian children and a little donkey. Lloyd achieved a perfectly lovely painting that you might enter the room without even noticing at first.

"But my kindergarten teacher was insistent that she wanted a blackboard. My heart sank! A row of blackboards in that lovely little building and all its charm would be gone. It would be just another school room. So I pondered and pondered and at last came to an idea. We took some old blackboard slate and had it cut into kindergarten size. We arranged a little railroad train on a child's more or less winding (and up and down a little) railroad track. We arranged our little slates gracefully along the wall and surrounded each with the outlines of a railroad car, with bright red wheels, and a locomotive with a big stack, and they rolled along the uncertain tracks, taking the children to the place where dreams are born.

"The little building was eventually outgrown by the school population, but once dreams did grow there, and the flowers grew too on the sod roof of the little porch. And in the blessed Christmas season, the flickering lights of dozens of candles in luminarios burned along the top of the wall each evening as they do in the old villages and towns of our great Southwest.

"We had already bought the old alfalfa field immediately to the west of the school and converted it into a larger playground, our athletic field. Now there was nothing to do but buy the property south of the road clear to the creek, and I started talking to the Stratton Estate   We frankly didn't want any more hangouts across from the school. We very much wanted the creek bank as a nature study area 'in perpetuity.' The Stratton Estate was very cooperative and gave us this land for school use for a very small sum.

"This gave us the land clear down to the old school house on the other side of the road. We built trails through it, we bridged it with a narrow little footbridge for those who wanted to use this route on the way to their homes in Broadmoor, and we built a theater-in-the-woods and finally a Scout house over on the creek bank.

"With the straight new road hacked through by the county, and a fine road it was, the expanded Cheyenne School ground simply cried for a new fence. But when we thought of a barbed-wire fence or a picket fence or, worst of all, a woven wire fence, my heart almost stopped. We wanted something as lovely as the school we dreamed. I began studying fences, and believe me, that is a discouraging job. I found nothing that suited me. It's all right for a little building or a little yard, to have a row of nice white pickets or redwood boards running up and down, but for a big school ground it wouldn't do at all. The dominant vertical lines simply ruined the effect we want to achieve. And most fences in that day were predominantly vertical.

"The more I looked, the more I worried. We wanted a fence with horizontal lines dominant, and I didn't know how to get it. At last I went up to Mr. Crissy of Crissy Fowler Lumber Company and talked to him about it. I even drew the sort of fence I wanted, and suddenly his face lit up. A dealer in Florida had just offered him some long cedar poles, and they would do the trick. The price was right. They would last practically forever, they would be rough and beautiful, and so I ordered a car load sent up for my fence. He agreed to keep anything that I didn't use.

"Mac was working for us then, a splendid yard man, as fine as they come, a man of great energy and imagination. We turned the main job over to Mac. He set the large cedar posts about ten feet apart and strung two horizontal slender poles of cedar, one near the top of the posts and the other near the bottom, to give us the dominance of the long horizontal lines. Then we placed two of the smaller more slender poles in each of these spaces, crossing each other diagonally in the middle of the space and fitting tightly into the four junctions of the uprights and the larger horizontals. He tapered each of the smaller poles carefully and bored holes in the upright poles so they would fit exactly. We had achieved a masterpiece.

"But now the gateways had to be considered, and we gave more and more study to them. We decided on large stone columns, built of rough stone from our own grounds, and each one topped with a cement block that carried out the lines of the roof of the school. We put a pair of these pillars at the end of the long walk that had so lately been Cheyenne Road and now connected the schoolyard with Cheyenne Road at the west end and at the east end beyond our fine grove of yellow pines. On the north side of the building we had a little viaduct connecting with a little covered waiting porch at the street car stop alongside Cheyenne Boulevard. The effect was charming.

"On the south side, where we must have an entrance from Cheyenne Road, we laid out a great circle with huge rough granite rocks, taking in the width of the erstwhile road and a little more. Here, the few cars could park, or an overflow of little girls could jump rope. Between the two entrances to this circle we set a stone wall that dipped in the middle, sloping up gracefully to the posts that anchored them on each end, and we planted a little plot of grass inside this wall.

"Someone brought a great basket of violet plants, and we set them in between the big rocks where they flourished and furnished endless bouquets for teachers until the small newcomers learned, very gently, that they were for 'everybody to look at,' not just their for their squinched tight little hands.

"On Arbor Day we had a woodbine planting. Everyone who could rustle a few plants brought a basketful of them. The grades were ranged in platoons all along the fence, each covering a certain yardage, and in one joyous day we set out many hundreds of roots that grew, in a few years, to a glorious green drapery along parts of the school fence, making such a beautiful showing in the fall that people used to drive out from all over town to see this curtain of wine-colored leaves half hiding our lovely cedar fence.

Until the woodbine was well established, each grade was responsible for watering its yardage. You could see them marching out at recess with their little cans and buckets, each child carefully watering the roots he or she had set out.

"Across the road at the entrance to our nature study preserve we erected a large log gateway, with swing gates, which we ordinarily kept locked, with little foot gates open on either side, and over the top we had a large sign painted "Theater-in-the-woods" with a path leading to our outdoor theater.

"Several landscape architects, taken with the beauty of the little fence and the stone gateway, came to ask questions about them. One couple from Denver I remember especially, who had frequent jobs in Broadmoor, came to say that we had achieved the 'perfect fence' with its preponderance of horizontal lines. They were very enthusiastic. And it *was* a lovely fence. A ball batted above it would find a couple of youngsters scurrying through the fence and recovering it and throwing it back. Decades later after I left Cheyenne, the school district had to build the unsightly impenetrable fences of the modern school yard."

As for the funding for such projects, Lloyd wrote, "Money is never a question where there is enough love and enthusiasm. It just takes care of itself. Pass the hat and get more than you really need whenever you are short. You don't have to beg. You only have to mention it where the spirit is right. As long as you are perfectly honest, and they are convinced that you will use the money only for the needs of the cause in which they are sharing, there is never the least question raised."

Once the little woodland called the nature preserve was acquired, bird study became a school-wide passion, one that would last for the 35 years of Lloyd's tenure. He started a bird club, which meant that the children would feed and study the birds in the nature preserve. They built a little bird hospital for injured birds and learned how to set broken wings. One student was designated to take buckets of bird seed through the little woodland and fill all the bird feeding trays. At the same time the nature preserve served many other purposes. The amphitheater built there was the scene of many a play, musical concert, and dance production.

Having played football in college, Lloyd thought the next step was to form a football team. "We had an up and growing spirit, and I decided that the best thing to tie it to was a fine football team. Football was fun, and the handicap of small enrollment at Cheyenne School made it that much more challenging. With fewer than 50 pupils in the four grades of high school, with more than half of them girls, it left us about 20 boys from which to pick a team. Some of them obviously couldn't play, so we actually had to include a few boys from our seventh and eighth grades. But we had a good team, a rather startling team!"

They managed to beat the teams at Cripple Creek and even Pueblo, a much larger school. The Colorado Springs newspaper made so much of these victories that even big Colorado Springs High School was goaded into scheduling a game with Cheyenne School the following season. In the intervening year Lloyd read everything he could find about football strategy, settling on a limited number of plays, including a forward pass that he invented and considered a work of art. For practice he had to divide his 17 or 18 boys into two teams to practice offense and defense.

The next autumn when the team was to meet Colorado Springs High School, Lloyd told his team, "You'll win the toss. Do the unheard-of thing and choose to kick to them. Then play so hard, tackle so clean and so hard that they fumble the ball. Get it and I want a touchdown from you in the first minute of play. Let's beat them before the game gets started!" His team followed instructions, scoring within the first two minutes of play, and won the game 29-0, the worst defeat for CSHS in five years. As the little team's fame spread, the larger schools became reluctant to risk defeat at the hands of such a small school.

The school fielded an equally determined basketball team, and Lloyd also made a study of basketball strategy. The team played well but lost to teams from some of the larger schools. Lloyd reminisced, "And so our year of inter-scholastic triumph just sort of poofed out. I came out with the difficult announcement that we would play no more such games. In fact, for a few years, we would not play interscholastic sports at all. (We would later resume interscholastic basketball and track.) Dozens of parents in the community immediately started a terrible howl! They seriously recommended that we close Cheyenne School completely—just fold it up and admit that we were done. But my loyal school board stood by me and said not a word in public except to express complete confidence in how I was running the school.

"Somehow or other I had a very stubborn idea that games should never become more important, for instance, than the study of English or Latin. I had the feeling that athletics didn't need to completely blot out a genuine love of mathematics. We were there first for the purposes of running a school, and these other things had simply become a little too important with us. So we would go on with the job of running our school for a while, and we would wait for this furor to die down a bit.

"Incidentally, I realized that the girls had nothing much to do in a strong athletic program for the boys. There was no development for them that was at all worthy of serious consideration. There was nothing much for them to do but to become somewhat self-inflated worshippers of the team, strutting their whipped-up enthusiasm before a great crowd of people. It somehow didn't seem quite right to me.

"Some of the more aggravated egos on my team moved up to Colorado Springs High School. It amused me somewhat to see how few of them ever made a team up there. After the first wild furor of their departure and all the predictions of the end of Cheyenne School, we soon settled down to our own delightful enthusiasms and began having more fun than we had ever had before.

"It was up to me to turn the activities of the school into some line that would be more rewarding. So we took up skiing, just then being started in this country. We were practically the first group in this part of Colorado to indulge in this famous sport. We soon rented the old Crescent Ranch, an old ranch house up by Divide, 30 miles west of Colorado Springs, and spent weekend after weekend up there, skiing in that high and glorious country. We carried on this sport for years.

"We also started a Mountain Club and began putting registers on the tops of all our mountain peaks, but the Colorado Mountain Club, which had been in operation for a little while in Denver, soon heard of us and absorbed us into their membership. We became the Pikes Peak Branch of the Colorado Mountain Club. We had to change our board of directors to all adult members, and it was not long until the school, as such, had lost all connection with it.

"Our school was growing very rapidly now. We were fast approaching a count of a hundred pupils in our high school alone! We had to build new rooms onto our building to make room for them all, and we added a gymnasium and an auditorium. We were definitely going places, but I didn't know quite where! Then the students decided to buy a cabin that was up Cheyenne Canon about three miles above the school.

"The purchase of the cabin was one of the finest things Cheyenne School ever did. It was a large cabin, with a front porch clear across the width, hanging high above the steep slope on which it stood. It gave a magnificent view of South Cheyenne Canyon, Cheyenne Mountain, and the plains lying out beyond. Close by was a beautiful little waterfall. The cabin had a large fireplace at the end opposite the porch, and around the corner from this big room was the kitchen with cupboards and a big stove.

"The cabin had been beautifully built by a group of young bachelors in town, artistic young men. They had subsequently gotten married and decided to sell the cabin. We paid them $1000 for it (it was on government land) and put several hundred more dollars into improvements.

"It was quite an undertaking for us, for the school board, of course, could give us no help. We managed it by borrowing the money from ourselves. We gave the students and the teachers interest-bearing notes, and the students advanced the funds mostly from what they had saved for college. We fixed each note so it would be completely paid back, including interest, by the time the student was ready for college. We never failed on a single note. We gave plays and special events at which we could make a little money, and we managed the whole affair with no strain.

"We decided to build in under the porch, which was completely open to the wind below. So we built a bunk room there. Then we built a long bench clear around the big room and built it well enough that it would hold all our bedding and supplies. We built folding tables and a place to store them so we could seat 50 or 60 at a meal. We got really busy.

"It was over a mile from the streetcar line to Seven Falls. Then the long hike up the hundreds of steps, and then a trail for three or four miles up to the cabin. There was no road that a car could travel. Oh, what carrying parties we had at first! Carrying the lumber and the mattresses up to the cabin, carrying them all the way up this long, steep trail—we did it! Youngsters were thoroughly used to hiking then. There were few cars in the world, and the students had practically no access to them. We were a walking generation.

"Two husky boys with two long boards (1"x12") from 14 to 16 feet long, tied by a rope over their shoulders and hanging on each side of them at arm's length, would take the four or five miles up to the cabin, going up the long steps of Seven Falls, twisting and turning on the narrow trail, and they would deliver their boards at the cabin without a word being said. Or the huskier boys would take a mattress and roll it and bind it carefully as tightly as they could and rig up a tumpline over their heads like an Indian and carry the thing clear up to the cabin. This was too much for one boy, so he always had another big fellow hiking along with him ready to take his turn on the heavy load every now and then. I'll never forget the big Victrola I packed up on my back and how the weight of the thing increased incredibly as I got higher and higher into the mountains.

"But we were all used to climbing and thought little of it. Nearly every weekend there was a party of some kind at the cabin. And some of the faculty had to go as chaperones—often just up to the cabin for a supper party, with the committee carrying all the load of food. And after supper, what singing around the fire. And after that, what a wonderful adventure coming down the trail in the ink-black night or under a friendly moon. Often a weekend party involved carrying more food and sleeping at the cabin for a couple of nights. It was part of our routine. We all loved it!

"Committees of us would work on the trail, widening it and straightening it, with pick and shovel, saw and axe. We even built a couple of miles of new trail, gradually widening it until we made quite a path. At last a family at Sweetwater, down the next valley, built a road over from the Stage Road on Cheyenne Mountain. So we built a sort of road taking off from this for over a mile up to our cabin. It was some road! We even built a narrow bridge across Cheyenne Creek. Eventually I had a Ford with a Moore's auxiliary transmission that could make it clear up to a spot behind our cabin. But we had trained our Ford to shut its eyes and not watch where it was going—just trust to the wheel, and we'd get there.

"Dorothy and I, and our two children, spent several summers at the old school cabin, with high school youngsters running up the trail every now and then to see us or to spend the night with us. It was a glorious spot and one of the richest memories I have of the old Cheyenne School."

BLESSED ARE THE PURE IN HEART
(Dorothy)

The new young superintendent sat and looked across his orderly desk at the group of mothers who faced him. He had asked them to come, and they did not know why, but they sensed trouble and were on their guard. He felt inexperienced and inadequate, but he could not dodge what he had to do, and the sooner the better. He wished he knew more about mothers, and especially these mothers, whom he had chosen carefully in order that the presence of the obviously blameless might disarm the possibly guilty.

It was such a little while since he himself had been 13 or 15 or 18. He knew perfectly well about the biological urges of young human animals. But he didn't believe in human animals of any age. He didn't believe that the mind and the spirit ever had to give over the reins and let the animal fraction run away with them. He believed that the thing to do with an unruly energy was to sublimate it into some creative action of the spirit or translate it into some vigorous and meaningful action of the body. He felt desperately in need of help about this. Out of some small inner cupboard of his mind he drew forth his pedagogical vocabulary.

"I thank you for coming," he said. "You'll think me very presumptuous to be diagnosing problems so early in my administration, but the fact is that I do have problems and I need your help. Please understand that you are just a representative small group that I have asked to come because I am afraid that a meeting of all the mothers might degenerate into a free-for-all. I'm not implying that your children are involved. I just have to tell you that I have been carefully sorting out rumors and proven facts for some weeks now, and I can't avoid the conclusion that our boys and girls, some of them, have some thoroughly wrong ideas about their relationship to each other, and they have been putting those ideas into action."

It was very hard for him to say, and there were some little embarrassed gasps as his meaning came clear, and then a shift to the defensive. He went on.

"I just wanted to tell you that I won't have it. I want you to know right now at the beginning where I stand, that there is no compromise and never will be. I want you to realize that I am likely to talk to your children pretty earnestly. As long as I am in this school, or any other school, I am insisting on a wholesome bunch of kids. I will not tolerate inappropriate talk, and I shall fight inappropriate behavior (which I realize I cannot control outside of the school grounds and school hours) at the first inkling of it within my jurisdiction."

He was remembering with fresh awareness the warnings about this community that had been so earnestly sounded by his friends. He knew he was walking on eggs. And he was comforted to see that, while some of the women looked as if they might be about to explode, some of them were looking grateful and were nodding their heads a little bit.

"We all need help all the time," he said, "and that goes for the children first of all. They need help from you as well as from the school staff. They haven't anything to do with each other. There isn't any mutual activity for the boys and girls on a reasonable, wholesome basis. They don't seem to have any conception about how to play together, and here they are, day after day, shut up in a school house together, and all they are doing is thinking about each other—and what they are thinking is not healthy. I may not be able to change their thinking, at least not right away, but I intend to change their behavior if it is the last thing I do. There is far too much talk about all this among the children and in the community, and first of all I want the talk stopped. Please, you can help to stop it. I want the mothers to stop talking about other women's children and to start thinking about their own. Could you spread the word around? And if anyone says it isn't my business, just ask them, please, what they *do* have me here for—just to transfer information from books into their children's heads? Or have they a right to expect me to try to help make civilized and decent human beings out of these children? If you must talk to someone, talk to their fathers. And if their fathers would like to talk to me, I should welcome them—although I do have a lot of faith in mothers.

"I intend to fight this myself in every waking minute as long as a child is close enough to be under my control. And I've got one plan so far. It always worked for me and my friends when we were this age. If you don't mind, I'm going to try to keep them so busy they won't have time to think. Will you be patient with me if it seems to you that I have them doing projects and taking part in activities for hours, where you and I will know what they are doing, even if they are out until nine o'clock? I don't know yet what I will think up, but I wanted to tell you that whatever it is, this will be the *why* for it. We've got to teach these kids to play together and to work together. And that's what I mean to try to do. Don't you see, this will be good for all of them at once, without having to single out the ones who have a behavior problem and who are causing us this anxiety. Will you go home and think about it? Don't *talk* to somebody—think about it first. Think what you can do to help.

"And this is definite—no quarter. I have just told the boys and girls this separately: people who write anything inappropriate on anything on these school premises will be dealt with right now, and that means expulsion. And students who say anything inappropriate will be severely disciplined, if I catch them, and that goes for anyone whose behavior is vulgar. You'll be hearing about a lot of things that I won't stand for as time goes by and the occasions arrive, but this is the first one—and I've told your children today—we're going to be clean! Clean bodies, of course, clean speech, clean minds. Think about it. You do agree with me, don't you?"

Some of them exploded. *Their* children were as pure as the driven snow. Some of them knew whose children weren't and wished they could talk about it. Some of them wrung his hand and said "Thank you."

"Thank you for coming," he said and closed the door behind him.

He stopped and faced himself. "You idiot!" he said ruefully and not aloud. "Now you are going to have to spend the rest of your days thinking up things for them to do!"

"What fun!" he answered himself, perfectly rationally.

BUILDING A SCHOOLHOUSE (Lloyd)

What fun in our youth to build our dreams! But I am sure that in my wildest day-dream I never planned to build a schoolhouse! As we turned into February of 1920, we realized that we simply had to do something about our school building. Our enrollment had increased 300 per cent in three years. So we sent out a letter to all our patrons, describing the plight in which we found ourselves. The letter, taking the one chance in four years to use such a date, was Feb. 29. The response was excellent, and we immediately called a general meeting for the next week and discussed the whole business. We stated our plight and answered all their questions.

We had decided to add, besides our new classrooms, a gymnasium, an auditorium, a domestic science room, a dining room, a library, and even, at this first meeting, a swimming pool. It took us three more days to survey the situation and to decide the swimming pool was out of the question. So we immediately posted our notices for an election on a bond issue for $100,000. (How little that would build today!)

The publicity was immediate and wonderful! There was even an editorial in the paper entitled "Cheyenne School—the Model." In it they said, "Right now they have one of the best schools in the state, the best in many respects, but they are not content with it . . . They want to make it an institution unique in the country . . . a model for education." We passed the bond issue with only six votes against us, in just 30 days, on April 17. The Parent Teacher Association gave a big chicken supper with everybody invited, to help celebrate this "unique" victory. We were very happy!

Now we faced the problem of time. To start building, to have the school ready for entrance the next fall, would hurry us, so we decided to concentrate everything on the additions to the classrooms and the remodeling of the old building and leave the gymnasium, the auditorium, and the new building completely until we had finished the first job. So, quickly we went at it. The plans were drawn, and the workmen were already beginning their preliminary changes before we finished school that spring.

We had to increase the window sizes on the east and west sides, for we were completely eliminating the windows to the north and south. This proved more expensive than we had figured, but what wide sunny vistas it gave us. When it came to tacking the six new classrooms onto the south end of the building, I immediately became interested in the possibility of split-level architecture. What a wonderful chance for half-flights of stairs, with my office and the classroom above it between stories. And how parents of recalcitrant children learned to hate them later on when they had to climb the flights in full view of all the hallways. ("Hey, Bill, your mother's in the office!") On the other hand I could see almost everything that went on in the whole building. Perfect!

Blithely confident that 20 was the ideal class, I figured that a room designed to hold but 20 would keep the enrollment at that figure. Imagine my chagrin later when we had to crowd from 30 to 40 pupils in each of these rooms.

At the north end of the building we had to build completely new staircases, split level again, and where they ended, we roughed in a partition to hold until we got the rest of the building completed. This left us a small room, later to be the coach's office, and we built a crude lean-to against it that could be used for a shower room, since abundant plumbing ended there, waiting for the real locker room of the new building.

Otto Engelking, our contractor, put his heart and his whole imagination into the job. He decided that he could slide the great slate roof of the original building to the south and cover the addition, thus saving the expense of tearing down and rebuilding this great angled slate roof. He finally convinced me, and I secured the permission of the board. So when the new south walls were completed, he bolted in the 2x8s that were to cap them, and rolled the whole roof south on short pieces of two or three-inch pipe until he had it in place. He watched for dry weather, and we got only a few drops of rain, which did no harm. A real downpour would have ruined all the ceilings in the naked rooms below. But he got away with it, and the new roofing, which he had ready and waiting, was up almost before the old roof had completely taken its trip and was almost immediately covered with tarred paper. He still talks about it with pride, and I don't blame him!

The old Cheyenne School was a brick building. The whole of the new building was to be covered with cement, or plaster, roughed up for looks. I liked the drawing very much, but the architect let the plasterer change the projecting line that ran about a foot below the windows. When I saw them chopping off the projecting brick of this line that I loved, I became alarmed, and I protested to the architect. He laughed at me until I brought him out and made him look at the building from down the road. Then he admitted that the windows would look like great footless arches unless the line was lowered to its original place below the windows. He agreed completely, and while he tried to get me to pay for the change of plans, which I adamantly refused to do, he had the original line restored at his own expense.

We were a few days late, but we started school in this new building on September 20. In the fall of 1922 we held the formal opening of the new addition to Cheyenne School. It was all finished outside, and the inside was completely finished except the gymnasium and the auditorium. The gymnasium had rough flooring and no railing round the balcony as yet. You could fall off easily if you didn't watch your step. And a few people did! The auditorium had only the rough flooring, and we still had to order the seats. But you could go in and look at it, and see what a wonderful place it was to be!

So we decided to have our formal opening. The Parent-Teacher Association had a great dinner prepared in the new dining room, and we prepared to open the whole building for everyone to see and investigate. We were all set to admire immensely what we had done and to marvel at our own accomplishment. It was a tremendous success!

We had to hold a second bond issue election in order to get $17,000 to finish the job. But that was a lark! There was not even a single vote against it. We were going places, and no one said us "Nay!"

We had begun to buy large oil paintings for the school, of which we were extremely proud. We had bought a great canvas of "the Arapahoe Peaks" by Charles Partridge Adams, as a memorial to Miss Hattie Evans, one of our beloved teachers who had died the spring before. It seemed somehow to catch her spirit. We had a large oil of "Indians Spearing Fish" by Bert Phillips of Taos, of which we were very proud. And we began acquiring a variety of prints of great value.

For instance, sometime later I heard of a set of prints from water colors of natives on horseback, ritual dances, and other intricate and truly Indian designs. They told me that these young Kiowa artists had been working as truck drivers and at whatever they could get in the world of the white man, and then the government had asked them to make these drawings for them. They were perfectly wonderful! No one could draw a horse as a Kiowa could! There were just a few sets left, my informant told me. So I raised the money and sent it to Washington and got one of the last sets and also an equally beautiful set of Pueblo Indian

91

designs. I have since been told, several times, that they are priceless now. But they simply hang on the walls of Cheyenne School without comment!

But the most valuable thing in the whole new building was the spirit of the kids. They were eager and unafraid! We had decided somehow to put a ban on that spirit of criticism, contempt, and assumed self-superiority that so many teenagers have. We were simply eager for all the marvelous experiences of life. Let other people sneer—we were going places for the fun of seeing what we could find. In the articles of the papers of that day, I am gratified by the tribute paid quite naturally to these fine youngsters again and again. I really believe they were unusual! They were as unusual as any youngster would be, who could be simple and natural and honest. They were just unspoiled American youth!

We had given our little Christmas play lovingly for the past several years, and the crowds that came to see it had grown larger and larger. Here we were with the little old auditorium just torn out and the new auditorium not yet finished, and we had no place in which to give our Christmas offering to the season. (The tickets were free, but when they were gone, they were gone, no matter how desperate some people were for additional tickets to materialize.)

Then one of the youngsters made the obvious proposal, and following his suggestion, we put on the play in our new unfinished gymnasium. We built a stage out of the lumber that was still on the site, we hung curtains where we could, we brought in truckloads of fragrant evergreens, we borrowed all the folding chairs we could borrow, and we put on our play. For several nights, until we were exhausted, we put it on to huge crowds that seemed to get as much of a lift from it as they ever got before.

In our regular plays, which we had given in the little auditorium, the group showed this same spirit. We built attractive approaches to the hall, we put on the plays with all the finish that we could. I had written all the plays for the school myself, taking advantage of the opportunity of adapting them to the possibilities of the then present cast. Our newspaper comments were positively exciting! And the crowds would often come out two or three nights to see our latest offering!

The last play we put on in the little auditorium was called "Timberline," and in it, after the first acts down on the porch of the cabin below, we set the final act at the mine itself at Timberline. A trail, a scraggly timberline tree (which we climbed up to our high mountains to get), and the tunnel leading into the mine! We had just built a room beyond the auditorium stage, in our new building, so I took advantage of this, and we ran the tunnel clear back across this room. Miners would enter the tunnel with their candles burning, and we would see them disappear farther down the dark tunnel. It was a sort of Cecil B. De Mille effect, and the papers raved about it! Our plays were very real! We gave them all we had!

[What is in a name? At some point the students began to call their superintendent and teacher "Pappy." At the current remove in time, the name sounds odd, perhaps countrified, but it somehow expressed their relationship to him. Any number of students have said, looking back on their school days, "Next to my father, he was the most influential man in my life." Later, generations of square dancers would also call Lloyd "Pappy."

There was another name that merited respect: Cheyenne Mountain School. It was named for a nearby mountain, and the mountain was named for people who had earlier lived in the region. As Cheyenne students participated in interscholastic sports, they adopted the team name, the Indians, and Lloyd took seriously the responsibility that came with the name. He believed that students at Cheyenne Mountain School should know and respect the people whose name they had taken—and whose land they occupied.

He approached the task on two fronts. First, as he wrote above, he began collecting artwork of the native people of the region. In addition to the paintings in the halls of the school, there was a collection of their headdresses, clothing, and pottery in display cases.

Then, since he couldn't take the entire school to visit a pueblo, he arranged to host at the school a Navajo weaver, a silversmith, and a sand painter. Before they came, Lloyd lectured to the students about the original inhabitants of the region and their traditions. Finally the day arrived when the artisans came, and all 12 grades of students spent the day watching them: the silversmith on the stage of the school auditorium, making jewelry from Mexican pesos and pieces of polished turquoise, and the weaver, who set up her loom in the cafeteria, carding lamb's wool and weaving a beautiful tapestry of color. To some the highlight of the day was watching the elderly sand painter. One student later wrote, "This was both art and religion, and we as students had been well prepared in advance that no pictures of the sand paintings were to be taken." They had also been taught to be perfectly quiet while watching the artisans. The larger lesson was understanding the cultural traditions of a people.

Another year a native American would erect his tipi on the campus and share his customs, stories, and songs with the students. There were also native American students who attended Cheyenne and were integral members of the student body. One of them, Joe Tafoya, danced through his willow hoops to a drumbeat provided by Lloyd as part of the Cheyenne Mountain Dancers. Howard Jones, son of the school bus driver of the same name, recalls the day that Maria Martinez came from the San Ildefonso pueblo to demonstrate how she made her internationally admired black-on-black pottery.

Lloyd also brought nationally known figures to speak to the student body. Graduates remember listening to George Washington Carver, Carl Sandburg, and, Edna St. Vincent Millay

Sandburg came more than once and is remembered by one graduate as a man with a shock of white hair who spoke while sitting on the edge of the stage with his feet dangling.]

DAVID RODNEY SHAW, 1917-1926
(Enid)

Lloyd and Dorothy became parents on June 16, 1915 when their daughter Doli was born, her name being the Navaho word for "bluebird." (She began her life as Winifred Doli but dropped the Winifred quite early in her childhood.) Sadly, there is little to report about David, Lloyd and Dorothy's beloved second child. He was two years and a few months younger than his sister. Like all children in the neighborhood, he enrolled in Cheyenne Mountain School. The one anecdote about him that has come down through the generations is a story that Lloyd recorded in his newspaper column.

"In the fall of 1923 we put our little boy, David, in the first grade. Wonderful Miss Lucy Nowels, his teacher, told me that she was delighted with his attitude. He was eager for work and was unafraid. So it rather surprised me early in the year to have her come to the office, with a little puzzlement on her face and ask me to come down and see what David was doing. I moved into the room and saw that all the children laying out plans for houses on their desks with little colored building sticks, slender and long. Each one had laid out a plan on the desk top and was delighted with the number of rooms to be had, regardless of whether most of them had doors or windows or not. They were very busy and very happy, and I enjoyed seeing them work.

"But gradually I moved over to see what David was doing, and I'll admit that I was baffled. He had a great pile of little sticks on his desk top, and they apparently made quite a heap and nothing more. But I stood and watched him, and while I was still puzzled, I had to admit that he was working intently and very happily on his great pile of unorganized sticks. Still, I could make nothing of what he was apparently building.

"At last I spoke to him gently, 'What are you building, David? I don't quite get you.'"

"He answered, 'A house!' He worked on quietly for a minute with the great patience children sometimes have for us, and then I asked, 'Who is going to live in it? I don't quite understand.' He looked up and answered, 'Beavers! It's a beaver house. Miss Nowels asked us to build a house, and it was the only kind of house I could think of built out of sticks like these. But it's awful hard to get an entrance hole, and to get it hollowed out so the beaver can go inside. But I'm getting it!'

"'Good work!' I said. 'Keep it up until you finish.'

"I drifted on and looked at the plans for houses the other children had built. I was a little proud of my boy and his sense of reality. So I slipped by his teacher on the way out and said, 'He's building a beaver house! Don't stop him.'

"'But it's such a mess,' Miss Nowels laughed, 'it has no plan, no order!' And I answered, 'No, it doesn't look like much. But after all, it looks more like a real beaver's house than the things the other children are building look like the houses we people live in! Praise him and commend him for his work when he is finished; flunk him if you think best, but don't let him know that he has flunked the assignment.'

"I have thought a good deal about it since! How early we learn to build and to draw things that have no resemblance to what we think we are drawing. Take a child's drawing of a man. Just a circle for a head and two eyes drawn in it like little circles, a triangle for a nose, and a big curved line for a mouth. Under this circle they draw a bigger circle to indicate the body. From the upper part of this second circle they draw a straight line for an arm on either side, terminated by five fingers, flaring out like a little brush. Add two more straight lines for legs, each ended in a little oval, which stands for the feet. It is just the crude plan of the general shape of a man, and if you are really ambitious you draw a dozen little stubby lines at the top of the skull, and that indicates the fact that most men have hair.

"It is very primitive! It is a diagram of a man, not the picture of a man. And it is absolutely necessary for children to begin to understand the world around them by drawing these schematic pictures of its creatures.

"But if a child should chance to misunderstand your intention and, instead of drawing the outline of a little house with the sticks you have given him, he sets himself to building the only house he has ever seen that is actually built of little sticks, I believe he needs encouragement. He is beginning to create something. And he will find it fascinatingly difficult to do. Walking out of the first grade room that day, I learned something about education. The expanding life always keeps moving into another dimension!"

In March of 1926, David became ill. Dr. Bortree, the family doctor, did what he could for the child. It was before antibiotics had been developed, and there was little the doctor could do to fight rheumatic fever. He attended David at home and signed the death certificate on March 25, 1926. A small funeral service was held in the home the next day, and David was buried in Evergreen Cemetery. Neither Lloyd nor Dorothy was a church goer at that time, so a complete stranger came into the family home to conduct the service.

Dorothy's memories of attending the Methodist church in Denver as a child consisted of getting motion sickness on the streetcar ride across town to church and then having her stomach further upset by the cigar smoke of the uncles back at home after the service. Lloyd grew up in a Baptist church where his father was superintendent of the Sunday school, both in Los Angeles and subsequently in Denver. Lloyd later wrote, "All that I distinctly remember is that I attended seven regular religious services a week and soon decided that I was paid up, in full, for my whole life." Nonetheless, he, Dorothy, and even their ten-year-old daughter Doli felt the lack of a church home when they faced the tragedy of losing David.

The grieving family spent that summer in Europe. Such a trip was not anything that they could have afforded had it not been for a generous friend. Bill Jackson, the stepson of the Colorado Springs author Helen Hunt Jackson, had become good friends with Lloyd at Colorado College. The two had hiked and climbed together all over the region. Coming from a wealthy family, Bill had been able to travel the world and thought it a pity that someone of Lloyd's education and intellectual curiosity could not afford to travel abroad. Tragically, Bill was killed while climbing above Seven Falls when he was still a young man. In his will he left $5000 to Lloyd and Dorothy to be used exclusively for travel in Europe. It was enough money in 1926 to pay for two long summers of European exploration. The family of three traveled that summer by ship to England and from there through Ireland, Scotland, Norway, Sweden, Germany, Switzerland, Italy, and France. It was a healing time for the little family as they adjusted to the loss of David. Four years later they would spend a second summer entirely in the British Isles.

On their first trip the family experienced an Anglican service read by the captain of the ship as they crossed the Atlantic. In England they attended an ambulatory service in Stratford on Avon. Doli, at least, liked even the sense of tradition that came with kneeling on a cold flagstone floor. Back in Colorado Springs, the family was interested in checking out the Episcopal Church. One day Paul Roberts, the rector of Grace Church, spoke at a Rotary meeting, and Lloyd found him interesting. Paul invited him to attend an evensong service. The two proceeded to have many a debate about religion. Lloyd protested that he couldn't believe all the claims stated in the creed. Paul replied that the creed was like a church banner, a proclamation of the church but not something that he was required to take literally. The important thing was to lead a good and generous life. The family did respect the heritage that had come down through the Episcopal church, and they ultimately joined Paul's church and also became dear friends with the Roberts family. Their daughters Elise and Doli became the closest of friends.

SPRING (Dorothy)

The miserable month of March grinds and slips and shrieks and stumbles along toward the equinox. Throats are raw, dispositions edgy, and the littlest ones begin breaking out with measles—first by ones, then by threes, then by dozens. Days break blue and crystalline, and before noon a black cloud is rolling down from the plain, and the wind whips up like ice. Nights show a clean starred zenith, and before dawn sleet pelts the roof. Snows are likely to be deeper and wetter than winter snows. Only the lengthening days hold promise.

Basketball season is nearly over, and the boys who have played too hard in a closed gymnasium look pallid and soft, quite different from the same boys after six weeks of skiing. The girls look different too. The colorful sweaters of last fall are tired-looking, and it is too early for the fresh bright cottons of spring. Scarcely anyone is at his or her best in March; it is a dangerous time for a schoolmaster.

Hold them down to the earth, throbbing its way through the seasons. Make each fragment of the year somehow precious for something. Make them remember March and April and May as vividly and as dearly as they remember October and Christmas.

In Colorado there is a flower that everybody but pedants calls an "anemone." It is not one, really, but a sort of first cousin, whose scientific name is "pulsatilla" and whose proper everyday name is "pasque flower," but scarcely anyone know that "pasque" means "Easter." So we call it an "anemone." It is the first flower of any consequence to appear in our wild spring—a little woolly tulip, deep or paler lavender, soft as a pussy willow to the touch, putting up an inquiring gray fur nubbin just at the edge of a snow bank in a field of dry grass—a probing little nose that opens out into a furry collar that hold a blue-lavender bud, a bud that opens soon into an amethyst cup filled with clear gold stamens. At first it wears its fur collar close around its neck, but as it grows taller and sturdier, the blossom lifts until the little ruff of fur is like an upside-down hula skirt around the middle of its stem.

But it is the *first* one that is miraculous. It is the deepest in color—truly purple. It opens, in its haste almost stemless.

Before we became so mechanized and so worldly in our town, people used to greet each other, around the end of March, with "have you seen an anemone yet?" There were people who had grown up knowing that soon there would be one, along the oaks in the little rolling leas to the south and west of Cheyenne School. After they had come out in fields-full, everybody went to gather them—but *someone* would find the *first* one!

He called them together in the auditorium—all of them, from the smallest to the tallest. He told them it was almost time; any day now someone would find one. He told the littlest ones the sorts of places where they would grow and how they would look. Their fingers could almost feel the woolly softness, just thinking about it. He reminded them that the first student to find one would receive, as always, a copy of his book, *Nature Notes of the Pikes Peak Region*, autographed with love and admiration by the author. "It could be you." He made it seem as if the finding of this flower, on the bleak hills of March, was somehow terribly important.

I can recall a raw afternoon, with snow beginning to filter down, and twilight coming early, when I looked out of the window to see three small and fiercely separate children flying up the hill to our house, each one with a hand suspiciously clutched around something precious. "Oh, Lloyd," I cried, "three of them have found one at once!" And so they had—and in separate places too. It would be risky to wait until morning; all three had decided that they would deliver their treasure right now—before supper, before it grew dark. They had converged at the bridge across the creek, and from there on it was a race hard run; they reached the porch three abreast. Three flowers: one, eagerly snatched up, most admirable for stemlessness; one, carefully pulled from the very bottom of the leafy duff, most admirable for tallness; one, found almost buried in leaves, most admirable for blueness. There was a great ceremony the next morning in the auditorium when three books were presented to three children who would never forget. The book? Oh, no, they may not even know what became of the book! The flower? They will never forget the flower.

A letter that came from one of these grown-up children ends by delightfully reproducing the experience of the three runners bearing flowers. Bob wrote: "I wonder for how many of us an anemone might be our first thought with regard to Pappy and Cheyenne School. In a way, our anemone ritual possessed a deeper and longer lasting significance than did the Christmas play, for we did not actively enter the wonderfully imaginative process of the play until fourth grade or later. But even as first graders, the anemone had for us a special meaning, and the search for the first blossom of the year, even in that first year, had something Grail-like about it. In my mind the first anemone has always stood for *challenge*, and the Christmas Play for *fulfillment*.

"The anemone ritual, incidentally, is one that we observe in our family each year. We go as a group as soon as we think the flowers might be out, visiting one of the many little hidden valleys we've discovered and explored since we moved to Boulder. We began the custom with Giga, and the added participation of each of the others has made the ritual more joyous.

"It is thus: first we pause along the stream and cut some red willow twigs which we weave into a sort of coronet. Bearing this, the Medicine Man (that's me) and the Woman of the Mountains (that's Kate) sniff the four winds, study the sky for magic signs, and then point the direction the searchers are to take. Suddenly we are childless as the small ones vanish as completely and quickly as young cottontails. So we walk sedately (a gait befitting our medicinal ranks) in their wake, making bets with each other as to which voice we'll hear. And we hear it almost at once, a high triumphant yell. The winner, of course, is crowned with the willow coronet, designated as Child of the Sunrise, and honored for the rest of that day. This year, because the small ones aren't so small anymore and because the anemones were blooming everywhere, we designated *three* Children of the Sunrise, wove three coronets, and then tried to maintain an uneasy peace as three separate honored wills vied for dominance . . . Spring is never official here until we have somewhere about the house a bowl of anemones."

What a gift Lloyd gave them—a lavender flower, growing gallantly next to snow under rough young pines and scrub oak! More durable, really than Boyle's Law or the history of the Holy Roman Empire (although they had those too). Children who come with a lavender flower and lay it in the hand of a man whom they love and respect and fear, as if it were the most important thing in the world; children who seek this flower, year after year, poking in the edges of old drifts, sniffling in the harsh wind, wiping their nose on the back of a grubby mitten. One of them, grown up, sends me poems sometimes.

He wrote:

We came to him with Pasque flowers,
wilted in our eager hands.
We came to tell the wondrous news
Blown from other lands.
We put flowers in his hands.

We came in breathless wonder,
spring in our still-stained hands.
The words we sought we did not know;
No small boy understands.
We put flowers in his hands.

And one of us was King then,
of our own and of all lands.
As Easter came and spring came,
we put flowers in his hands.

Because of some special dispensation we never understood, St. Patrick's Day was always a pleasant day. It never stormed, and the wind was just enough to give a good burn. Just at the end of the first period, the gong would ring on the high school speaker system, and an unexcited and business-like voice would announce: "As you all know, this is St. Patrick's Day. Those of you who would care to play hookey may be dismissed at this time to go home and put your rough clothes on. We shall meet as soon as possible at the east end of the big mesa near Pat's pile. Everybody is to go on foot, and please be sure to bring a rock to put on the 'pile.' Mrs. Bissen is preparing lunch—will the juniors please form a committee to help carry it over and serve it. Anyone who does not care to go may not go elsewhere; you may stay here and work in the library.|"

It served. It accomplished the necessary relief until spring vacation. With a whoop they were off. In no time at all, bright jackets and sweaters dotted the low swales running up to the big mesa. In less than thirty minutes the diamond was laid out and the baseball game was on. Flossie Mae tried to leap a steep-sided gulley, missed by two feet and went flat, with her chin hanging on the far edge of the gulley. Joyous helpers dragged her up—"Come on, Floss, you're shortstop—hurry!" There was no difference at all between boys and girls on this wonderful day—the same warm old jackets topping the same shrunken jeans, the same smeared faces, grimed with charcoal, dust, greasy hot dogs, and sun. The game went on and on, with no quarter asked or given, and then they played kick-the-can. But first all put their rocks, as big a one as each could carry, on the great cairn we called Pat's Pile. It had gone on for years—they even called the celebration the Pat's Pile Picnic. No one could begin to reach the top except the tallest boys. What, I wonder, did the millionaire who finally developed the land and built his own house right on that spot, what did he do with all those rocks? And must he not be haunted on St. Patrick's Day by the ghosts of teen-age celebrants, screaming their equinoctial spirit back into control. We always thought that perhaps St. Patrick knew about it—and approved.

A mother would phone the school office: "There is quite a large herd of deer in Sweet Potato Gulch" (the half-tamed wilderness that was in our very back yards.) Instructions to Woody: "Please get the bus out in front." Instructions to Miss Botting: "Do you think the second grade would like to go see a herd of deer?" The seven-year-olds bundled into coats and sweaters and into the bus. Pappy sitting on the arm of the front seat, talking back to them, talking past their lifted faces to their inside eagerness—still sitting there for a few minutes after the bus had stopped at the outlet of Sweet Potato Gulch, to be sure that everyone understood about deer and how beautiful and how shy they were. Two dozen small Indian-type beings, going soundlessly up through the scrub, coming to the edge of the little park-like valley—shhhh! Two dozen creatures of another kind, rough in shedding coats, lifting lovely heads watching cautiously, sizing up the situation and going on grazing. I can see it.

One day I called the office: "There is a huge flock of cedar waxwings in our crabapple tree." "Good! I think I'll bring the third grade up!" "You'd better stop the bus at the bottom of the hill and have them sneak up," I warned. Presently I saw them coming, Indians again. He would have had time to tell them what

106

beautiful creatures these were, these gray satin birds with their spiky little crest and the bits of scarlet wax on their wing quills. The children moved without a sound; they came close; they gathered around the tree. The waxwings didn't move. The children drew very close; they were able to see the satin of the feathers, the spots of scarlet wax. Still the birds did not move; it was a superb "observation." Long after the children had gone, even when darkness came, the birds were still there, taking a desultory peck now and then at the crab apples that had hung all winter on the tree alternately freezing and thawing. It was only the next morning that it occurred to us that they were inebriated on an extraordinarily potent brand of applejack. Pappy stepped into the third grade room that morning and told them why the birds were so easy to observe. He explained how alcohol is made by the fermenting of the thawing fruit. He pointed out how foolish it was of the waxwings to lay themselves open to all their enemies by taking all this alcohol. "Anything could have caught them!"

And one day the second grade missed flash card drill. One day the third grade missed arithmetic. Every day it was spring.

Among the pioneers who had homesteaded the original acres in the valley of Cheyenne Creek were several English families. One lovely woman had sent back to England for roots of the common English buttercup and planted them along the little spur of the creek that ran through her place. Nothing even resembling an English buttercup had ever grown in this environment before, but the immigrants were perfectly at home. They grew mat-thick, rich-foliaged, covered in May with a pattern of golden flowers, positively varnished with shining. High water and birds carried them the full length of the valley, and in the school Nature Preserve, where they were cherished, they were one of the great springtime joys.

Let Bob Cook tell it:

"But the buttercups come first in my mind because it was in my kindergarten year that Pappy first took my class on a nature walk. It was in the spring, and we followed him across the road into that enchanted forest and nearly walked our little legs off trying to keep up with his strides. And we picked buttercups that day, great golden armloads, which we took back to Miss Anderson, nearly smothering her in them. And Pappy laughed, and suddenly we all fell in love with this great roaring man who, until that buttercup day, had been something huge and awe-inspiring, seen usually from a distance.

"The loss of childhood, while never total, is a heart-breaking thing to experience, and I think each of us keeps looking for it as we go on through life, as though we might just have misplaced it somewhere. How else to explain the loveliness of children and the mingled wonder and despair they arouse in all but the most warped of adults. Or the joy felt by those of us in whom childhood seems to have survived more strongly than in others when we seek into our memories and unearth all manner of half-forgotten glints and glimpses? There have been times when, sitting up here in my crowded little room, I have actually smelled Cheyenne Creek, the smell of last year's decaying leaves, the rich earth smell that accompanies the sprouting of new plants, and the blooming of the buttercups . . .

> *He came to us with buttercups.*
> *Knee-deep in buttercups we stood*
> > *and heard the water of the stream*
> > *sing of another higher wood.*
> *And the day was good.*

> *He came in pussy willow time*
> > *to cheer the birds in flight with names:*
> > *junco, nuthatch, pale waxwing,*
> > *the jay the towering crest proclaims,*
> > *the hawk that nothing tames.*

He found us in our spring of youth,
showed paths through an enchanted wood,
and gave to everything a name.
Knee-deep in buttercups we stood
and everything was good."

Only ten minutes from the center of a city, he gave them spring—great chunks and shining splinters of it. Or, rather, he set them to finding it for themselves, and along with it, flowers and silken-feathered birds and holidays and picnics and solidarity. What he *gave* them, because he was very anxious for them to grow up quickly and wisely, was their childhood, to keep.

DEEP RED ROSES (Dorothy)

The first–grade teacher sat quietly at her desk, methodically arranging the work for the afternoon session. Morning sun streamed slantingly through closed Venetian blinds. The air was fresh; it was still early. The room was very still. Twenty-eight bits of concentrated humanity were writing—writing wonderful things: words. Each miraculous letter was being born laboriously from the end of a stubby pencil. Here, there was a small shuffling sound as a little body readjusted taut muscles; here, there was a tiny audible sigh; here, a pink tongue-tip poked purposefully from between clenched teeth; here, a brow was frightfully knitted.

The first-grade teacher looked charming this morning. She was wearing one of her prettiest dresses; her hair had been carefully "set" the afternoon before; around her neck was a fine chain of beads that had been the gift of a first-grader long ago; and a gay corsage of tiny flowers was pinned against her shoulder. It was her birthday.

She hadn't told anyone it was her birthday—there were so few left before she would be "too old" to teach any longer. Too old! It was a ridiculous idea; she dropped it. She just wouldn't have a birthday! But she knew she would. Something in the back of her consciousness was waiting, with childish eagerness, for something that would almost certainly not be forgotten. (They would be coming soon!) The purposeful bits of humanity shuffled and sighed again.

The door opened. Twenty-eight pairs of eyes shifted from the miracle of the written word to behold two high school seniors, beings from that unimaginable world upstairs where beautiful almost-grown up people did such wonderful things. A tall boy and a lovely girl. Coming down the stairs the girl had been allowed to carry it, but as they came through the door, they were both holding the long prickly stem of a half-blown red rose. They marched to the desk, grinned proudly, and made their speech together, "Happy birthday, Miss Nowels!" and they handed her the deep red rose as it if were the Nobel Peace Prize.

Her heart melted. It was yesterday that they had sat before her, with these same stubby pencils clutched in cramped fingers, half-disciplined little bodies squirming in these same seats. And they were still hers! They would always be hers, and some part of her had become theirs, and would be always. Tears were near to brimming; it was a dangerous situation.

With a dramatic rightness far from accidental, the door opened again, and the office secretary, with her secret shining smile, came in with a tall glass vase filled with water. "Happy birthday, Miss Nowels," she said, as if this were the only birthday the world had ever witnessed, and she placed the tall vase on the desk and was gone. The first-grade teacher put the deep red rose in the tall vase while 28 radiant faces were turned with wonder and delight toward it and toward her. Most of them knew what was coming next: it had happened last year in kindergarten; they looked gloatingly at the new ones who did not know.

Two jolly juniors—a slender dark girl and a boy with a brush of red hair and a twinkle: "Happy birthday, Miss Nowels!" Hers too! Two red roses in the tall vase. . . Four sophomores, who had persuaded their geometry teacher that two people were not nearly enough to carry out so important a mission. . . and then, a true commotion in the hall, and the whole freshman Latin class, the tiniest girl marching in front with the rose. Innovators, these— they always had been, even when they too sat in these seats. They lined up along the wall, carefully pulled the door shut, and burst into enthusiastic song—"Happy birthday to you! Happy birthday, dear teacher, happy birthday to you!"

And so on, through the morning. The concentrated small humans relaxed and watched this lovely ceremony with all their hearts. The children who brought the roses grew smaller, shyer. They came upon the heels of each other, or they left long gaps, but the tall vase was filling—it was a great bouquet.

While the emissaries from the third grade were in the room, honoring this teacher of a long past time when they were "little," Dr. Shaw himself opened the door a crack and beckoned to two who sat near. She did not see them go. In her happy excitement she did not even miss them; they could have been kidnapped. After the second grade from the room next door had sent their rose, gigglingly delivered by a pair who were still not quite sure whether they belonged to Miss Nowels or Miss Botting, or both, the door opened—slowly, mysteriously, and her own two entered, almost beside themselves with rapture. He had given them the biggest and tallest rose of all, and she let them put it in the vase themselves and hugged them, being by now completely inarticulate.

There were a dozen roses in the glass vase. People didn't usually get more than a dozen roses, but the little ceremony was not quite over. With customary regard for their littleness and inexperience, the big man had gone himself to the building across the yard where the kindergarteners were working their magic of colored papers. He had chosen two cherubs, blond and dark, shy as stars, and holding their small hands in his two big ones, had brought them back to the "big building" where they were to wish the teacher they would have next year in the first grade, a happy birthday. He pushed them gently through the door himself, and they whispered it with paralyzed voices, "Happy birthday, Miss Nowels." She could scarcely hear them, but they too would be hers, a bit of herself to go along with them. ("Dear God, thank you for folding this place around me. Thank you for giving me children to teach. And thank you for this birthday.")

Finally he came himself, Dr. Shaw, taller than trees and a little terrifying—but very safe too—and even he had a rose. He laughed his big laugh and said, "Happy birthday, Miss Nowels, from all of your colleagues."

The morning was gone, lost, useless. She sent them out to recess. Perhaps—after lunch. No one was ever missed, none of the teachers, nor the custodians, nor the nurse, nor the secretaries, nor the lunchroom staff. For those with summer birthdays, the roses appeared on their "half birthday," six months from the summer date. It was a little world of birthdays. The small drama never came out twice quite the same, for, should it be the birthday of the French teacher, then almost all the children were shy and incredulous, finding it hard to believe that they would ever slide into a seat in the corner room and find themselves conjugating the verb *aimer*. They were her future rather than her past, and she was theirs. But the past was in them both. So was the present: youth and wonder and good will.

Sometimes, at the end of a month replete with birthdays, like November or April, the Shaws would contemplate their personal florist bill with a happy little sigh, hoping that the budget would include it, and turning the backs of their minds on the unimaginative and cruel, who complained, "He even spends the taxpayers' money to buy roses for his teachers on their birthdays!" The florist was in league; he loved this ceremony himself, and he kept a list of birthdays too, and saved his nicest red roses or great yellow Madame Pernets, or whatever was best, and allowed a little discount to someone who bought 30 dozen roses in a year. And, of course, after a couple of seasons, a great vase of roses appeared magically on Dr. Shaw's desk on *his* birthday. And also a gourmet's shower of home-made jams and jellies in jars and glasses gaily bedecked with shy affectionate notes tied on with ribbon.

113

What could matter half so much? What if a morning was spent? Suppose a man, grown perhaps a little gray, perhaps a little paunchy, a man who always was and is even now a tiny bit slow with seven times eight and eight times nine, a man over whose head the subjunctive mood swept as unheeded as water over a surfer's head—suppose this man, leaving his office at five o'clock, were suddenly to remember how lovely, how altogether right it felt to hold a long prickly rose stem in a small hot hand and surreptitiously take a deep breath of its fragrance and know with excitement that he was about to give it to someone!

I saw three such this morning. They were sitting in front of me in a hushed room where a quiet man stood in front of a bank of flowers and spoke earnestly about a teacher named Lucy Nowels. And suddenly we were not there at all, but I saw the three of them standing in a semi-circle around her worn and shining and ineffably tidy desk, and each one held a tall red rose, and they said, as loudly and as brightly as possible, "Happy birthday, Miss Nowels!"

[According to Lloyd's records, this tradition began in November of 1934. The faculty promptly replied in kind, each teacher bringing him a rose for his birthday on September 29th.]

CHRISTMAS IS A PLACE (Dorothy)

For some people, Christmas is not a date on the calendar, nor a week in the liturgy, nor a mad merchants' festival, superimposed upon the gentle season of Advent. Christmas is a place. A "house," Chesterton called it, "the house of Christmas."

For some people it is indeed just that; they go home to it for a day or a week or a fortnight every year. But for others it has wider boundaries; the journey is longer; they wander there, perhaps for long periods, perhaps throughout the year, and they can be said to "live" there. These are those who, casting aside both doubts and dogmas, have come to know that *something* that most people call by one or another of the names for God does come and dwell among humankind—and dwells among us over and over again, and that it is His house in which they dwell together. This place has many names (one of the most popular is "The Kingdom of Heaven"), but from the solstice until Twelfth Night, its name is "Christmas."

For Lloyd Shaw, Christmas was the place where he most truly lived. It may be that this went back to the days when he was a little boy living on the edge of genteel poverty, with the almost-empty stocking by the fireplace and the chicken-instead-of-turkey on the table; and to the later days of unfulfilled longings when he studied mink fur pieces in the shop windows and vainly imagined his mother wearing one of them.

But there was also a deeper sense that the "place" was inhabited by a holy Child and visited by some wise kings and some simple peasants; and that, one and all, they brought gifts to some presence that they could not truly see. Once when he was 11 years old, he had been assigned a Christmas composition in school, and he had sat down with one of his short pencils pressed fiercely against the blue-lined paper and had written a little story about a boy 11 years old who was the son of shepherds and had encountered three wise kings as they journeyed into Bethlehem, and conversed with them about a mysterious great star, and was told what it meant and whom they sought, and so must go himself with a gift also; and, lacking gold and frankincense and myrrh, took with him a little bag of shiny stones that he had gathered in the brooks and on the hills, and gave them to the Holy Child. He had felt the impact of this work of art so mightily himself that he was astonished when the teacher had merely remarked it was "a nice little story, Lloyd." He filed it in his memory.

His whole life was to be deeply entangled in the giving of gifts, although the surface man always found that it was not only more blessed to give than to receive, but also it was easier—and more fun. When he came to Cheyenne School, he brought with him a treasure of gifts that might have required a whole caravan of camels to carry, save for the fact that these gifts had no substance and were invisible. Anything he truly possessed must be given away, at once, or be lost forever. There was neither piety nor unusual virtue involved—just simple grace. He could not possibly help it. He found himself in a situation in which children of all ages waited wistfully to be given something. He knew all about this, for so he himself had been, and was still. His obligation was to give them things, as gifts, as if these things were not a largesse that they had already possessed from the beginning of their days. When the buttercups came into bloom along the creek in May, he took the little ones by the hand across the wood and down to the bank, and he *gave* them the buttercups without anyone needing to touch them and as if they were his to give. When the first good snow of the season fell, he took the tall children, almost as literally by the hand, forth into the maroon-walled canyons, and he gave them the treasures of the snow while they flung it wildly at each other in hard-packed balls and shouted for joy.

When he found a wonderful poem he had not encountered before, or a lovely song, or an astonishing fact, or even a willingly entrapped person—be it poet or cowboy or Indian chief—he was more than likely to ring the bell and call the high school into the auditorium (or the primaries or the junior highs or even the whole school, faculty and all) and to give them this gift which had cost him nothing but love and enthusiasm. In the very giving it became treasure, capable of being passed on from generation to generation. He gave them his great laughter, and they always laughed right back, in proof of the transaction. When he felt the need to give them tears, they wept, although he did not. Best of all, he gave them a sense of something for which there is no longer a meaningful word, since we have become so careless with all words.

We shall have to call it *holiness.*

He lived in a place called *Christmas.* And he *gave* them this place.

Of course there was a Christmas at Cheyenne School when he went there. It was perfectly typical and unselfconscious, for this was several decades before the sweetest of festivals became involved with "freedom of worship" and constitutional rights. It was manifested by Christmas trees in every room, and children eagerly devising ornaments, and the old simple carols. It was to be some time yet before the great medieval carols were rediscovered. There was the making of gifts; it was a time of whispering and humming and secretly smiling. The Holy Child was perfectly welcome as a guest at the party, but, since it was a public school, it was not quite *His* party. It was ours. Nevertheless, He came, being blithely beyond the jurisdiction of courts and constitutions.

Included in the fine staff of teachers was Mrs. Brown, the music teacher, who was very good indeed and managed the difficult small voices into a surprising degree of certitude and control. There were programs and playlets in all of the rooms with candy canes and paper hats; and there was a carol service for the whole school on the last day before the holidays.

But this man was capable of rapture, and the sweet little program was neither deep enough nor high enough, not nearly. It left the high school students untouched, carried along only by their gentle concern for the little ones. Their place in it was awkward and inept. Before another year he would have to devise something bearing wings for flight, something to remember when you were old. And this would certainly entail inviting the Holy Child to the party as guest of honor!

Late the next fall he went one day into his little study in the white house at the top of the hill, taking with him the little boy who had fitted into his skin when he was eleven years old. He had the same sort of a soft short pencil and the same kind of blue-lined paper and the manuscript of "a nice little story, Lloyd" in his head. He was gone a long time. When he came out, it was with orders: "I need some poems to go with this play. Look! This little shepherd boy needs to express things that he can't possibly have words for. He can't even think them—they are just something he knows in his heart. There isn't a part in the cast that should speak them, so they will have to come from off-stage, sort of like a Greek chorus—the voice of the wind—something like that. Can you write me some poems like that? I'll need four: one at the beginning and one for each scene, when this child is staring at the Star and listening. . ."

"What about?"

"I'll tell you" he said, "as I go along."

And so I, who was used to cutting and fitting, polishing and re-polishing, omitting and re-admitting in order to get a poem somewhere near right, found myself writing four poems that

118

simply ran off the point of the pen onto the paper, exactly the way he wanted them, for his voice to read.

It was surprising how little revision was necessary in *The Littlest Wiseman*. He had taken some of the dialogue from the book of Isaiah and from the Gospel of Matthew, and the remainder took on the same grace and nobility of speech. There was the little shepherd boy who was capable of rapture and his brother who was not; there were the traditional shepherds, gauche and uncomfortable; there were three wise kings, a puzzled Joseph, a multitude of winged angels; and there was Mary. And a great light shining from a crude manger. Just the usual trappings and the usual plot with variations, but somehow born in magic. For, in a way that has not been quite defined, it was utterly different.

The music was almost right—it was all almost right, from the beginning—but as the years went by, one at a time the details perfected themselves. There was the gift of an authentic costume from which to copy others; the discovery of a song; a *right* way to move the angel who beckoned; a better way for the small attendants to enter before their kings. The great miracle took place when we found exactly the right music to go before the little play: a collection of five medieval carols, newly published. And a fine composer made us some music for the chorus of angels, music of our own, set to re-arranged words from Isaiah. And then, one day, our new music teacher who had grown up in Cheyenne School, discovered that Gounod's "Bethlehem" fitted the pageantry and pauses of the final scene as if that blessed gentleman had foreseen our need and composed this piece to fit it!

The angels were trained by our dancing teacher in *porte de bras*, and by Lloyd in inward shining, and they completely lost their identity as ordinary school girls. They moved as they had never moved before, and they looked as they had never dreamed of looking. They wore great wings, designed by our physics teacher (who had also designed a famous viaduct) with strong steel frames and a cheese-cloth base on which to sew thousands of curled tissue-paper feathers. It was a sweet and startling sight around Thanksgiving time to see a slender 16-year-old in skirt and sweater, walking home along Cheyenne Boulevard with big white wings sprouting from her shoulders. You knew that she had just won her part as an angel and that she was taking her wings home to be re-feathered, but there was something hair-raising about her too. She was surrounded by implications. If you were to tear the feathers from a pair of those wings today, you would find, written in pencil on the cheese-cloth, the names of all the girls who in their turns had worn them. On several pairs, you would find the dim name of a mother and the fresher one of her daughter!

I came across a photograph of the choir boys of a long-lost year. They had just come down the aisles, carrying their tall white lighted candles and singing, "Be we merry in this feast *in quo salvator natus est,*" and they had lined themselves up across the stage, their bright red cassocks and clean white cottas glistening against the blue velvet curtain. They stood singing with the tallest two in the middle and ranging down to the littlest on the ends, and I noticed that the two in the middle were the present governor of Colorado and the United States Air Force colonel who is in charge of the project called "Operation Survival."

Operation survival! Before you go very far into the story of the Cheyenne experiment, it is necessary for you to understand this: without a survival kit, we perish. We perish young. Oh, my childhood and something from its dreaming! Throw me a line or the sea engulfs me! Oh, Mother of my littlest years, toss me a pick against this ice, or the cliff takes me! Oh, Teacher that I loved, tear apart this net, for I smother! Oh, song that I sang—song that I sang! Sing in my ears against the whisperings of witches! It was as if all children who entered Cheyenne Mountain School were given a small invisible knapsack, strapped securely on their shoulders, and thereafter, surreptitiously, items were dropped into it for survival by their teachers, by their playmates, by their experiences, their surroundings, by the steps they danced and the

120

games they played and the miles they climbed and the books they read and the songs they sang. And by the Cheyenne Christmas. It was the heart and the hub of the wheel. Cheyenne alumni are likely to be asked, "What was the secret of the Cheyenne School experience? I suppose it was the dancing?" And they are 89% likely to answer, "Oh no! It was Christmas!"

The Cheyenne Christmas began its evolution with the first grade reciting "'Twas the Night before Christmas," lined up in their flannel pajamas with candlesticks in their hands, and it ended with a noble carol that became a life-line and an anchor. The evolution was gentle from year to year; nothing was ever lost. (If you want the detailed story of *The Littlest Wiseman* with the names of many of those involved, and the stage-by-stage changes, you will find that Lloyd has presented this beautifully in the foreword to the 1951 edition of the book, *The Littlest Wiseman.*) From the cutting of the greens on a bitterly cold Saturday morning to the carol service for the whole school on the morning before the Christmas holiday, the procedure finally became traditional and hence soul-sustaining. One boy wrote home from the anguish of Okinawa: "I could never have borne Christmas at all this year if it hadn't been for the fact that I suddenly seemed to smell the fir and pine as we loaded it onto the truck up above Twilight Canyon, and I heard the kids shouting and laughing, and for half an hour I was home."

Another lad, grown and troubled, told us about having navigated a plane flying a lonely mission across the North Pole in deep and dreadful darkness. Suddenly he remembered during a lull in his radio signals that it was Christmas Eve, and a darker hour centered the dark night of his spirit. The world seemed to be falling apart beneath him, leaving him high above the Arctic Ocean, detached and forsaken. He cried out in silence, and suddenly the cabin of the plane was filled with music—great trained voices singing in English and Latin, "*In dulci jubilo!* Let us our homage show! Our hearts' joy reclineth *in praesepio.*" He didn't ask any questions until afterward—he simply wept while the heart returned to his body and the polar night throbbed with the song. Later when he was able to investigate, he found that what he had heard was a radio broadcast by the Tabernacle Choir in Salt Lake City, somehow involved on his short-wave length.

It takes a long time to obliterate 33 Christmases that extend themselves to second and third generations even now. "Do you know you are a *cult*?" one young woman said recently to another. "All you people who experienced the Cheyenne Christmas and took part in *The Littlest Wiseman*. . . when you are together, several of you in the same room during the Christmas season, you start talking and remembering things too good to be true, and the rest of us are left out."

It is perfectly possible that the pouch of pebbles that the Littlest Wiseman carried to the Christ Child contained nothing but *touchstones*. A touchstone is described as a smooth and shining stone, usually jasper or very dark quartz, by which one can determine the quality of gold and silver alloys by the nature of the marks they leave on the stone when rubbed across it. Symbolically, the term is sometimes used to signify a test for the quality of anything, a poem or a song or a life. As little Zarah told over his handful of pebbles, "Here is one all pink and white I gathered in the brook of Hebron. I always loved it most. And here is the agate imbedded with moss, and this shining crystal of spar and this black one and this one of many colors. Would they do? The king is such a little king, he might care for them almost as much as for gold. . . . They are all I have . . . I could slip them in under the manger. . . I will do it!" But the Holy Child, who was a touchstone himself, had no real need of them. Still, a good survival kit could use a handful. So at least one of the touchstones that were slipped into the little Cheyenne knapsacks is a song. It was a "shining crystal of spar."

By the time some 15 Christmases had come and gone, the Cheyenne Mountain School's "Christmas Gift to the Community" had settled into a pattern that scarcely varied. The wing with the auditorium and library and gymnasium had long since been built, and the audiences could be accommodated in the theater in five performances a season, instead of seven. There was a fine stage with high fly galleries and adequate switch boards. The auditorium could be banked with fragrant fir and pungent pine and lighted by eight-times-seven candles. There were chimes ringing changes in the attic while the people quietly assembled. Then after all was quiet and eight o'clock had struck, the organ began playing things like Debussey's "Little Shepherd" and an ancient Scottish carol for which the score is lost, until the carols began. There were five of these. Four of them were *macaronic*, which means that they were sung in two languages: Latin and English. They were very beautiful and very difficult for young untrained voices, and so they practiced them as they never practiced anything else—over and over until they sang in the blood itself. The first of them was sung at the very beginning by the choir boys as they came down the aisles, shining like cherubs, after standing for what seems like eons, against the back wall of the auditorium while the fifth grade teacher, whose task this always was, lighted their great wax candles. (How frantically and unwhisperingly they waited!) The high school chorus joined in the refrain each time, partly to keep the youngsters on track but more truly because they loved this joyous song beyond all reason: "Be ye merry, in this feast *in quo Salvator natus est!*"

But once the choir boys were safely through the blue curtain, the deep magic began when the high school, unseen, started to sing:

> *In dulci jubilo!* Let us our homage show!
> Our hearts joy reclineth *in praesepio!*
> And like a bright star shineth *Matris in Gremio!*
> *Alpha es et O! Alpha es et O!*

123

What did it mean, this old song, so simple and so profound: Did they *think* what it meant? Certainly they loved the taste of the Latin on their tongues, and they did know what the phrases meant and how quaintly they described the Nativity as people saw it in the 15th century, but it is likely that few of them ever got very far beyond that first phrase: *In dulci jubilo*—in sweet joy!

In sweet joy! Is this not the natural country of the young? Are not the puzzlings and the rebellions and the self-imposed exiles of the children a confused intellectual reaction to the experience of being somehow outcast from sweet joy? When they sang it, a new ingredient entered into any situation with those first three words. Then it became for a while just a lovely song, but when they came to *alpha es et O!* You could hear it between the lines and under their voices—that young certainty. Whatever it meant, this "the beginning and the end," it had a battened-down feeling, as if one were safely fastened at both ends. "Alpha es et O" melted into the most lovely harmonies.

> *O patris caritas! O nati lemitas!*
> Deeply were we stained *per nostra crimina,*
> But thou hast for us gained *coelorum gaudia.*
> O that we were there! O that we were there!

> *Ubi sunt gaudia,* where if that they be not there?
> There are angels singing *Nova cantica,*
> There the bells are ringing, *In Regis curia*
> O that we were there, O that we were there.

It was that refrain that told them . . .
"O that we were there, O that we were there!"
Where? Where was it that they so desperately wanted to be? Kneeling at the manger in Bethlehem? That would do for a symbol. But, really, where? At home—where I belong—in sweet joy!

…Where if that they be not there?
The song rose with angels and bells—and sloped into yearning:
"O that we were there!"

Is *longing* a bad thing for the young to know? If they do not sometimes yield to simple longing, may they not forget how to long when they grow older? To long with all their hearts for goodness and grace—in sweet joy? Perhaps our greatest educational disaster lies in having failed to teach them what to want—to be there.

If you are interested, you will find the words to all the songs and their sources and arrangers in the 1951 edition of *The Littlest Wiseman*. But this song you will have to take with you clear to the end of this book, for it was the touchstone. Rubbed against gold or steel or silver, it shimmered into sound, and it sliced through the tawdry like a blade.

Even thus Clark heard it over the North Pole, and the earth steadied itself on its spindle. Even so, as Lloyd wrote, "Once when I had a group of my students doing a dance program at the University of California, we rode out in our bus late at night on the ridge above Berkeley to see the magic of the lights spread out over the cities and the bay below us, stringing across the gossamer bridges and piled and spilling over the many distant hills of San Francisco. The students were deeply moved by the scene, and when one of the University faculty who were with us asked if we could sing one of our school songs, one student asked me, "Can we sing 'In Dulci Jubilo,' Pappy?" and they did, filling it with extraordinary tenderness and love.

Ever since, it has been their very special school song. Whenever triumph or trouble has overwhelmed them and left them without words, this old 12th century carol has brought them back again to a simple strength and faith. While rolling along over the almost empty highway beyond Dodge City, Kansas, one cold and rainy morning, our bus turned over into the barrow pit. A score of us were tossed and pitched amid the flying baggage and bits of glass, but, miraculously, no one was hurt. After the fire in the engine was extinguished, a passing motorist took me to find some sort of sanctuary for us all. Days afterward, I asked some of them what they had done during the half hour that I was gone. He answered, 'We crawled back into the overturned bus, to get out of the wind and rain, and then somebody started to sing "In Dulci Jubilo," and we all joined in, and everything was all right again.'"

Christmas is a *Place*. It is not the sort of place that can be flattened by a hurricane or bull-dozed off the map by developers or washed away by floods or blasted by bombs. The little campus where the Cheyenne Christmas took place is doomed. It has been replaced by five separate units. The new high school that stands on the old horse pasture is very elegant indeed, and within a year the original building will be torn down to make space for a new junior high school, also very elegant indeed. Soon no one will ever be able again to walk through a door into Cheyenne Mountain School, and those who walk into other schools with that same name over the door will find it hard to believe that the things that are recorded in this book ever happened in a suburban public school such a short time ago. If they are able to feel compassion, they may feel it for those alumni who have no longer any place to which to come back; no longer a "there." This will be nonsense.

For the door through which they enter into a place called Christmas has not been torn down. It stands. And if they cannot find it, it is simply that the road is washed out or the forest has thickened or they have lost the map. They will know the door when they see it—it will have a wreath on it. They may even do what Francis did.

It was Christmas Eve. There was a wreath on our door, and someone knocked. There stood Francis, bleak-eyed. We had not seen him for several years.

"Come in, Francis!"

"Dr. Shaw, can you help me? I'm on an assignment and I only have about 12 minutes. I just stopped off between planes to

126

see my mother, and my plane leaves in an hour." He pulled a dog-eared copy of the old paper-bound edition of *the Littlest Wiseman* out of the pocket of his Navy officer's uniform.

"Will you read 'How Far Is It to Bethlehem' to me?"

"Why, yes, Francis, of course."

And Lloyd opened Francis' book and slowly and lovingly read the poem that comes just before the blue curtains open on Zarah and his star. He read it in two voices: an asking voice and an answering voice.

> *How far is it to Bethlehem*
> *By way of the seven seas,*
> *By Joppa – and Jerusalem –*
> *And the Mount of the Olive trees?*
>
> *How many leagues by water and land?*
> *Half of the world's wide space*
> *To where the dull, small houses stand*
> *About the market place.*
>
> *One takes the sea in a mighty ship,*
> *One rides with a caravan,*
> *Till the dusty palms of Beersheba dip*
> *At the edge of the desert's span.*
>
> *And I may not stand in Bethlehem,*
> *Nor feel the touch of his hand,*
> *Nor hear the stir of his garment's hem*
> *Through the dreary little land!*
>
> *How far is it to Bethlehem*
> *Maid-mother of all the towns?*
> *And must one go by Jerusalem*
> *And the gray Judean downs?*

How far by way of a man's own heart,
Dull with the world's old sin?
Only as far as one stands apart
To let a star shine in!

Francis had not even been seated. He stood, lean and tall, in the doorway between the hall and the living room. He took back his book and put it in his pocket.

"Thanks, Pappy. I feel much better now. And it's Christmas." And he was gone into the snow-still night.

HE WAS RESPONSIBLE FOR THEM
(Dorothy)

He was responsible for them. It never occurred to him that any other viewpoint was possible. People were responsible for each other—as sons, as playmates, as brothers, as parents, as teachers, as students—people were responsible insofar as their relationship made it possible to help, to guide, to watch over. He could remember when he was a small boy in Denver that his brother Glenn caught him and two other ten-year-olds valiantly smoking something of their own manufacture in the traditional location behind the barn. The others listened to a brief and bitter speech, but for Lloyd there was a stern and painful spanking from the tall brother who was barely too old to be spanked himself. "Gosh, Glenn, it's nothing but corn silk!" And Glenn answering, "Yes, and what will it be next time, if someone doesn't tell you where to get off?" "Glenn, don't tell Mother." "Heck no. Why should I tell Mother? *I'm* raising you, kid!"

"There's a thing called 'noblesse oblige,'" he once said to Dorothy, at that time his college sweetheart, as they walked in the snow-patterned park below the college after the holidays. "I don't know how you achieve 'noblesse,' but even if you don't, there's probably somebody who thinks you possess it, who looks up to you in some small way. You just can't be a school teacher and not remember that all the time. A school teacher is *not* free to do as he or she pleases any more than a clergyman is. For that matter,

129

neither is a parent, which is something else I hope to be. You have to watch your step every minute, for there is always somebody you are responsible for. I hope I can remember it."

When he received his first teaching assignment, he went to one of his former high school teachers, a man whose techniques and controls he admired, and said, "Mr. Barker, you're a remarkably fine teacher. Would you have any rules of conduct to pass on to a beginning one?"

The expert scarcely hesitated. "Yes, two," he said. "First: be definite. If a kid comes to you and asks, 'Do you want this assignment done in red ink or black ink?' don't say you don't care. Say "red" or "black" positively. Then he feels safe; he doesn't have to worry; he can go about the important thing—the contents of the assignment. And second: never make a threat you are not prepared to keep."

The first rule was simple. The second one loomed, a tower of responsibility. A threat was dynamite: if you do this, I shall do that. And yet discipline was a part of responsibility, and discipline called for punishments. If you said you would, you had to, or you had failed the sinner. He announced at once to his biology classes at the Colorado Springs High School, "I shall tolerate no cheating in this class. This is definite, and final. Anyone caught cheating in this class will be dropped from the class. I mean this. Is it clear?" They looked owlish and said that it was. He did not say, "I owe it to you to see that you do not cheat," but that was what he knew.

He made no further issue of it, but he was watchful. And then it happened, where it seemed least likely. She was a lovely girl—well-bred, attractive, intelligent. Perhaps he was mistaken; he kept watching. And it kept happening. He repeated his general warning. And then one day he walked quietly down the aisle and picked up from the seat beside her the small crowded paper on which she had written the answers to the likely exam questions, looked at it briefly and stuck it in his inside coat pocket.

His mind quaked as he whispered to her to go. "You mean I'm dropped from the class?" she said with big eyes.

"You're dropped from the class."

At the noon break his principal wandered in. "What's this I hear about your kicking Ellen out of the class?"

"Yes, sir. She's kicked out."

"Why?"

"Because that's what I said I'd do if anyone cheated. And this was the semester final."

"She's an awfully nice girl. Couldn't you overlook it this first time?"

"No, sir, I couldn't. I have 29 in here I'm responsible for."

"Do you know who her father is?"

"Yes."

"He's an important citizen in this town. This is going to raise an awful rumpus—in fact it's started already. Darnn it, Shaw—why did you have to pick her out?"

"I didn't, Mr. Hill. "She picked herself out. And I'm awfully sorry to have made any trouble for you. You can always fire me, you know. Right now I sort of expect it."

Mr. Hill roared with laughter and threw an arm around the young man's shoulder. "Of course I can't fire you. You're right! But you're a nuisance. But I'm with you. That's one of my fixed rules—unless you know he's wrong, stand by your teacher. You can't have a good school unless the administrator stands behind his teachers." And the young man made a note of that.

"But you know what they're going to say, don't you—all sorts of people are going to say it—that your job is to teach 'em biology, and their characters are none of your business."

"I'm afraid I think that biology is pretty incidental to my job, Mr. Hill. I think my job is to do my bit toward *educating* them."

The principal gave him a pat; it was an encouraging pat. All the same, this was quite a thing, this business of teaching

131

school. He was learning, but there was scarcely anything in those education courses he had taken that was of any use to him on the actual battlefield of the classroom.

Now at Cheyenne School there was no longer anyone to stand behind him, except his hard-headed school board. As the weeks went by, he was coming to love them—their cautious thrift, their honesty, their open minds. But he was the administrator, a sort of combination light house and fortification, surrounded by surging parents, school board, childless reactionaries, and the children themselves, all ages and sizes, all made up of their own particular recipe of talents and capacities, lacks and shortcomings. And never for one hour did he forget that he was responsible for them.

He had a fine arsenal of weapons for the battle. A wonderful childhood and boyhood packed with innocent mischief. An endless capacity for invention. A deep sense of the humanities when most people didn't know what the word meant. An almost passionate devotion to the idea of keeping things beautiful. A will to act. A swift and creative imagination. A sense of play that could transform hard work into what felt like a holiday. A deep and inexhaustible instinct for teaching in any situation, seizing the method at hand for the opportunity at hand. And, above all, that life-long purity of heart.

His great gift of eloquence was the centrally activating power plant. Speech was his most personal weapon. He could wheedle and exhort, plead and cajole, observe with pride and point with scorn, whisper and roar, harangue, tease, expatiate, pray and preach. And laugh! His silences could be long, lonely and brooding; mostly they were mine. His laughter was for all the world. He used this eloquence shamelessly. He talked them into things, and this called for prayerful decisions about just what it was that he should talk them into. And he sometimes used his silences for punishment or praise.

A treasured former student, by that time a woman with tall sons of her own, had an opportunity shortly before his death to talk for a long time to both of us about how it had felt to be the object of his sense of responsibility.

"Pappy," she said, "you were a very cruel disciplinarian."

"I, cruel?" He laughed. "That's a libel. When was I ever cruel?"

"You were terribly cruel to me once. It was a punishment that just kept going on and on from that day to this. You never put a period to it. I don't know to this day where I stand."

"That really does sound bad," he said. "Tell me about it."

"This was Miss Morrow's English class. I sat behind Russ, and even then, you know, Russ was big. I could sort of hide behind him. There was a pin on my desk, and there was a little split at the toe of the sole of my shoe, so I stuck the pin in the split head first. It held solidly and I had a useful weapon—for what? Well, the piece of Russ that was visible between the back of his chair and the seat of his chair looked vulnerable, and I just reached up with my toe and stuck the pin into Russ. And Russ went right up to the ceiling with an awful shriek. Miss Morrow—and what a wonderful teacher she was—just said, 'Dena, go to the office please.' You see, she didn't even ask me what I'd done, or *if* I'd done it, and that was unnerving to begin with.

"So I went to the office, completely terrified, and you looked up from your desk and said, 'Hello, Dena. Anything I can do for you?' And I said, 'Miss Morrow sent me to the office.' You said, 'Oh? I'm expecting someone in a minute, Dena. Do you have your books? You can just sit down at the end of that table and study for a while.'"

"Well, I sat there; and parents came and teachers came and kids came, and you talked to all of them. And then the class bell rang, and you didn't say I might go, so, of course, I couldn't. Then you dictated some letters, and then more people came, and once in a while you would look up and smile and say, 'You all right, Dena? Do you have everything you need?'"

"And by that time I felt as if I would die if I couldn't tell you why I was there and get it over with and get *sentenced!* Finally the bell rang for school to be out, and the kids went home, and the stragglers went out to the playground, and you just sat there writing letters as if I were invisible. Along about five o'clock, when your secretary started closing up her desk, you put yours in order and you said, 'OK, Dena, let's go home.'"

"So we walked up the boulevard together as far as my house, and talked about everything on earth except me. And from that day to this I never got to tell you what I'd done!"

"And I never knew! In fact, I remember nothing about it. It does sound cruel all right: withholding the privilege of a confession—a quarter century of continual suspense!" He roared with joy. "It seems to have been effective."

"Effective! It changed my life."

He grinned. "For the better, I hope?"

"You were always changing our lives for the better, Pappy."

He was thoughtful. "I wish that were true. In this case, though, if you could have told me about this horrible crime, I would probably in all honesty have had to tell you that, under the circumstances, I would have stuck a pin in Russell too. You were the wrong person to whom to tell this. I must have been inspired."

"Do you remember," said Laurie Margaret to me, when she had just come home from working on her doctorate at the University of Salamanca, "about the time we messed up the lunch line on April Fool's Day?"

"No. Tell me about it."

"It was April Fool's Day of our senior year, and Charles and John and I were sitting on the platform outside the auditorium, studying together. We were all Rangers and could go where we pleased, and we had all been Rangers for four years, and if we could hang onto our status for two more months, we would get gold Ranger pins set with a diamond, to keep. Of course, we were acutely aware of the fact that besides losing your A average, you could also lose your ranger pin for a failure in citizenship. I was the last person in the class, unless it was Charles, to lose it on that account. I had been a conscientious 'good citizen' for about 17 years.

"Well, it was April Fool's Day, and it was almost lunch time, and Pappy hadn't done a thing about it—you know he usually did pull a joke on all of us. We decided *we* had better do something, and we dreamed up this fine plan. The lunch time was staggered, you know, so each class would have time to get through the line before the next one got out. We simply canvassed all the high school classes and the junior high study halls. One of us went into each room and said, 'Will you please dismiss your class for lunch at 11:45 today. I was asked to tell you.' 11:45 was when the 6th grade was supposed to come upstairs to lunch. You see, we did not offer any authority for this—we had asked each other to do the telling. And only one of these intelligent teachers even questioned the idea or seemed to think it unusual that messengers were being sent when announcements from the office always came over the speaker system. The one who protested was furious and flatly refused. He kept his students until the regular time and then went storming down to the office to find out why this fantastic order had been given.

"But by that time the beautiful damage had been done. We hurried back and sat on the platform to watch, and it was the grandest mess you ever saw. It was just chaos. Mrs. Bissen in the cafeteria and all her staff were in a complete tizzy; the halls were packed with kids clear down the stairs; the teachers were wild; and everybody was blaming Pappy at first. Then somebody began to catch on. 'Teach' Johnson came down the hall from the study hall and spotted us and said, 'Oh, but you're going to get it!' Mr.

Patterson was organizing things like mad. It was a total and terrifying success. I kept thinking how I had thrown away my whole career. They might even withhold my diploma. I was sure to lose my scholarship to college. I saw my ranger pin fly away before my eyes. And I had broken my parents' hearts. Charles was simply white with fear. And then, finally, just as people were beginning to shout 'April Fool!' along the halls the gong rang and Pappy's voice, like the voice of doom, said, 'Will the officers of the senior class please report to the office.' Then he read off our names: John and Charles and Laurie Margaret.

"I don't know when I have ever felt so finished. We went down to the office and went in and shut the door. Outside the windows Cheyenne Mountain stood in the spring sun, and there were a hundred finches on the feeder in Pappy's bird window. He looked at us, and I died, and then he tilted back his swivel chair and grinned, and then he threw back his head and *roared* with laughter! And he said, 'Congratulations! That was a beauty!'

"We blinked. 'Well,' he said, 'you saved me the trouble of thinking up something, but I would never have dared pull *that* one.' He grinned again. 'May I suggest that you limit your careers in crime to this one complete success. If you are less than perfect just once between now and commencement, I can't think of words to tell you what I'll do to you. Go on, get out of here and get back to work.' And as we went out, he called after us, 'April Fool!'

"We found out afterward that it was the teachers who got scolded—for not being alert to the calendar and for being caught off-guard. But he fooled us by not doing anything to us, and he put his whole punishment into calling the entire school's attention to us by saying our names aloud, and by pointing out that we all held positions of responsibility. Long afterward he preached us a little sermon about *noblesse oblige.* "

[Lloyd's disciplinary tactics didn't change much over the years. Norm Brown entered Cheyenne School in the mid-forties as a high school freshman. At his previous school he had run with a tough crowd, and on his first day at Cheyenne he managed to find a fight. He reported that he "filled the air with some nasty name calling, mostly aimed at the other fellows' moms." From his office Lloyd overheard, opened his window, and instructed Norm to come to his office. Norm later wrote, "Superintendent Shaw briefly and very clearly let me know what the words I had used meant and that I had no business calling someone's mother the names I had used. He did not speak to me again. He just let me sit in his office. All day.

"Pappy changed my life and taught me respect in one day and with very few words. Pappy Shaw was clearly the most influential man in my life."

[Norm performed all four years with the dance team and helped teach in Lloyd's summer classes.]

"QUESTION IT, HORATIO" (Dorothy)

The seniors came into the library a little shyly. They had used it for years, happily, familiarly, but this was new: never before had they approached it as the citadel of Senior English.

"You just wait," they had been told by their betters when they had been freshmen, sophomores, and juniors, "you don't know *any*thing about a tough course! You wait until you get into Senior English!"

The state of Colorado required only three high school years of English, in the 9th, 10th, and 11th grades. The fourth year was optional, and no curriculum requirements were set for it. This was Lloyd's opportunity to rectify what he considered gaps and lacks in the English literature curriculum, to insert some sly slices of ethics and philosophy, to spread before his youngsters their native language, beautifully and lovingly read aloud. Once initiated into this amazing course, the victim cheerfully passed down in his or her turn the legend, "You just wait! You don't know <u>anything</u> . . .."

The seniors had picked up their books along with their other texts the day before. They looked ridiculous on top of the stacks of large, business-like textbooks: little duodecimo volumes bound in discreet brown cloth, small enough to slip into anyone's pocket, labeled in black block letters along the spine *Hamlet*. They accepted them diffidently; the legend was effective.

They had the little books now. The library was empty, the long, long table completely clear. Outside the open windows

September was radiant. Pappy came in; he came in confidently—pleasant, business-like, formidable. "You may sit wherever you like," he said. The senior class averaged less than 30 in those days; there was plenty of room for them. They quietly took seats around the long table. Pappy sat down at the head of the table with his back to the magazine rack with its rows of bright covers. Behind him was the wall of reference books and the shelves labeled "Religion," "Philosophy," "Sociology." The legend had it that in Senior English he actually took such books off the shelf and read out of them!

He smiled cheerfully. "You know, of course," he said, "you have undoubtedly been told that this is a snap course." Someone gasped aloud; someone snickered. "That's quite true," he continued, "it is a snap course. There is no textbook; there are no lesson assignments; there is no home work in the usual sense. All we do is read. In fact, all you have to do is listen.

They were listening.

He went on, serene and casual, as if it were not the end of the academic world. "You have probably heard rumors that you have to pay for your seats in this course. That may sound shocking, but it's true. However, it needn't inconvenience your parents or cut into your allowances. Arrangements have been made for you to earn the money." They all knew about this; they had seen the long green checks, drawn on the "Quasi-National Bank, Ltd." and made out to their senior school mates of other years. There was really no excuse for their expression of alarm, except that here they were at last, gobbled up in the legend—it was actually happening to them.

"We have a magazine." They knew about it. They had sat at the long table and read it and admired the masterpieces of their betters. Now it was happening to them. "We have a magazine called '*The Tyro—a Magazine of Literary Miscellany.*' You will find copies from previous years on the table. You can earn the necessary money to stay in the class by submitting manuscripts to the editor of the *Tyro*. The editor will appraise this material and pay you for it on a basis of what it is worth. It will cost you $15 a week to rent a seat on Acme Avenue, $10 to rent a seat on Broadway; $5 for a seat on Cuckoo Alley."

"Isn't there a seat for a D?" someone piped up.

"Sorry, our cheapest seat is $5."

"What if we can't even pay $5?"

"You will be evicted."

There was a discussion about just what that entailed—absence from the class until the rent was paid, and interest piling up on the indebtedness until they got back in. There was a discussion about the nature of the material, and a gentle reminder that it would be judged on quality rather than quantity. "For instance," he said, "you could write pages and pages of junk and get $7.50 for it when you might get $20 for a good, well-crafted sonnet of only 14 lines." Potential poets blinked.

"You won't have to read a word in class or prepare for the class," he said. "We shall have some outside reading, though. We shall expect three average-length books of good literary quality for each six-week period. The librarian has a list from which you may choose these books, and you may consult her about others. We want you to learn to enjoy a truly great book. In order to save you the trouble of writing out reports on the books, you will make your reports orally to the librarian. She will arrange a schedule of the times when she can take them." Good heavens! *Oral* reports! You couldn't fool her in an oral report. And 18 books a year! "Oh, it wouldn't necessarily be quite that many," he said cheerfully, "I should think Tolstoy's *War and Peace* might do for a whole six weeks." What about mysteries? The librarian was listening. (She loved Senior English.) She looked up. "Willkie Collins' *The Moonstone* is on the list," she said.

"I also want you to learn to feel comfortable reading articles in good magazines—I mean articles with literary value and lasting content. We'll read three the first six weeks, four the next, and five the next; and in the second semester, we'll read one a week." What kind of articles? What magazines? *Colliers* OK? "These," he said and ran his finger along the top shelf of the rack—*Atlantic Monthly, Harpers, Yale Review, Saturday Review. . . shoulder to shoulder they stood, and onto the next shelf and the next.

No *Colliers*? No *Colliers*. No *Readers' Digest*? No *Readers' Digest*—those were mutilated reprints. No *Sports Illustrated*? No *Sports Illustrated*. Why are they on the rack if we can't use them? "For your information and for research. We expect you to read them anyway."

"You may turn in written reports on the articles," he said. "They may be quite short." The librarian smiled lovingly to herself, suddenly remember a beloved girl who had once turned in quite a short report on a fine article in *Harpers*: "This would have been a good article if you liked it, but I didn't."

"Gosh, Pappy," cried an uninhibited one in despair, "have you forgotten that we have three other solids, one with lab?" He grinned.

"Oh, yes, I almost forgot. I do want to you get the feel of good verse as a final little kick in your literary pants. The best way to do that is memorize. Will you please pick up a notebook like this." (It was blue, a big page with clear wide-spaced lines.) "The class meets right after lunch on Fridays. Each Friday you will have memorized and will record in class in the notebook a poem of literary merit—a poem of your own choosing of not less than thirteen lines." (That thirteenth line ruled out many a trite bit of poesy built in three four-line stanzas.) "Consult the librarian about your choices, if you like. She will be glad to help you."

Why did the librarian love this so, I wonder. (She was also editor of the *Tyro* in later years.) Senior English was almost a full-time job for her by itself. The poetry was graded more on the quality of the poem than on the accuracy of the memorization. Why did she rake through the repertoire for a poem that might appeal to a particular child, while all those books waited to be filed and returned to the shelves, and the fifth grade would be in in a minute, all on fire about Indians?

A tiny moan escaped a hockey player. Suddenly Pappy laughed. He stopped being polite and businesslike and threw back his head and roared: they looked so miserable. "You know, you kids are awfully lucky. All this and *Hamlet* too! But you don't need to worry about *Hamlet*; that just turns up on the final examination." You see, Senior English was required for graduation in Cheyenne Mountain School!

"Please open your books to *Hamlet* at page one."

They were ominously docile. They opened the little books at page one and laid them flat in front of them on the table. They knew all about Shakespeare. They had listened to themselves read, year after year, *Julius Caesar, As You Like It*, and *Macbeth*, taking turns boring each other with their words, words, words—stupid archaic, incomprehensible words. Well, one more year, and they would be through with Shakespeare forever. What did teachers see in him anyway?

"Hamlet, Prince of Denmark, by William Shakespeare, Dramatis Personae." He was reading it in a dry monotonous voice, exactly as it was written on the page. He read the Dramatic Personae: "Claudius, King of Denmark; Hamlet, son to the former and nephew to the present king; Horatio, Friend to Hamlet. . ." He read it as if he were reading proof on the Montgomery Ward catalogue. They followed in their books, stunned into silence. He finished the Dramatis Personae and started on the play: "Bernardo. Who's there? Francisco. Nay answer me; stand and unfold yourself." He could hardly bear to read that line without letting them hear in his voice how much he loved it, how wonderful it was. But he went on with as much expression as a cuckoo clock until it was time for Horatio to come in; he couldn't bear to do this to Horatio.

This should have been a part of the legend, but scarcely anyone ever told. The occasional ones who came into the class knowing that this was going to happen held their peace. Eyes grew bigger, faces rigid. A year of <u>this</u>?

He stopped abruptly. He glared at them. "This *is* what you think Shakespeare is, isn't it? This is what you expected. It's the way you would read it to yourselves. This is the way you hear it when you think of Shakespeare! Good heavens! You poor dears! Shakespeare! No wonder you hate him, when you listen for him to sound like that! Now—listen!"

He took them north along the sound from Copenhagen to Elsinore. He took them past Hans Andersen's little bronze mermaid sitting in the sun and watching blue sparkles on bright water. He took them along the green coastline and through the town of Elsinore and into Kronborg Castle, properly towered and turreted to this day. He reminded them that perhaps Will Shakespeare had been on a ship that was held up for toll in the little harbor and that he had picked up his story at that time. The drawbridge dropped and they crossed the moat; they climbed to the platform on the great square corner tower; it became close to midnight—thick dark—fog coming in from the sea; it was cold; they shivered but they went with him. There was something strange and lonely about it all—something sinister, but something brave and loyal too. They went. There was a sentinel on the tower, Francisco, pacing to keep warm, startled by the voice of Bernardo, crying out sharply, "Nay, answer me. Stand and unfold yourself."

"Like a flag," Pappy said, "rolled up on its staff. And then it unfolds itself and you know that it is the flag of Denmark. You know it is Bernardo." It was eerie waiting with Francisco and Bernardo, and Francisco sick at heart. What could be wrong here? The fog was thicker, wetter. They were waiting for Horatio and Marcellus. Suddenly Francisco cried out, "Stand! Who's there?" And Horatio called out, "Friends to this ground," and Marcellus called out, "And liegemen to the Dane," and the class bell rang! And so they went to live for a while in Kronborg Castle, hard by the Danish town of Elsinore, 400 years ago. They shivered on the platform, and the ghost came and Marcellus whispered, "Question it, Horatio," and Horatio cried out, "By heaven, I charge thee, speak!" And they argued long and earnestly about whether or not they would have had this sort of courage. "Never be afraid of a ghost," Pappy said, and spent the hour discussing how many kinds of ghosts there are. "Whatever it is, speak to it; question it!"

They sat by day and looked across the narrow sound to Sweden and watched Ophelia at her embroidery; they wandered in the church yard and down a hundred halls; and all the time the story tugged at their minds—was he mad or not, this slight young man in black velvet? Was Horatio easier to love, who was so sound and so steady? What, what, *what* would they have done? Sometimes it took three weeks to read Hamlet, sometimes six. It depended. At the end they closed the little brown books, variously touched, or not at all. They had survived *Hamlet* and they were part of the legend. They would never be quite the same, for greatness makes its own demand. There would always be a flash of sudden comprehension of how difficult it is to be a human being—difficult for them as well as for the Prince of Denmark. There would always be a corner of the world where there was a darkened platform with a ghost walking; a noble hall with a queen walking; a garden with a sweet maid walking; a maelstrom of the mind with a man walking—all walking toward doom. And weaving it all together, tendrils of their native tongue at its lovely best—little scraps of phrases to linger until the end of their days: "Absent thee from felicity a while, and in this harsh world draw thy breath in pain to tell my story."

And then they went round the Horn with Dauber. For 160 pages of Masefield's vigorous verse they went with Dauber and learned another kind of doom and the running joy of a windjammer at sea. Inland children—they tasted the sea and the reek of the ship; indolent children—they experienced the terrible need to communicate their wonder through the Dauber's terrible need.

> *There the four leaning spires of canvas rose,*
> *Royals and skysails lifting, gently lifting,*
> *White like the brightness that a great fish blows*
> *When billows are at peace and ships are drifting. . .*

How Pappy read it! Like a song. . .

> *There the great skyline made her perfect round,*
> *Notched now and then by the sea's deeper blue*
> *A smoke-smutch marked a steamer homeward bound,*
> *The haze wrought all things to intenser hue.*
> *In tingling impotence the Dauber drew*
> *As all men draw, keen to the shaken soul*
> *To give a hint that might suggest the whole.*

There was also doom—Dauber's, and triumph—Dauber's. They sensed and held it, meshed in the lovely pattern of the words.

When the bosun finally offered to teach Dauber square sennit, Pappy took from his pocket sash cord that he had woven into square sennit that morning at his office desk, to show them how it looked, and then he took another bit of cord and showed them how it was done, and how fine it was for a lanyard or a quirt. Someone asked, "Pappy, when did you go to sea?" and Dauber was lost for a day while he told them about Bunny, the erstwhile ship's cook who had turned up as cook on the Wildflower Excursion that the old Midland Railway ran from Colorado Springs to Spinney in South Park, and on which he, Pappy, served as photographer and nature guide. Bunny's mouth was full of oaths, but his mind was stored with the orderly beauty of a hundred knots, and his fingers were fleet with them. And Lloyd learned them all with pure delight in the patterns, the same delight he found later in the patterns of the dance and in the amazing order that appeared on a properly strung warp when a shuttle was thrown.

"And so I went to sea over in the middle of South Park, Colorado," he said. But the librarian remembered a time on a lake-still Atlantic, sailing to Ireland on a one-class boat, when he sat rather wistfully on the after deck watching the four quartermasters and a passenger who had been a telephone lineman taking turns showing each other knots—craftsmen's bits from a lost past. Visibly suffering from the need to get into this excited and exclusive conversation, he waited discreetly until an argument arose about a certain sort of hitch that some of them had seen and none of them could remember, one that you tied as you took the rope from the deck, but much more complicated than any sort of circus or sailor's hitch. He slipped lightly from his deck chair, stepped almost shyly into the circle. The rope lay straight on the deck. "Could this be it?" he said and lifted the rope with swift hands, tied into a beautiful knot. From then on, all the way to Eire there were six men in the very exclusive knot-tiers club that met on the after-deck of the *Arabic*. And finally the captain himself showed him how *he* tied a crowned Matthew Walker.

But they always went back to the book, no matter how far afield it led them. The Dauber had yet to fall from the fore-topgallant yard, and this had somehow to be made plain as a right and beautiful thing; and the ship had yet to come into Valparaiso Harbor without him—

> *When in the sunset's flush they went aloft,*
> *And unbent sails in that most lovely hour,*
> *When the light gentles and the wind is soft,*
> *And beauty in the heart breaks like a flower,*
> *Working aloft they saw the mountain tower,*
> *Snow to the peak; they heard the launchmen shout*
> *And bright along the bay the lights came out.*

"But, Pappy, Mary said, "this is terrible! The Dauber was the one who should have seen it! He was the one who would have loved it!"

"Of course, he answered. "And how do you know that he wasn't there?"

I think it never occurred to them that they had listened raptly to 160 pages of poetry. They listened just as raptly to the 90 pages of this poet's "Everlasting Mercy," full of earthy wisdom and as simple as the morning paper. They learned that there is poetry in a boxing match. "Sea Fever" turned up in their memorization books.

It was November. Quarterly exams were over. They had survived the legend. They had written, received bogus checks instead of grades, paid their "rent" and remained in their seats. They had read books—and survived the book report. But it was time for a big boost. "Is it *Cyrano* now?" the librarian asked as he came into the room ahead of the class.

"Yes, *Cyrano*! Where will I find it?"

"It's on the table. I laid it out for you."

Cyrano de Bergerac! The repertory of Senior English was deliberately and unashamedly designed to ignite, if possible, the souls of persons approximately 18 years old. It was not afraid of being romantic or poetic or exciting. It simply bristled with morals, only half revealed, with guide-posts never quite pointed out, with old-fashioned virtues like courage and integrity and gentleness. So here came Cyrano, swashbuckling down the streets of Paris!

How Pappy set the stage for that enchanting first act! (Did anyone ever write a first act so delicious as the first act of Rostand's *Cyrano de Bergerac*?) He filled the invisible stage with people—beautiful, elegant, trivial, intelligent people. They spoke their preposterous lines with pure joy. The gay little pages fished

147

for wigs from the gallery; the musketeer pursued the flower girl; the common folk picnicked on the floor of the theater; the ladies and the titled gentlemen entered the boxes, incredibly suave and self-satisfied. Roxane came, lovely Roxane, and Christian cried out, "Ah!" And everyone was waiting for Cyrano. Cyrano came. Was there ever anyone invented as perfect as Cyrano for boys and girls turning 18? How they loved him! How Pappy loved him and the splendid lines he spoke!

These children had been listening daily for almost three months to iambic pentameter, and I think it never entered their heads that this was so. I think they never thought about the fact that they were being taught poetry. They were being confronted with a man, a human entity so different from that slim Hamlet in the black velvet doublet that it seemed unlikely they could have lived in the same world. Whatever world it might be, here was certainly a different way of facing up to it. Hamlet's way, Dauber's way, Cyrano's way—they all took courage and a kind of fierce honesty. Do you remember the place where foolish Valvert starts out by taunting Cyrano:

> *. . . look at him, not even gloves?*
> *No ribbons, no lace, no buckles on his shoes—*

And Cyrano makes that wonderful speech:

> *I carry my adornments on my soul.*
> *I do not dress up like a popinjay;*
> *But inward I keep my daintiness.*
> *I do not bear with me, by any chance,*
> *An insult not yet washed away—a conscience*
> *Yellow with unpurged bile—an honor frayed*
> *To rags, a set of scruples badly worn.*
> *I go caparisoned in gems unseen,*
> *Trailing while plumes of freedom, garlanded*

With my good name—no figure of a man,
But a soul clothed in shining armor, hung
With deeds for decorations, twirling—thus—
A bristling wit, and swinging at my side
Courage, and on the stones of this old town
Making sharp truth ring, like golden spurs!

Wonderful Cyrano! Composing the ballade about the duel while he was fighting it! "Then, as I end the refrain, thrust home!" How they loved him—and grew an inch thereby! Drama, romance—pure corn in the jargon of today. So much to say about courage and the high heart and standing up to be counted!

And fighting! This peace-loving man chose the most magnificent fights in literature with which to rejoice the hearts of these just-past-seventeens. Real fights: Hamlet's bewildered battle with his own brain; Dauber, at last licking the fore-topgallant mast; Saul Cain and that terrible boxing match, a fight won that was lost and, at the end, a lost fight won:

O wet red swathe of earth laid bare,
O truth, O strength, O gleaming share,
O patient eyes that watch the goal,
O ploughman of the sinner's soul.
O Jesus, drive the coulter deep
To plough my living man from sleep.

After the semester changed, there was Lear and the dreadful all-but-hopeless battle of simple goodness against unmitigated evil. He almost always broke it at about this place and read them Barrie's *Dear Brutus*—prose at last: silly sensible people at war with their own selves. But when spring came, and the blood ran too thick, and lethargy set in, he took James Stephens re-telling of the ancient Irish story of *Deirdre and the Sons of Usna* from the shelf. For once they groaned when the class bell rang,

149

squarely in the middle of that greatest of all fights: beautiful Deirdre and Usna's three sons against the whole of Ulster! Blood dripped from the pages of the book as Pappy read, but here were love and courage and a loyalty as clean as a spring morning.

In between there was a considerable repertory of shorter bits to suit the temper of the particular class. Sometimes he even read selections from the Baghavad Gita (when the quality of the class permitted) and a number of psalms. And often he read Kahlil Gibran's "Prophet," who speaks exactly to 17, in a voice that the hardening ear will never hear so clearly again. Seventeen, rushing headlong into the prison of the world, needing so demandingly to be told: "But you, children of space, you restless in rest, you shall not be trapped or tamed. Your house shall not be an anchor but a mast... For that which is boundless in you abides in the mansions of the sky, whose door is the morning mist, and whose windows are the songs and silences of night."

Courage and honor and love—he rubbed their noses in them. Love! He loathed the fools' gold counterfeit they were so willing to accept. Love did not happen—it was built; it was not given—it was giving; it was sacrifice and an inconvenience and an everlasting wonder. Watching them, listening to them, he would interrupt himself furiously to snatch the great Bible off the reference shelf and read the 13th chapter of Paul's first letter to the Corinthians—"suffereth long and is kind. . . vaunteth not itself . . . beareth all things, believeth all things, hopeth all things, endureth all things."

"Your silly little namby-pamby hand-holding, eye-rolling affairs," he would cry, "you haven't the courage to really *love* someone!" Fiercely he would whisper to the librarian, "Get me Shakespeare's sonnets," but she would have them ready to put in his hand, having watched the storm rolling in. She had the book opened at the page he would read:

Love is not love

Which alters when it alteration finds . . .

He talked about that. "If so-and-so did thus-and-so, could you still stand fast?" He made up situations; he spun plots; he argued; he pleaded.

> *O, no! It is an ever-fixed mark*
> *That looks on tempests and is never shaken*
> *It is the star to every wandering bark,*
> *Whose worth's unknown although his height be taken.*
> *Love's not time's fool . . .*
> *Love alters not with his brief hours and weeks,*
> *But bears it out even to the edge of doom.*

He was utterly intolerant of "puppy-love." Deep life-time love *could* happen between two very young people, sometimes did. He was amazingly helpful about it when he was convinced. But if it lacked dignity—if it ever embarrassed anyone else, it wasn't real. "Bears it out even to the edge of doom."

He was in vigorous disagreement with the psychology of educators who argued that the successful teacher was the one who kept in mind the student viewpoint, who was "simpatico," who "spoke their language." "Nonsense," he would say. "You play with them, work with them, love them: but you don't speak their language—you speak yours. Every year you are a year farther away from them than you were the year before, for they are always 17. Bring them the vintage of that additional year, but don't speak their language! Make them understand yours."

Some of them rebelled, of course. Some rebelled vigorously, some stupidly. He loved the vigorous rebels. It was a constant duel, and time had sharpened his weapons. Hartley was brilliant, ingratiating, and lazy. He lived by his wits, not by hours of conscientious preparation, and he was convinced that one could pass Senior English without paying his "rent" regularly. One could get by with anything, as long as one was pleasant and full of promises. Monday morning came and Hartley had less than $5 in his balance at the "Quasi National Bank." In fact he was stone broke. He presented the evidence cheerfully and took his accustomed seat at the far end of the table.

"Goodby, Hartley," Pappy said.

"Sir?"

"I said goodby. We'll see you when you're solvent."

"You mean I'm kicked out of class?"

"Let's say you are evicted for failure to pay your rent, and don't forget your interest begins today."

"What'll I do?"

"I'd suggest that you go back to study hall and start writing."

They were in the middle of *Cyrano*, which Harley was loving, but he held out for weeks. His "indebtedness" reached a fantastic sum with interest compiled upon interest. When he finally surrendered, it was like an autumn tree whose leaves were theme paper, closely scribbled. They fell steadily on the table of the Editor of the *Tyro*. Compositions on every conceivable subject, all brimming with Hartley, frantically piling up against imminent disaster.

Horton was different. He resented the time it took. He had a superb and beautifully organized mind. "I resent all the time it takes to do this reading and writing. I can't see where it is going to be useful to me in the field of science. I won't break my straight A record, and I have to write an awful lot to be sure of it and read a lot too."

"Read a meaty book, a long one," said the librarian. "Try *The Brothers Karamazov*. And Horton, you don't have to write a lot to get a good grade. Why don't you try a sonnet?" (A sonnet, she thought, is not a poem; it is a scientific exercise that sometimes turns out to be a poem as well.)

"Me?" muttered Horton, "write poetry?"

"Not poetry, Horton, just a sonnet. It's a little like math." She showed him where to find the best instructions.

Friday came round again. The editor of the *Tyro* wearily gathered up the great stack of manuscripts submitted "To the Editor of the *Tyro*—at your customary rates," and stowed them in a dossier to carry home. On Sunday evening she came to Horton's single sheet of paper with its fourteen lines of flawless pentameter, neatly typed. She read it incredulously. It was Horton most certainly; no one else could have exactly that to say. Horton had written a poem; he would write other poems; he would go on, please God, all his life blowing this sure spark into a tall fire. He would be a great scientist, but not that only—he would be a poet too, a maker. She took it to where Lloyd sat in his big chair, reading a Spanish novel "to keep from forgetting my Spanish."

"Here's your scientist," she said.

The teacher's face reflected the light of the student's little candle. "Good," he said, "very good!" He chuckled. "Saving himself time. I wonder how long it took him."

On Monday when the manuscripts were returned with the checks and the "letter from the editor," Bill leaned over Horton's shoulder to read his check. "Gosh, Hort! Twenty dollars! For that little bitty thing?"

"It's a sonnet," said Horton diffidently.

"Gosh, Hort, *is* it? Gosh!"

Pappy read it aloud to the class.

Not very long ago a letter came in the mail from the Medical School of the University of Utah from Dr. Horton Johnson, research pathologist of the Medical Faculty. The editor of the *Tyro* opened it to find that it was indeed addressed to her in a long-ago capacity. "To the editor of the *Tyro*," it said. "Dear Mrs. Shaw: Just wanted you to know that I still whittle away at a piece of verse once in a great while. But how I miss the comments in red ink! If you feel inclined to so decorate the enclosed sonnet, I'd be delighted." She unfolded the sonnet.

Autopsy of J.Y.C.

How soon the academic question dies
And I, the white robed priest, am left to stand
Alone, with neatly opened heart in hand
And helpless hear, where brave Adonis lies,
His thin young soul, which pounds the chill damp walls
In grief, and, seeing his many dreams congeal
In shapeless pool on sterile stainless steel,
Runs screaming naked down the morgue-gray halls.

But we were boys just twenty years ago!
I think I could have caught his shirt-tails then
And brought him crashing down. "Come back! You know
It's just a game." And shaking hands like men
We could have shuffled home beneath that sky
Where time stood still and only clouds passed by.

"Here's your scientist, darling," she whispered, and aloud, "Thank you, Horton."

Shuffling home from school along the dusty boulevard, with the wild plum coming into bloom and the lilacs in bud, and almost done with Senior English! Touched or untouched, or just indifferent—who could say? This was no special experiment for a self-chosen group selecting an elective course; this was everybody. This was a second-class district public school, and they all had to "take" Senior English, and to some of them it must have been a delicate kind of torture, being brow-beaten and cajoled, whispered at, sung to, laughed at, wept with, and exhorted. Bombarded by a thousand star-bright atoms, the great voice warm or husky or sharp—the bits striking hard to be remembered forever. Fat books lifted suddenly from a shelf, words spoken—"Which of us has

154

known his brother? Which of us has looked into his father's heart? Which of us has not remained forever prison pent? Which of us is not forever a stranger and alone? Remembering speechlessly we seek the great forgotten language, the lost lane-end into heaven, a stone, a leaf, an unfound door. . ." Ah, yes, we know, at 17! A slim book lying open on a table beside a slender vase with one red rose. "Edna St. Vincent Millay died yesterday," he says. They have just finished "Conversation at Midnight," eloquent, fluent, bitter-bright. Now he is reading:

But the music of your talk
Never shall the chemistry
Of the secret earth restore.
All your lovely words are spoken.
Once the ivory box is broken
Beats the golden bird no more.

Why must we be forever obliged to try to keep from weeping—at 17? Why was the librarian so delighted when we memorized: "This is the shape of the leaf, and this of the flower and this the pale bole of the tree"? We didn't understand it; we just liked the way it sounded.

Hammering, hammering, hammering, trying to break through to them; "breaking through to you on waves of joy," someone wrote later, "because he was always breaking through that way."

And always, in the midst of everything, two men to take home up the dusty boulevard: a puzzled man in a black velvet doublet—Hamlet, Prince of Denmark—saying gravely, "Question it, Horatio," and an altogether unpuzzled man wearing a rakish hat with a white plume, swinging his sword in great circles in the middle of a street in Paris, and crying,

What's that you say: Hopeless? Why, very well!

155

But a man does not fight merely to win!
No, no, better to know one fights in vain! . . .
You there—who are you? A hundred against one—
I know them, my ancient enemies—
Falsehood! . . . . There! There! Prejudice—compromise—
Cowardice—What's that? No! Surrender? No!
Never!

Was it hopeless? School teaching is always three parts hopeless.

Did anyone ever pick up Cyrano's white plume and stick it in his own cap? Often, I think. There are a number of business men and lawyers and doctors and poets walking American streets, discreetly concealing long sharp swords and dashing and un-profaned white plumes that they picked up from Cyrano de Bergerac when he dropped them in Senior English at Cheyenne Mountain School.

They are completely aware. Bob wrote, "It has taken me a long hard time to begin to grow up, and throughout that time, even when I was most confused and childish, Pappy has always been with me looking at me with the cold, deflating look when I was foolish, smiling at me with the wide glorious smile when I did something good. So long as I live he will be riding in my head, judging me and what I do with a look, with a smile, with a sharp word, with a thunder of laughter, with quiet words of wise understanding and compassion. Some of us took a long time to realize that he had been right in something he said, or that he meant something better than we thought it sounded. But Pappy's way was always that of pointing something out to a person and then letting that person work his own way out of the dilemma. It is what he once read to us and what has recurred to my thoughts again and again: a great man, smiling, laughing at the stars, and telling the world that he still has 'my white plume!'"

THE BEGINNINGS OF DANCING
(Lloyd)

We had been in our new gym only a couple of weeks when the daily paper carried a story that Miss Elizabeth Burchenal, head of the American Folk Dance Society, would be in our city, and would hold a class for the directors of the Women's Gymnasiums of the region and anyone else who was interested in coming. "Girls have forgotten how to play," she said. Not only girls, I thought, but their brothers and parents as well.

Groping in this direction a few months before, I had led my youngsters out into the yard and started them in on some old English folk dances. I knew nothing about dances of this sort, except that the people who lived in the old villages simply loved them, and I thought there might be something in it for us. The youngsters were most cooperative, and we worked hard and laughed a lot. We sort of enjoyed it, but somehow I didn't know enough about it to put it over, and so we cheerfully dropped it until there was something within our reach. Here it might be—and I was curious about it.

So I sent Miss Marion Elser, who was in charge of our girls' gymnasium classes, to Miss Burchenal's class, and she brought back an enthusiastic report.

Miss Burchenal had another story in the paper saying that the realm of folk dancing was a little kingdom lying just around the corner, waiting for some of us to discover it. (America had not

157

really discovered it yet.) She said that it could only be appreciated by someone who was *doing* it but that it was a much-needed form of recreation. Then she left town and went up to Denver. When I found that she was going to have a general session in one of the big gymnasiums, I decided to go and see for myself. I found her delightful and was much taken with her dances. This might be what I was looking for. So I had a long talk with her and got her promise to return to Colorado Springs and have a session with us. I had to raise fifty dollars for her trip. But that was nothing if she proved to be real.

So, she came, and my youngsters fell in love with her. We danced for her with wild enthusiasm. She loved us as much as we loved her! We entered into her program with our minds eagerly wide open, and we suddenly discovered that we had found something precious.

On Wednesday night of each week throughout the year we had a folk dance in our gymnasium, just for fun. We did all the dances Miss Burchenal had taught us. We got copies of her books and worked out a lot more. We had a wonderful time. We were dancing for pure joy! There was nothing else to dance for then!

It was only natural that some of the kids began to wear bright scarves and bits of color. Everybody enjoyed them and began copying them. We all laughed and dressed up more and more—just for the fun of it. No one laughed at us. Not a single pupil tried to razz another for the costume he or she contrived. We all loved it! We were dancing for pure joy!

One of our teachers, a real musician, enjoyed playing the piano for us. She would study out a tune and get the swing of it so she could make it live again as it had lived before for centuries. It was glorious!

Between sessions I would prowl through Miss Burchenal's books and pounce on another dance that looked inviting. I would study it and master it and teach it to my joyous group. They were not just youngsters in years but in viewpoint. Several of our faculty were also dancing with us with the same kind of enthusiasm. They would put on a touch of color, and they would take hands and laugh and move in perfect joy.

We found that we were touching the magic spring of action that had flowed down through the centuries. Indeed, we were swimming in it! The folk spirit that had seeped into the very bones and minds of a whole village of people had seeped into us, too. We came out onto the gym floor in the long winter nights, as the villagers had come out onto the green in the long summer nights, and joyously danced our hearts away.

I am sure that our ancestors had no "Directors of Physical Education," and probably no committees were in charge of anything. So we danced simply too, naturally and for joy. We never gave a great deal of thought as to who was better than whom. We were simply having a good time—we were following the impulses of our hearts.

What fun we had! In the Danish dance, "Little Man in a Fix," we soon found that when the two men ran with left elbows hooked and the two women ran with their partner's right arm around their waists, it was soon possible for us to lift the women clear off their feet (and you can bet the Danes had discovered that before us.) It was all a matter of balance. The two boys swung around and around with their girls riding on their free arms, arched well back, like pretty shawls with heads and feet. It was beautiful and thrilling!

We had entered into Joy. And we guessed that we had found something that might fill our very lives with meaning. We had started on that long and delightful quest that would at last carry us back through all the old dances of America, and then would lead us slowly back and back to more and more faraway ancestors, dancing their prayers and their weddings and their harvests.

We were having such a hilarious time that word about us began to spread. More and more parents would come down on Wednesday nights to watch us dance, to laugh with us, and to

marvel at the wonderful time we were having. They would find themselves suddenly
laughing with us in contagious joy. It was they who proposed that we hold an exhibition for the rest of the parents. The idea appealed to us, for we were eager to share our joy. So we arranged a program and had copies of it mimeographed for our audience. We put all the chairs we could find around our gymnasium, both downstairs and up in the balcony. We dressed in our very best, and we added all the legitimate color that we could possibly find. Our faculty and our students, all who had joined in on giving our program, put together a laughing, hilarious, and at times seriously moving and beautiful program. We danced our very hearts out for them.

An old ticket from that performance is dated May 4, 1923—only a few weeks after we had started to dance!

Early the next year Miss Burchenal's book on American Country Dances was published, and we jumped in and learned to dance a lot of them with particular joy. I think it was in this volume that her Uncle Steve's Quadrille, an old American dance in square formation arranged in several parts, was first introduced. We seized upon it, dancing it immediately, and it was always a great joy to us. And we found such old contra dances as Money Musk and Hull's Victory, and we danced them with enthusiasm.

It happened that a few years before, our local County Agricultural Agent had decided to put on a square Dance Contest at our Annual Pure Seed Show in the city auditorium. I had gone up and watched it from the first and was quite interested, but I couldn't see any possibility right then of incorporating this brand of dancing into the work at my school. There were no available books then, and it was a little too complex for me. We weren't quite ready for it yet, so I just kept it in the back of my mind and kept brooding on it every now and then.

The next year on December 12, 1934, one of the best callers in the county, Mr. Guy Parker, called me from his ranch and asked me if I could furnish a few dancers to fill out his two sets of squares that he wanted to enter in the contest that year. He would of course teach my students the dances. I was delighted and immediately agreed. So he brought his dancers up to my gymnasium a few times, and I filled out his sets for him with some of my best dancers. He didn't want a general dance, just enough to fill out his sets. In fact he didn't want any audience at all. So with this chance to study the square dance, I jumped at the opportunity he offered me. Guy, unfortunately, would always manage to leave out one couple in his calling, at least while he was practicing on our cold gym floor. But we got the idea and enjoyed this form of dancing immensely. We went up to the auditorium that year and helped him win a prize, which we insisted on his keeping. But we had our start at last in the square dancing of our own West. And we loved it!

So I arranged with the winners in this particular contest and their caller and small orchestra to come out to my school on the next Wednesday night and teach us all how to square dance. We had to pay them something, but the chief thing I had failed to think of was what a terrible ordeal it would be for them to be there at all. They were simply country folk and would be coming to what they considered to be a "city school," a rather famous city school if you looked at it in a certain light, to teach them their old and familiar form of dancing. It was actually quite unthinkable. So some of them took a friendly swig of something to brace their spirits up, and others borrowed the bottle, and by the time they got here they were all quietly inebriated. They couldn't dance very well by then, and they couldn't, alas, teach us much of anything. So we were the very nicest we could be to them and let them go home early, and after they were gone, we had a good long laugh.

I didn't know where to turn! But somehow we had to master this form of the dance. A couple of years later I heard of a young man down south of Fountain, a rather well-educated chap, who had been brought up on these dances. My friend Bob Collier, a teacher at the South Denver High School, had chanced to meet him and, becoming interested, had invited him to come up to Denver and teach his form of dancing to his youngsters. Bob had an enthusiastic group of youngsters that he was sponsoring, and they were getting along very well with this new —for them—form of dancing.

So I got in touch with Bob and went up with a bunch of my youngsters and joined in on one of their sessions. It was just what we wanted! Through Bob I learned the dances he had found, and I taught them to all of my youngsters. We had his enthusiastic club down to Colorado Springs and took them up to our school cabin for a night where we had a great time together. I was very sorry, a few years later, when Bob left his high school position and became interested in other things.

As we broadened our scope to include these American folk dances, we at first relegated them to the junior high while the high school kids continued with their showy international folk dances. Indeed some of my high school dancers were just a little superior at first about doing mere American dances. It is perfectly natural, I guess. At least I have found this to be true from many years of sad experience. We might discover a very valuable gold mine in our own back yard, but it wouldn't appeal to us at all. It is a mere hole in our back yard while if we found an old sawdust pile a thousand miles away, it would be quite wonderful because of the enchanting distance. It would charm us with its many possibilities, but of what possible use could a hole in the ground be in our own back yard even if it contained gold or diamonds in abundance? We human beings are strange animals! It took us years to work our way through to where we could see this truth clearly.

We let the junior high, poor kids, dance Uncle Steve's Quadrille, and Pop Goes the Weasel, Money Musk, and Hull's Victory. They were too easy for us! So we did the French Jibi-di-Jibi-da, which is nothing at all to dance but sounds good on a program. And we did the Danish Little Man in a Fix, carrying our

162

girls proudly draped over our held-out arms, the Czech Kanafaska, the Portuguese Vira, the Swedish Dal Dans, the Irish Siege of Ennis, and a host of other European dances.

By the next year we had gotten sort of famous! Word was getting around about us. We were even invited to dance that fall at the southern division meeting of the Colorado Teachers' Association down in Pueblo. After we danced there in the morning, there was so much excited talk about us that they asked us to dance that afternoon at the big general session meeting in the large auditorium. They changed their program at the last minute to fit us in somehow. So we went up and danced a half-hour program for them with all our enthusiasm. We were a tremendous hit, for it was something entirely new to them.

Invitations began to come to us from every school in that part of the state. Within that busy month we were invited to the annual dinner dance and the big program of the local Kiwanis Club at the Antler's Hotel in Colorado Springs. Our inexperienced kids were thrilled at finding their names printed on the "swell" program at each place. Every weekend we had to go to another school. It was quite exciting. But still the dancing itself was much more fun than the trips. We had stumbled on something that proved to be invaluable to us.

Within a month we were invited back to the high school in Pueblo where the state teachers' meeting had been held. It was one of the largest high schools in the state, and their pupils had been wanting to see us dance since everyone continued to talk about us. A writer for the school's student paper wrote the following article:

"Dancers delight students! They came, they danced, they conquered! Surely this   describes the enthusiasm with which the school received Mr. Shaw and his eight couples of folk dancers who so thoroughly captivated our entire audience. After the assembly everybody was doing it! Staid faculty members, dignified seniors, and rollicking under-classmen! They got everybody to dancing with them down in our gymnasium. Even "Dutch" Clark [who later became the most famous half-back in college football in this part of the country] succumbed to the rhythm of the dance or   to the lure of the little siren visitor dressed in red. The colorful costumes of the Cheyenne Dancers added a great deal to the perfect picture they made in the long and   beautiful repertoire. These high school students and Mr. Shaw are to be sincerely congratulated on having perfected so many artistic and difficult dances and on the utter joy that they seem to be having in doing them."

Ah, it was this joy at which the high school writer could only half guess! We had found something tremendously joyful and good, and we had started in eager pursuit of it. We thought little then of how the people reacted to it. We were off, with our eager eyes set on a distant and shimmering goal!

Lloyd's school diary, which he kept from 1932 to 1935, continues the story. On March 20, 1935: "Mr. Guy Parker came at 7:30 and taught us four new quadrilles. The pupils are catching on fast and love it." The next day Lloyd wrote, "Started noon practices on quadrilles so the whole school could learn them. This is a rare opportunity to learn this authentic folk activity." At their regular Wednesday evening folk dance on March 27 he reported, "Guy Parker and his daughters taught us four new dances and Varsouviana, Rye Waltz, etc." The next day he wrote, "Held an auditorium to stress costuming of Square Dance contestants and discuss [the] whole opportunity. Had a tryout and chose twelve semi-final couples for [the] Square Dance Team." The following day Lloyd and his dance team headed for Lamar and Las Animas in southeastern Colorado, dancing in the morning for students in Lamar. In the evening they performed in Las Animas: "made a big hit before a big crowd."

The next week on April 3 Lloyd noted, "Dinner for Guy Parker's orchestra at 6:00, square dance practice at 7:30. How hard it is to call with a country orchestra!" The next day his Cheyenne students competed in a square dance competition in the city auditorium, where some couples made the finals in the couple dances—the Rye Waltz, the Varsouviana, and the schottische. The next night at the same venue, "At the end of the program about 20 sets danced the Waltz Promenade. We picked it up and loved it. What a night! We danced The Girl I Left Behind Me and First Couple Promenade the Inside Ring."

"CHEYENNE MOUNTAIN HIGH SCHOOL" (Wenngren/Enid)

It was in this busy period that a Swedish educator came to visit. He was spending an extended time in the US to learn about its educational system. The resulting book that he wrote turned up in Lloyd's dance library. Here is his description of his day at Cheyenne School.

from
Fostran för Nutid, Framtid och Democrati
(*Education for the Present, Future and Democracy*)
By Robert E. Wenngren
Translated by Enid Cocke, 2010

[Translator's Note: In Lloyd Shaw's library I came across a book in Swedish in which I found an inscription written to Lloyd Shaw by the author. I looked in the Table of Contents, and, sure enough, there was a chapter on Cheyenne Mountain School. Lloyd Shaw's diary, which he kept in the 1930's, places Wenngren's visit on April 30, 1935. Wenngren, as he reports in his book, spent several years studying educational systems in the US.]

I had certainly heard talk several times about Cheyenne Mountain High School. But one hears talk of so many things that are the biggest or next biggest, the best or next best in the USA, or "in the world," that one pays little attention and soon forgets what was heard. And I had forgotten Cheyenne School. But then I came on my way westward to Denver, Colorado, a city with a splendid climate, wide open streets, a wonderful nature park with Buffalo Bill's grave, and with various things of interest concerning schools and education, among them an especially well known system for adult education. It was Dr. Essert who is involved in the latter who reminded me of Cheyenne School's existence. "You're traveling west. Have you been in Colorado Springs and seen Cheyenne School? Don't think of traveling farther west until you have visited it. It is the world's most wonderful school. Don't people talk about it in Sweden? You simply have to go there."

And so I had to. And so I traveled south to Pikes Peak, the Garden of the Gods, and Seven Falls. When one starts early and drives fast, one arrives like the early bird. It wasn't much later than sunrise when I stopped in Colorado Springs and asked for directions to Cheyenne School. Everyone knew where it was. "Just three or four miles and you're there." And so I was there. Given its unusual qualities, one could not miss it.

Dr. Shaw, the superintendent, immediately puts one at ease. He is extraordinarily likable. One feels welcome and completely at home in his school. Here I meet one of the most charming personalities that I have met in the world of education. "Bad luck," he says, "I was just getting ready to drive to the Colorado College chapel to give a talk on 'My Religious Experiences.' People are gathering already, so I can't cancel." "Good luck," I counter. "Now I can share in the experience." In this way I experience one of the most memorable hours of my life. The Dean of the college takes me around and shows me the chapel. It is a donation of a Mr. Shove, who wanted to introduce some of the old culture from his fatherland, England. The style is pure English and some of the building stones are even brought from old English ruins. Mr. Shove built himself a monument, and his genealogy is carved on the wall of the choir.

The chapel begins to fill with college youth. They throw away a cigarette butt hesitantly after a last inhalation, some outside but a few inside. They make themselves comfortable in the American manner: sit on their backs, put their feet up on the nearest available place, and let their heads disappear between their shoulders. Not everyone does this, but some do.

And so it begins. They sing in unison without full participation. The Dean says some words of welcome and gratitude to the donor, who sits nearby—and then Dr. Shaw.

He opens his heart and gives a gripping picture of a person's internal and external fight with the devil, the church, religion, and God. He captures his audience. They sit up, gather together their extremities, collect themselves, and listen intently. Here is something to think about. Dr. Shaw gives something of himself, and they appreciate it. "I didn't get any further than the introduction," he says on the way back. "One gets no further when he speaks freely from the heart and the heart is overfull."

"Tell about your school."

"Oh, there isn't much to talk about." He is modest. "Cheyenne Mountain School is a public school, District No. 12. We have a kindergarten here, elementary and high schools. It's the usual organization. But you can look around, and perhaps I can show you something a little surprising later." One of the school's older students, a courteous, knowledgeable youngster, takes me around and explains everything as if it were his own school. I ask him. He answers, "Yes, it all belongs to us." The whole school and everything in it. Even Dr. Shaw is ours.

We should go over and visit the kindergarten first. It has its own playground with a sandbox, shovels, swings, slides, trapezes, and next to it is a lawn for dancing and doing somersaults. Inside, the school is a child's paradise. On the walls are bright colored and fanciful paintings of the lives of the Cheyenne Indians who not long ago often had their campgrounds here on their way to the buffalo grounds. Here are peaceful paintings of locomotives, cars, and stations, which can be whitewashed over and conjured up again. There are children's books in abundance, children's furniture, and a children's piano, which they play with perseverance. A rich collection of costumes and clothes is found in a capacious wardrobe. They are used to make the children's plays and tableaux more realistic. There are also radios, film equipment, and music boxes.

"Now we'll go over to the nature preserve," says Fred. "It's just across the road here." Now here is something unusual. A good friend has donated a large area for a "Nature Study Preserve." Cheyenne Creek winds along beside it. In this moist environment the vegetation is unusually rich, even jungle-like. Trees, bushes, and flowers of unusual kinds flourish in abundance, and many of the mountain flora have been transplanted down here. In bird houses and nesting boxes the winged creatures appear to be thriving. And in the middle of this glory of nature wander the small children as if in paradise and the older students as if in a researcher's herb garden. Here is peace, beauty, and harmony.

In a clearing there is an open-air theater. "We regularly produce *The Littlest Wiseman* at Christmas and *The Harvest Moon* twice a year. It's Dr. Shaw who has given the plays their plot, and Mrs. Shaw has given them form. You have perhaps heard of this American Oberammergau play. But we produce even other things in addition—little things that we write ourselves.

"But let us go up to the corral on the mesa before we return to the school. We don't have so many horses right now. The terrible dryness has made it impossible for us to feed so many. Under normal conditions we have about 30 head. Now in the heat they are for the most part very docile." With practiced ease, competence, and elegance, he mounts a horse, which is not the least bit disturbed.

With our return to the school, it is lunchtime. As with most American schools, there is a special lunch room where both teachers and students can get their noon meal. Here is a lunch

169

room of an unusual sort. It is tastefully painted, and the wealth of artwork surprises me. "Here our school has so many friends," says Dr. Shaw. "We get help with the things that we can't manage ourselves. And the teachers are so interested and manage to find so many things."

We take a tour of the school. One sees, senses, and marvels. How can this be possible? Here is an altogether ideal school. Library, museum, laboratory, costume studio, and set workshop—all are so strangely artistic and pleasant that one can hardly describe it. It has to be seen. No, it has to be known. Dr. Shaw seems to understand my reflections. He says, "The spirit is more important than knowledge, teaching more important than the method, and more important than everything else is to live, yes, live and let live."

A youth comes and reports that all is ready in the gymnasium. "Please go up in the balcony. I must go down there," says Dr. Shaw and disappears. What is this? One of the small surprises. Skansen! *[An open-air park/museum in Stockholm where the folk arts are preserved and practiced.]* A pair of violin players and youths in folk costumes. They tune up and begin to play. Swedish folk tunes! Vingåkersvals, Fryksdalspolska, and Oxdans! All this at the foot of the Rocky Mountains, 1900 miles from New York where one can occasionally see a folk dance performance. From Holland, Scotland, Hungary, and Poland. A Russian dance ends the performance. Never have I seen a group of young people dance with such joy and insight in spite of the tropical warmth! But there stood Dr. Shaw in the middle of them, directing and dancing with them. He explains later that they have over 100 different national dances on their program and that he saw some of these dances at Skansen. "What a wonderful place," says Dr. Shaw. "And Stockholm. Both my wife and I fell in love with its beauty, surrounded by water."

"You have so many old cars in the parking lot."

"Oh, I must explain. We have a 'Five-dollar Ford Club.' The name tells what it is. It's simply a group of Ford owners, but each Ford must not cost more than five dollars. For that matter, you can see for yourself. You will see them in action. Come!"

After a few minutes I have a "Ford formation" in front of me. Five-dollar Fords. A motor, four wheels, a gas tank or a can of gas, something remaining of a body, usually only a seat, and a boy with a sense of humor. I get a seat in one of the better ones so I can come along and not sit on top of someone. And so we head straight out into nature. We drive over stones, hollows, grass clumps, puddles, bushes, mud, and creeks. Uphill and downhill in winding serpentines. It is a damp but refreshing ride. There one turns over. But what does it matter? Two boys are there to help, and it is quickly back on its wheels again. There is another one stuck in the mud. A chain-clad wheel whips mud up in the air. But it doesn't help. The car just sinks deeper. But willing boys' hands easily lift it up. There goes a tire. It doesn't matter. It doesn't mean anything. Just so the car rattles and goes. Especially rattles. Next we come to a steep slope with a fairly solid surface. Here the goal is to drive as high as possible up the slope and turn without overturning. I am a bystander. One needs to know exactly when it is time to turn. No one has an accident. Beautiful. And so we come back. I am shaken, jolted. But it certainly is enormously refreshing.

The Ford seems however to be less in style than the horse and bull. The students ride both of them. Beginners have old calm horses and bull calves, but one who is skilled and brave will mount a young stallion or a full-grown bull. Then the rider raises his lasso in a wild-west manner and feels free, happy, and strong. This is truly living for a youngster. This is rodeo sports.

A few years earlier Cheyenne Mountain High School awakened attention in the world of American football. They had a team in the state's highest league, and nonetheless decided that they shouldn't participate. Football was too dangerous, and they

171

should devote themselves to rodeo sports instead which, says a newspaper article, is thought to be less dangerous, although Dr. Shaw fell and broke a rib while on a ride with the boys. The media had a field day over that. It is to abandon the field of glory to give up football. When I see the boys play ball, I ask about it. Dr. Shaw explains, "We didn't give up ball games, but we got out of competition. A few years ago we went in for football with all our might. We had a group of strong and sturdy boys, but the school was so small that we could get only 14 boys even though we drew some from the lower grades. We had exceptional luck and beat teams from the biggest schools in the state. When our little school had such a success, the news media began to praise us to excess. I became afraid that if we continued to play with these smaller boys from the lower grades, someone could easily get seriously hurt. We discussed the issue, the boys and I, and through a vote, decided that we should give up the competition. Now we play among ourselves and less for glory than for the sake of enjoyment and fitness.

Dr. Shaw and his colleagues seek to develop a natural sport and to that end use the land around the school. Mountain climbing and skiing are the most popular sports. Above Seven Falls the student association owns a log cabin, and, as a ski lodge, they rent a ranch house, which lies on the back side of Pikes Peak. The students even have their own bus and a set of tents. Together they have earned money through their dramatic productions and competitions with Fords, horses, and bulls. The students travel by bus with skis and tents on holidays and on weekend outings over the state's imposing mountains. They participate in sport for its own sake, not for first prize. They don't work for medals or recognition.

Basketball, in which students are eager to compete, occupies an honored status at Cheyenne School. They think it is a fine and decent sport. As far as physical training is concerned, one can say moreover that it is an individualized system. Students each

172

choose two or three sports that they want to participate in each term. They must devote a minimum time to each but may spend more time on them if they want to. The school has the opportunity for all sorts of physical training. They have an excellent gymnasium, six surfaced tennis courts, an area for golf, a track field, and a running track. Way up the mountain they have access to a swimming beach and a swimming pool. In the winter they skate and ski. They have even tried flying gliders, which interested the boys mightily. Thus they satisfied their desire for challenge and daring.

One sees how far they have come in Cheyenne School. But how have they come there? A cheerful temperament and a fresh perspective. Much is done among the students themselves. They realized that they needed substantial financing to have riding lessons. But then they needed a corral. They got permission to use an area behind the school. The owner was obliging. The streetcar company, which had dug up a lot of rails, donated 100 of them for posts. The US Forest Service let the boys go into the forest to look for timber to make hurdles for riding competitions. Meanwhile they had a wonderful and strengthening activity. They don't mind digging, and they know that physical labor is a useful activity.

"What do the parents say?" They are typically interested, pleased, and enthusiastic. But all the boys who want to ride must have written permission from their parents. In general the community supports Dr. Shaw and his school. When some sort of animal protection society comes to a rodeo to protest that animals are being used for riding, they overlook the fact that the animals have it as easy as the boys.

Dr. Shaw himself thinks about this healthy ranch sport and says, "In this day of 'paved' civilization, it is something wonderful for a boy to learn to handle horses. I believe that we have hit on something that will prove to show itself of exceptional worth for developing character and fitness by providing such an experience to boys. And that offers us a fascinating way out of the over-organized and overemphasized sports system of today."

Dr. Shaw has received all sorts of evidence that the public is interested in his school and his program. He has received a lot of help. The school has received free use of 700 acres of pastureland in the winter where there is room for practice and exhibitions. They have also gotten free use of horses to ride for the winter. They have even gotten the loan of saddles and bridles, so about 30 horses with tack are available for the school's use.

It is not hard to understand the joy of living that 30-some youths know when they get on a horse's back and climb through open meadows and over mountains to reach some beautiful outlook to take their lunch break. There they gather for their meals around their elders, cook their food, tell of their adventures and observations, and study their maps while their horses graze nearby. It is a healthy wilderness experience, which surely has major implications for both physical and mental development for the foundation of a healthier outlook and way of life than the study of all of zoology's orders and classes. Through this open-air life is created an intimate knowledge of nature and a love of the same, which is evident in students in Cheyenne Mountain School.

Dr. Shaw has every reason to be pleased with his school, and that he is. He has been offered many prominent positions, but he refuses to take them. When I ask him about it, he says, "I will stay here as long as I can. It is so good to be here. I have to a certain degree achieved what I was working for. Of course there are many private schools that have stables where students can buy or rent riding horses or bring their own and pay for their upkeep. But I am warmed with satisfaction and gladness when I think that fate has let us, without expenditures, have a pasture full of horses where my public school students can go out and have the enjoyment and use of them."

There is an attraction of Indian story romance and wild west adventure over Cheyenne Mountain School, but this attraction is controlled, cultivated, and fine. It is like the kindergarten's colorful and idealized paintings of the Indians' lives compared with the privations and strains of existence.

A couple of years later I met Dr. Shaw again in Berkeley in California.* He had come in the school's bus with his folk dancing students the long 1300-mile trip from Colorado Springs. In the University's gymnastic and sports hall they demonstrated folk dances before more than a thousand spectators. There were folk dances from the most diverse countries. Among others represented were Sweden, Denmark, Poland, Russia, and Spain. The costumes were colorful and the dances were performed with a rhythm and precision that showed much practice but also insight. Here again was the same contagious enthusiasm as I had witnessed in Dr. Shaw's school. The audience was enchanted with both the costumes and the dances. Dr. Shaw directed from the microphone while his students danced. When they finished up with the Swedish weaving dance, Dr. Shaw said many lovely words about both Sweden and the Swedish folk dances, and he asked me to give his greetings to Sweden and the wonderful Skansen. Perhaps I can carry out my assignment here.

[The dance team visited UC Berkeley in 1940. Lloyd's entry for the day of Wenngren's visit to Cheyenne School also refers to his speech at Shove Chapel as "a difficult assignment and always a difficult audience." A later diary entry indicates that Lloyd did manage to get an English translation of Wengrenn's chapter about Cheyenne School.]

THE ACCIDENT (Lloyd)

One of the ironies of Lloyd Shaw's story is that the man who climbed mountains all over the state, popularized skiing in the Colorado Springs region, and helped get the country dancing, himself became crippled. Here is the story in his words.

In 1928 we bought our first school bus, a big second-hand bus from a firm in Salt Lake City, and we had our name beautifully printed all along the sides. It was better for our great variety of school trips, and we all enjoyed it immensely. It was quite a purchase for us, and we had to buy it all by ourselves with no helping contributions from anyone. We were quite frank about the fact that we were to use it also for our dancing trips, but we would use it even more for all the other uses of our busy school program. We had a little money in our treasury, and what with the money that we made on our plays and by arranging a temporary student loan to our bus fund, we had no trouble in financing the purchase. At last it was all painted for us, and they phoned us from the garage that it was ready—would we please come up and get it.

I recall the excitement with which we rode into town that evening to pick up our new bus. One of my teachers took me in his car since it was planned that I should drive the new bus back to the school. As we were driving along down Cheyenne Road, a woman in her car suddenly darted out of a little side road on our right without even looking, without any warning at all, and

176

smacked full into us and turned our car completely over. Marvelously, she was not hurt, and my driver, as soon as he crawled out of our car, found that he was not hurt. Making sure first that I wasn't seriously hurt, which I assured him that I was not, he turned hurriedly and started to argue with the woman about how it had all happened.

I was pinned beneath the car and lay bleeding in the ditch. I was severely cut, but I couldn't tell how bad it would be. At last a neighbor, who had stopped his car to investigate the accident and to listen to the argument that was going on, discovered me. He helped me to get loose. He was greatly concerned and helped me up into his car. I assured my companion that I was perfectly all right and for him to go ahead and take care of the accident. And I was hurried home! I had lost so much blood that I passed out as I staggered through the front door. But they picked me up and dragged me to a bed. Doctors were there soon, and they got my bleeding stopped. I assured them that I was quite all right, except for a terribly sore and battered body.

I didn't want to talk. I just wanted to lie there. And in a few days I became aware that my doctor thought that I was all right except for a nervous shock. Me, with a nervous shock! He decided that my nerves were all broken to pieces. So since he encouraged it, I pulled myself together and got up and forced myself back to the school. But a couple of days were all of it that I could possibly take! My hips swelled terribly, and the pain was simply getting to be more than I could bear. So I admitted that I was whipped. I went back home and crawled into my bed again.

I became a nervous patient to my complete disgust! They even had to brace up the covers of my bed and build a sort of box up over my feet to keep the covers from touching them there. They kept me in bed for weeks and for weeks, and I became fully aware of the fact that I had become a great disappointment to everyone who knew me. So I crawled in and waited until they let me go back to school again.

This was more of a disappointment to me than most people could realize. For within a few days after my accident we had an important engagement for my dancers planned, the most important engagement we had yet been invited to fill. We were to go up to Denver to the main section of the Colorado Teachers' Association and dance for them in their convention in the big city auditorium. It was our biggest invitation to date, and I was simply going to have to miss it. And miss it I did!

But I finally managed to limp back to school and to lead the dancing with all my heart. I still had a little trouble with my hip, but I refused to let it interfere. In fact it was years later when I had bought a very fine big saddle for my horse that I noticed one morning that I had to let the stirrup out one notch farther on one side than the other. I spoke to my doctor about this the next time that I saw him. I suggested the possibility that I had really broken my hip in the auto accident. He laughed at me, but, swearing by the evidence of my fine saddle, I insisted. Laughingly he agreed to take an X-ray of my hip and to pay for it himself if the hip was really broken. We had the X-ray made, and may I report that he paid for it! The hip was definitely broken. It was the first of a series of accidents that eventually put me onto a couple of canes in order to be able to walk at all.

[By the 1940s Lloyd was walking with the help of the two canes. He would put them aside briefly to puzzle out the steps to a new dance, but he had to rely on the canes with only such brief exceptions. He and Dorothy never considered moving from their beloved house with its flight of steps to reach the front door and a second flight of steps to reach their bedroom. Over the years arthritis developed where the hip had broken, and it became increasingly painful. He was remarkably upbeat, but he would never consent to use a wheel chair, for example when he was in an airport. In his last decade he may have compensated for his disability by choosing to drive an Oldsmobile 98. On the highway my brother and I would chant, "Pass him, Granddaddy, pass him!" when we came up behind a car. He would roar around the slower car, and our grandmother would softly say, "Oh, Lloyd."]

THE DANCE GOES ON (Lloyd)

At the performance for the teachers assembly in Denver, it seems that the youngsters danced and made a tremendous hit in my absence, and that the next number on the program was a speech by the great American sculptor, Lorado Taft. He had been so taken by our dancers and their program that he started his talk by making some extraordinary comments about them, saying that they perfectly illustrated the great field of art about which he proposed to talk. He said, according to the newspapers that were shown to me, that they had found the so-seldom-seen essence of true art and had displayed it remarkably.

Invitations for us to dance for crowds began to pour into the school after the Denver appearance, and as soon as I was out of bed again, we began to accept them. We had danced once before at the State Agricultural College at Fort Collins, but now everyone seemed to want us all over the state, and we began to accept invitation after invitation. We had our new bus, and it was very easy to take our dancers almost anywhere in it. So we accepted all the invitations that we could without stopping our other activities in the school that called for the participation of all the other students. We found ourselves terribly busy!

And what fine invitations we had to dance! Big schools, college assemblies, and Chambers of Commerce. We danced for men's luncheon clubs—Rotary, Kiwanis, Lions, and so on. Large convention groups would invite us. We were busier than we had

180

time for! Joyously and happily we kept hitting the road again and again in our new—and to us—our almost perfect bus. We were always paid enough for every engagement to more than cover our expenses. We danced for every college in the state. We squeezed in most of the bigger high schools. We loved the dancing for itself alone—all these marvelous trips were simply added payment for our shared joy that simply knew no bounds.

At first when the invitations began piling in on us, I lost my head and postponed a play we were rehearsing and finally never gave at all. To be sure, some of the leading members of the cast were on the dance team, and they were pleased to give up the play. But what of the others—those for whom we didn't have room on our dance team and who would still have enjoyed the trips and the dancing? Not only would we be unable to take them on the trips with us, but the very things that they could do very well we had decided that we didn't have time to do any more. Would they grow to love our dance program, or might they be expected to turn against it?

I thought this out and came to a firm decision. We would limit our trips to the fall and spring of the year and keep as many of our other activities as possible going full blast at the same time. To be sure, all of the general public's desire to see us dance could not be channeled to only these two dancing seasons, but finally if we were careful, we could get to the place where we could accept an important off-season engagement without anyone's realizing that we were gone. We could hold a couple of practices after school in the afternoon and then slip away for the evening without saying much to anyone. If it was to be an over-night trip, we could, by careful arranging, put it on a Friday when the school was not busy at some other special activity and return quietly on a Saturday without anyone's being aware of our going.

We carried on with our folk dancing, of course, and at last I definitely decided to include a great deal of our western square dancing. I had been studying and researching it, as far as I was able, and had found it to be very good. But of course there were some dissidents on the faculty who didn't feel that it was worthy of inclusion in our exhibitions. It seemed to be fine to me and very real, but perhaps it didn't have quite the appeal of the international dancing. So at first I let the school concentrate on its European dancing and just slipped in enough of our own American dances at our private parties to let them get a thorough feel of the thing. I was of course aware of how much stronger appeal could be made to the average American audience by presenting to them the unfamiliar foreign dancing. Nothing is very exciting to us that springs from the local level. Take the old furniture, for instance, that was being abandoned from our American homes—the fine old things that were being replaced by the shiny, modern, and new. It takes a generation for people to realize the value of their own handiwork. Then, alas, when people become interested again, there are so few examples to be found that they demand a tremendous price, and they take on the dignified name of "antiques." So with our own dancing, we were still too close to it to recognize fully its intrinsic beauty.

This was vividly illustrated for us when on one of our eastern trips a little later we stopped on the way back to do a program for the University of Kansas. They loved our European dancing, but as soon as we opened up on the American section, we experienced a tremendous letdown from the audience. They felt that this couldn't be real dancing—for only a few years before most of them had been dancing it. We realized too late the mistake we had made in including these numbers in a Kansas program.

But in the East people especially appreciated these dances. They were far enough away from the homely source of the dances to appreciate their true beauty. To them they were striking and beautiful! They simply raved about them. But in our west they were still too close to be trusted. People were familiar with them, and so it stood to reason that they could not be good.

The introduction of these old American square dances always ran the dangerous risk of this sort of reception. But we kept right on. They were a definite part of our picture, and gradually we began to introduce more and more of them in our programs. We were presenting a complete picture of European dancing, as far as we were able, and we fearlessly brought it up to include the dances of America, which we exhibited with equal joy. For the most part, to our more sophisticated audiences, these dances were received with great enthusiasm.

I should remind you that square dancing was not in the 30s and 40s as it became in the 50s and 60s. It was not a common activity. Far from it! Most people had never seen a square dance, and they were very interested in this form of activity that had been so common with their ancestors.

And of course we compromised in the matter of our costuming for the European dancing, for we could not change costumes for each nationality that we presented. So different members of our group wore entirely different costumes, whatever was colorful, and they might dance a Scandinavian dance and follow it with a dance from a Mediterranean country. We would do an Irish dance, followed by a German dance, then an English dance, immediately followed by a Russian dance! It was all colorful and it was all beautiful. But all the time we kept introducing our old American dances with utmost sincerity, and for this part of our programs, we wore authentic cowboy clothes.

For dancing as part of our school program of activities, I found that it was necessary to establish different categories of dances that the different age groups would perform. There was no reason whatever to my assignment. The franker of this I am, the better it will be for all of us now, but then I had to assume a very important reason to make my decision stick. So the high school gradually became the center of traditional American dancing: the squares and rounds and circle dances of our ancestors. The junior high students danced the contra dances of New England, and a few of the easier rounds and circles that we didn't use with the high school students. And the grade school took over the simpler of the European dances. I am aware of the shock this will give some people! "But why give the most difficult group of dances to the youngest children? Are you not showing some prejudice?" In any category of dance you can find easy and difficult dances, so we found the simpler dances that the grade school children could enjoy—while looking forward to the day that they could do contra dances and square dances.

To be sure, we kept on dancing our program of European folk dances on Wednesday nights. We chose difficult dances and pretended they were years beyond the ability of the grade school youngsters. But it is all a matter of attitude. I suppose that quite a few youngsters brought up under my system think of European dances as being largely grade school stuff (except for a few really hard dances that they did in high school) and the contra dance as being junior high material. And I smile at the New England authorities who have raved to me about how difficult the contra is, that the only reason we don't dance it well enough in the West to get great joy out of it is because of its intrinsic difficulty. And my group thought the real adult dance was the square dance and its related forms such as we did in high school.

I cannot resist the temptation to make some reference to these early dancers. I wrote to many of them in the '50s and challenged them to stir up their memories and relive the old days for me. Dozens of answers came in. Jean McKinley was in the first group that danced for Miss Burchenal. She made a statement in her letter that is quite typical of so many of those who responded: "I don't believe that most of us enjoyed the wonder of the trips nearly as much as we did the greater wonder and joy of dancing." They all enjoyed the trips tremendously, but I truly believe that most of them enjoyed the dancing even more. The dancing had become a way of life to them, a precious thing beyond all reckoning.

Another of our girls, Mary Haney, admitted to me that the European dancing seemed much more precious to her than our mere American dancing picked from our own frontiers. But Mary said she took a course a few years ago at our local college from a well-known professor from one of the leading universities in the east. They touched on folk dancing in this course, and when Mary immediately proposed a project on European folk dancing, it didn't interest the professor at all. However, when he found that she had done old American dancing as well, he became all interest, pumping her with exciting questions. She ended up coming out and borrowing books from my library and finally wrote a fine paper on American dance. She even brought her professor out to the house to see me, and I felt at last that she had begun to see the glimmer of truth.

A HOME IN THE MOUNTAINS (Enid)

The nine months of the school year consumed all of
Lloyd's time. Many evenings were spent at the school with
dancing, basketball games, or play rehearsals. On weekends there
were camping trips and performances in other cities, and on
Sunday evening Lloyd opened his home to the seniors. With his
passion for drama, he loved to read aloud and then engage the
students in discussions or arguments, as the case might be. During
World War II he opened his home to soldiers at Fort Carson, and
they had discussions or listened to recordings of classical music.
One memorable evening a soldier spoke dismissively of the
interpretation in a recording of a Beethoven piano sonata. "Can
you play it better than that?" challenged Lloyd, to which the
soldier replied, "Yes, I think I can." He sat down at the baby grand
in the living room and proved his point.

The summers, however, were Lloyd's. For a while he got
away from book sellers, aspiring teachers, and all the
responsibilities of the school year. As a young man he was
determined, as so many are to this day, to climb all of the "14ers,"
the 53 Colorado Peaks that rise above 14,000 feet. He went out
alone at times. At other times he took his wife and young children
along, finding them a place where they could stay while he set off
to climb alone. In August of 1920, after summiting on Mount
Blanca in the Sangre de Cristo range, he found himself still high up
on the mountain when a lightning storm began. He watched in

186

fascination as the blue glow of Saint Elmo's fire rose out of his upheld fingers. Then he tried to hurry down the mountain out of the range of the lightning. He chose a route down Huerfano Canyon, making his way down a snowfield, using his camera tripod as a staff. He broke through the snow crust and lost his balance, falling 300 feet and breaking a couple of ribs. Farther down the mountain he came upon an old farm house where an elderly couple gave him shelter for the night and drove him down to the nearest hospital the next morning. He reported that this ride was more harrowing than the events on the mountain!

He was not deterred by the dangers of climbing alone or by the hardship and worry that it surely caused his wife. But finally he had a moment of truth. While heading up a mountain to claim yet another 14er for his list, he made a wrong turn, which took him up a different peak. At the summit he got oriented and realized his error. He also realized that it was a beautiful climb, one that was easily as challenging as many 14ers he had climbed. On his map this peak didn't even have a name, but he gave it one himself: La Verdad, the truth. He decided that his quest to climb 14ers was no more noble than aspiring to climb all the telegraph poles on Tejon Street in downtown Colorado Springs. So he turned his energies in another direction.

About 30 miles west of Colorado Springs beyond Woodland Park and the tiny town of Divide, there was a handsome lodge that Lloyd discovered he could lease cheaply for the high school boys and girls to use as a ski lodge. They could go up on Friday evening and ski Saturday and Sunday, all for the cost of their food. Needless to say, there were no ski lifts, so they simply climbed up the neighboring hills and skied down them—and had a glorious time.

In the summer Lloyd, Dorothy, and Doli would spend their summers at the lodge. From there they could ride their horses in every direction. There were fewer fences at that time, and the family befriended the local people who made their living ranching and raising lettuce and potatoes. Lloyd kept a diary of that summer and the following five. He wrote: "One day after circling the rocky point to the south of the lodge, we found an old timber road that led us down into a most delightful valley. Calypso, columbines, shooting stars, and ferns were tucked away in its stillness. Finally a tiny little stream joined us and chattered along over the moss, whispering to us as we all went down the valley together. Now a bit of open park land, then a clump of twinkling aspen; then an aisle cut through the silent slender spruces. Here and there a great pile of rocks, flower garlanded, reached up toward the ridge. At last a willow thicket, a swamp guarded by great aspen boles, black-eyed Susans on a summer picnic, and a little patch of potatoes proudly flaunting their purple and white blossoms.

"As we circled the potato patch, we had to climb the grassy hillside, and here we could look down a meadowed valley that spread from grassy ridge to piney knoll and that opened out to a gorgeous backdrop of mountains. Blue ridge after blue ridge of regal mountains, then purple peaks beyond and close beneath the sky the stunning radiance of Mt. Harvard and Mt. Yale, violet tinted pyramids of distant alabaster. Patterns of willow clumps led the eye softly through the flowering meadow on the softly tangled lines of the hills, to the piling mass of summer clouds above those distant, dreamland peaks. The Vale of Contentment! Love at first sight.

"To our surprise we found that we were on the ridge that marks the west boundary of the Crescent Ranch, and a short canter took us home. Our valley haunted us, and we soon returned at sunset to see our lovely valley fill with purple shadows and boil over with the colors of the sunset.

"A few weeks later our horses took us down another valley on beyond; we knew it to be different and yet it seemed the same. We were all confused. But at last we were certain it was a different valley. Then we fell to arguing which of the two was lovelier. We threaded an amphitheater of aspens, rounded a grassy knoll, and lo! There was our potato patch again! So our sunset valley divided into those two incomparable ridge-closed valleys, each with a little stream of its own to feed the swamp and flowering meadow below.

"Who did it belong to? Who planted that funny little lonesome patch of potatoes? Who could dare to possess such loveliness?

"We found ourselves in the autumn quite homesick for our mountain land. The aimless talk of the summer had crystalized itself into a definite decision to buy a bit of land we could call our own and to build a bit of a home somewhere there in the rolling beauty of Hayden's Park. With the flaming of the aspens our desire too burst into flame, and definitely, 'as soon as possible,' we wanted this place of our own.

"Early in October we went with the junior class to the ski lodge for a weekend of wood-getting and sport. And I, of course, led the party that wanted to hike to the sunset hill we loved at the southwest corner of the neighboring ranch, the hill that looked down to the sunset valley to where the view leaped lightly from the far peaks of the Collegiate Range straight up into the flames of the sky. This was the corner that we most often thought and talked about and we were simply indulging ourselves in another lovely look.

"Then turning back, we detoured through the adjoining ranch. I found a neighboring rancher getting out a fine crop of potatoes, and I had a long chat with him. I told him we had our eyes on the southwest forty and then hesitantly inquired if there might be any possibility of somehow getting these two lovely valleys that led down to the gates of the sunset. It was like inquiring the price of the moon! But to my surprise he said that a Mr. Holmes owned them and that he was quite sure that he would be glad to sell. In my excitement I tried to seem uninterested and to only hint at a possible price. And when he named the trifle that would turn the trick, I was terrified lest he see my surprise and delight, in case that might spoil the deal.

"My dreams were all aflame. I had somehow never believed that it would be possible to buy these little streams. I had only hoped to buy a plot somewhere near them. And now I felt I had them almost in my hands.

"Next morning with the boys I returned to the sunset hill to build a ski jump before the snow would fly, and all the while I kept appraising the two unbelievable valleys with the enraptured eye of the destined owner. Across the pasture below us a rancher came riding a big plow horse with a second one tied to the tail of his mount. I of course sauntered down to him for the chance of a chat. Yes, he knew Holmes well and thought he would be glad to sell, but to his mind my lovely valleys were worthless, all cut over and rocky and with hardly a tillable acre on them. But he had some land two miles west that would 'suit me to a T.' I let him talk, throwing in as many questions as I could in order to pick up tidbits of information about the values these hills might bring. Four or five dollars an acre, he told me—where I had expected anywhere from ten to forty as a price.

"That night I wrote to Holmes at Cripple Creek and offered him a possible five an acre for the forty acres where the two streams joined in them that looked down the long valley to the sunset. And while I awaited his answer my dreams all but got mixed with my food. At last he answered by long distance phone and we arranged to meet at the lower gate of the sunset valley on the following Sunday.

"Doli and I went to keep the engagement, leaving Dorothy and Pete Fezer at the ski lodge to prepare the lunch. We found Mr. Holmes to be a delightful old man. He told of his machine shop in Cripple Creek and of his friend Walter Hughes who had homesteaded the valleys and of how the title came to him to repay some debts owed him by Hughes, and on and on. He took us up to his ranch, which lay over the ridge to the south. We waited during the long recitation until we could come naturally to the little valleys of our choice.

"I made him see that I wasn't interested in anything but the little valleys. Finally we were squarely on it, and I almost held my breath. Would my bubble burst, would my dream come tumbling down at my feet? Yes! He would sell the forty acres at the price I offered. But he didn't want to quarter the homestead. He wanted me to take half of it and would therefore sell me the adjoining forty at half that price. I could hardly believe him! My castle was taking shape.

"On the following Saturday Mr. Holmes met me at the ski lodge and we exchanged deed and check and completed all the details of the purchase. Then we went over to the valleys and he located as best he could the corners of our eighty. We agreed on the details of a survey and planned to settle the exact boundaries at another time.

"I hurried back to the students at the ski lodge glowing with a strange new something in my blood. That little mountain ranch was mine, mine. I felt an exchange in the flowing current of life. I felt a security and a kinship with loveliness that I had never known before. The world had changed for me. I had opened the very source of living. I was happy beyond all comparison. Something epic had borne me off my feet. It was not that I possessed something, but that I was possessed!

"On the morrow we had a crowd invited for a 'ground warming.' We put up a rude table for the picnic in an amphitheater of bare aspens. Soon they came—teachers, school board members, and families, and soon my rude table was sagging under the steaming dishes they had brought. It was a lovely picnic—but to them it was only a circumstance while to us it was an occasion.

"They saw a little aspen valley threaded with a tiny stream—like a thousand other high valleys they had known. We saw a very special valley, a very lovely valley, redolent with the promise of its future. A valley that we hoped generations of our blood might call their mountain home.

"What a host of names we thought of. And every one we tried out by typing it, studying it, and trying it on our tongues as well as our eyes. But out of the welter slowly emerged the Welsh 'coombe' (cwm) a high mountain valley. And soon we added to it the old Scots "corrie" a glaciated mountain valley, for our valleys were two. It seemed appropriate to name the steeper, rockier northern valley the Corrie, and the gentler aspen-filled southern valley the Coombe. So Coombe Corrie we christened it and so it is." The family gave additional names to specific areas in the valleys, but they have not endured. The only one remaining is Aspengaard, a play on Asgaard, the Norse home of the gods, for the beautiful stand of aspens that runs up the Coombe.

The following spring in 1932 Lloyd was still contemplating what sort of structure to build. He had little idea of what would be feasible financially until he talked with Andy Kuhlmann, a neighbor down the valley who had emigrated from Germany. Andy thought there were still enough big spruce trees on the land to build a log cabin even though many of the tallest ones and the pines had been taken to provide timbers for the mine shafts in Cripple Creek during the gold rush of the 1890s. Lloyd asked him to name his price "for cutting and piling at location enough straight spruce logs to build a cabin with 18 x 24 inside dimensions. That evening he made his price--$18 to $20, and of course I took him up."

The next week when Lloyd was at the ski lodge for a school party, he went over to check on his logs. There were none. When he told neighbors of his disappointment, they laughed. Andy was "just that way." They said no one could work so well or so fast—once he got to work. Andy referred to his buddies as his "college chums"—companions he had met in jail. It was Prohibition time, and Andy was a moonshiner, among his other talents. But the next time Lloyd got up to his land, there were the logs, all cut in time before the sap got up to loosen the bark.

The next task was to determine the location for the new cabin. The family first considered some of the higher points on the land, but one of them was prone to lightning strikes and would have necessitated the building of a long road, and another was too wooded to permit a view down the lovely valley. They finally agreed on a south-facing slope near the confluence of the two little valleys. It looked down the long valley to the Collegiate Peaks, the snow melted there quickly, and only a short road would be needed to provide vehicular access.

The following Sunday the Shaws hosted friends at the ski lodge, from which they walked over to the cabin site. Lloyd wrote, "A soft, musty, lovely day. I wanted to stay on there and start on my cabin and my trails and the hundreds of things I have planned. If the cabin is a fraction as lovely as its dream, it will prove an abiding joy. I can hardly wait to begin it."

But before beginning the cabin the next spring, he laid out and planted a garden. He took a biology class to visit a farmer in the Black Forest northeast of Colorado Springs to learn about his methods for growing potatoes and to procure good seed potatoes. After commencement he planted peas, carrots, onions, radishes, lettuce, Swiss chard, spinach, cabbage, cauliflower, beets, turnips, and six varieties of potatoes. He gloried in the ritual of the work: "It is so ancient and fine a thing to do, and one's heart sings so contentedly when one looks back on the fresh turned earth and knows that his crop is in. And wrestling a plough and seeing the earth roll back from its blade and feeling the tug of the reins at your waist and calling to and managing your horses is all fundamental and deeply satisfying. One remembers Robby Burnes and all the others who ploughed their straight furrows. A bit of it is a fine antidote to all the concrete and paving and city lots of our age." Lloyd's diary logs the planting of a garden for the first five summers and tells of the promising crop as it comes up. The first year he reports harvesting 1500 to 2000 pounds of potatoes, which were shared among friends and faculty. Vegetables were planted in succeeding summers, but interest in gardening waned over time.

For their first summer on their land, the family established a camp: for Lloyd and Dorothy a "tent cottage with a wooden floor and frame and half walls—with a fly to help the coolness and to hold out the weather—and an awninged porch to eat on. . . and for Doli another tent adjoining us with an extra bed for her guests. . . . We may be a little crowded and at times a little inconvenienced, but this is our spiritual 'down payment' on the place. And we are living intimately with our sunsets and our valleys where the flowers are weaving a pattern of changing color through the growing days." After getting established, they had a neighbor bring his team of horses to cut a road to the cabin site. Lloyd wrote "the snorting of sweating horses on a steep hillside, the struggle with the plow cutting a furrow through rotten granite, the aching muscles, the dust of the drag all blend into a memory of a real day's work—satisfying but hard."

Andy Kuhlman was still busy on another job, so Lloyd got Bill Lubkin who was staying at Andy's to come over and help him. "He is a tall young German without a lazy bone in his body and a good companion. He is something of a musician—well raised by a school-teaching father, trained for an artist. The freaks of unemployment washed him up on Andy's strange coast." Together Lloyd and Bill excavated the area for the main room of the cabin and, upon Andy's return, they laid a concrete foundation. To have the front room jutting out over the hillside, they had to build a concrete support wall at the front and then dig into the granite hillside at the back. Lloyd was grateful for Andy's experience: "Andy is an old Cripple Creek miner and an incurable prospector and an expert with powder and drill."

Slowly the big room took shape. There were frequent trips to nearby Divide and Florissant and down to Colorado Springs for supplies such as cement and sand and a rented cement mixer.

Windows and casements were designed and ordered from a mill in Colorado Springs. Floor joists and flooring were laid, and then the log walls began to go up. Lloyd wrote that "the lifting of heavy logs and the chop, chop, chopping with my axe nearly did me in. I have never been so tired as deep down into me, and my hands ached till I thought the fingers would drop off." It took special talent to notch the logs so they fit tightly together at the corners. After Lloyd gained some skill in the task, "Andy indulgently let me fit up one of the front corners of the building exclusively. I cut and fitted logs in other corners, but my own corner is all my proud own."

Throughout these days of hard work, "company keeps drifting in to our joy and our inconvenience. Poor Dorothy sometimes has as many as ten of us at the tiny table on the tiny porch of the tent. And if it rains, her outdoor stove and her indoor oil stove are both inadequate. . and our whole living and storage and bedroom-parlor-dining room and kitchen [are] crowded into a tiny ten by twelve tent and its tinier porch. But though the work leaves her tired with always three hungry working men to feed, she loves it. She resents the days that take her away from here, the days that she must go to town."

By July 31, 1932, Lloyd sat on the front porch that jutted out over the hillside in front of the finished living room: "It is a few days less than a year since we first rode down through this valley and dreamed our dream. We hardly dared to include ownership in the dream, and a cabin like this was beyond all thinking. For it is unbelievably lovely, every line has found the right place against our sky. . . The great pillars supporting the porch make one's eye leap, the mottled blocks of the almost inlaid oak flooring are a constant cause of exclaiming. The porch with its circling sides exceeds our fondest dream. And when we stand in the garden below and see the cabin loom against the sky above us, it seems no cabin but some magic mountain palace fashioned of brown logs."

The interior of the room was spacious, with stripped spruce logs for the rafters. Doli, aged 17 and heading into her last year of high school, added a memorable touch to the new room. She decided that the horizontal rafter ties should be painted. Inspired by the Irish Book of Kells, which the family had seen on their trip to Europe, she teased the whimsical creatures out of the illuminated first letter of chapter headings and painted them on the rafter ties. Her painting continued with the south gable where she painted St. Michael with a shining sword (because Lloyd had been born on Michaelmas) and added a Celtic dragon on either side to further protect the laird of the manor. On the opposite gable she painted cattle brands, some of their neighbors' and some of them famous brands of the West. Centrally featured was their own brand, two quarter-circle connect, the closest the branding board would accept to their desired two C's for Coombe Corrie: 2 ‿ .

At the completion of the room, Lloyd wrote, "I cannot record my emotions. It is more than a cabin—somehow in this clean valley it is a sanctuary of loveliness. I feel strange forces outside myself guiding and directing and helping. Somehow it is a trust. We must rear some beauty here that will serve for others. Like a squire who had kept vigil by his armor, I feel a strange destiny of service before me—a trust, a duty, on the high road of beauty."

The family moved their table, stove, cupboard, and chairs into the new room, and colleagues came up from Colorado Springs to have dinner with them. Andy pronounced himself finished and that his salary had ended. He continued, however, to add improvements. As Lloyd wrote, "Since he is only happy when he is working, he kept on working—but as a free spirit to follow any prompting of his heart. He rocked up the well and cemented the top beautifully. . . Then he had me go with him and collect some great pitch poles for a gate. He had already collected the bars. 'It must be a good gate,' he said. 'I want you to have the best gate along the road. I think you can always tell what sort of a rancher a man is by the gates he keeps up.' When he finished, it was a beauty, the best gate along the road."

Bill Lubkin continued working for a few more days at Lloyd's request, and then he too formally quit. "But he too wanted to do something for us—wanted to leave something as a memorial. So he put in a day and a half of hard labor building a trail up to the big rock where he had had his tent. Bill said, 'Every time I turned the trail around a rock or under a tree, I would say, come on all you folks, and I would see you and all your friends, walking where I had dug, for years and years into the future.' Bill too has been a rare character and a prodigious worker. He was all broken up at the thought of leaving—and we shall miss him and Andy terribly. But Tuesday afternoon, his trail finished, he sat on the porch, looking at the view he loves so and playing my guitar while he sang one German song after another. . . Then he packed his bag and asked me to drive him down to Andy's cabin. How fine this world is when merest chance will let me pick up a reformed bootlegger and a moving picture scenic artist—and find them both high minded, clean in thought and dream—or is it the hills that attracted them and that is how I found them here?"

During the following winter there were many trips up to the ski lodge with forays over to the cabin when the snow permitted. The next summer the family was installed in the cabin by June 20. On another day Lloyd and Doli returned to town and rode their horses up to the cabin, with Doli's friend, Elise Roberts, riding Dorothy's horse. The ride usually took six to eight hours, with a stop for lunch. It is hard to imagine riding a horse up the highway through Ute Pass today with its busy traffic, but in the 1930s the road apparently accommodated all modes of transportation.

During this second summer Lloyd's diary reports gardening, fence building, entertaining, and horseback riding. There were also trips to Denver to visit "the folks," presumably Dorothy's parents, back to Colorado Springs for school meetings, and north to Cheyenne Wyoming for its Frontier Celebration.

Dorothy's sister Lorna and her family came down from Denver, and Lloyd's brother Ray came out from California.

It wasn't until mid-July that he began to work on the kitchen, which would adjoin the living room on the east wide. This time he felled his own logs and with the help of his aptly-named horse, Grande, snaked them down to the building site, where he again had to dig into the granite hillside to create the space for the new room. Finally on August 1 the actual building began, but even then it was fitted in between errands, school board meetings, and visitors, who came almost every day. On August 26 Lloyd moved the wood-burning stove into the kitchen and fitted the chimney pipe. On September 3, Lloyd, Dorothy, and Doli entertained the Cheyenne School faculty. He wrote, "A lovely cordial and eager spirit! A beautiful afternoon! And a glorious evening with a full moon. After supper some had to go down, and others stayed for a long visit by the fire, and a few climbed the rock, where I played Indian melodies on the flute while they watched moon shadows creep across the great valley. A perfect ending for a perfect summer."

By the summer of 1934 Lloyd's diary becomes more succinct. On Monday, June 4, he wrote, "Entertained the senior class at supper. Peanut hunt—supper—the rock—games in the cabin." It wasn't until June 21 that he wrote, "We are here for the summer. Home at last." There ensued the usual activities: gardening, riding, entertaining, and trips to other destinations in Colorado and again to the Cheyenne rodeo in Wyoming. There was also chinking, the process of filling the cracks between the logs in the cabin walls. For the first year or two after construction the chinking consisted of mud while the logs were still drying out and shrinking. After this process was completed, the chinking was done with cement, mixed with lamp black to achieve the desired color.

In August the summer's project began: building a fireplace in the corner of the living room. The family had settled on a design they had seen in Skansen, the open-air museum of traditional Swedish architecture, when they were visiting Stockholm. The fireplace would have a square footprint and sit in the corner of the living room. It would have a large sloping masonry hood that extended out over the footprint. They had never seen such a fireplace in the US, so there was an element of the experimental in this project.

They began by bringing up sand, cement, and steel plate from Colorado Springs. Then they went to Cripple Creek where they cleaned and loaded 1000 bricks from the lot below P.J. Holmes' shop. There is no diary entry about the actual construction, but Doli reminisced that they had no idea whether this unusual design would draw properly. They first tested the finished fireplace by putting a lighted candle in the front corner that jutted into the room. To their delight and relief, the flame bent obediently toward the back of the fireplace and the chimney. Since that time five generations of family and thousands of friends have gathered around that wonderful fireplace.

In mid-April of 1935 the family came up to spend spring break at the cabin. Though not as dry as the states to the east, Colorado was also becoming parched from lack of precipitation. On April 18 Lloyd wrote in his diary, "We awoke to a fine sifting of snow from a lowering sky. . At noon heavy wet flakes began to fall in deadly earnest. The thirsty ground drank them up as fast as they fell. Then the multitudinous white flakes almost blotted out the far side of the valley. The grass clumps became coral. The aspen catkins became shining clusters of silver. Then the meadow whitened—the parched ground began to slake its thirst and the snow began to lie. . . At about 3:00 o'clock through the myriad white flakes the sky turned mysteriously saffron and the falling snow was distinctly yellow. A great dust storm (which so darkened the city that they had to turn on all the lights) had blown into the upper air and the snow was a tincture of yellow Oklahoma." The family had a harrowing escape as the car slipped and skidded across the meadow and they stopped to help neighbors who were hopelessly stuck. They even considered staying the night in Divide, only two miles away, but word came that only a light snow had fallen farther east in Woodland Park, so they continued on to Woodland Park and down Ute Pass "though eight or ten cars were hanging in ditches or off bridges."

Now that the living room, fireplace, and kitchen were in place, Lloyd staged a more elegant dinner at the cabin for the seniors in the class of '35: "brought the seniors up for dinner—seated them at small tables and had two waiters from the El Paso Club wait table for us and take care of the kitchen. Had favorite books for place cards. (I have never seen a crowd of youngsters so radiantly pleased.)"

The family moved up for the summer in mid-June. As before, getting a garden in was the first priority, but the construction plan for the summer was the building of the first bedroom. Lloyd planned for two bedrooms that would be up the hill above the living room and kitchen, making a T-shaped building. But first he enclosed with wood the platform tent that he and Dorothy had occupied the first summer. It had become Doli's residence once the living room was built, and she, under her father's instructions and with her mother's help, completed the slabbing of the tent. She then painted designs on the canvas interior of the hut, using Norse figures from the books by Ingri and Edgar Parin d'Aulaire.

By mid-July the foundation for the new room was almost complete, "but how slow it has all seemed," Lloyd wrote. "Twice I have had to go to Denver to make speeches, several times to Colorado Springs for board meetings and school affairs. . . Excavating for the foundation proved another hard job in hard granite, then measuring and laying out the forms with nothing but the sky to nail to had me puzzled. . . last Wednesday morning I had my forms all finished and went after my first batch of water and gravel. . . I started the concrete, mixing in the wheel barrow and

Dorothy spreading and filling with stones after each load was poured. She was a real helper. And there is something fundamentally right about a man and wife working together in the face of this great view, building a shelter and a dream."

He worked with a neighbor and his horses to snake the logs down to the cabin site. . . "his horses are fine and reliable—they follow you up over logs as nimble as a dog, they can turn around in a three-foot space, and they'll try anything you ask them to. . . what a zestful day, crashing down through columbines and roses and rue and twin flowers, the smell of dead mold turned up and of crushed leaves, the strong urge of horses, the puzzles to solve, the logs to chop out, and at last the heavy lift and pry and leverage to get them loaded on the wagon." At the cabin they again used the horses to drag the logs two at a time up the hillside to the building site.

But there was still more excavating to do at the back of the room where it would fit into the hillside. Finally he "struck rock, so hard that a pick wouldn't budge it. So I got Andy, who put three shots of dynamite in it and broke it up." Finally ready to begin the log work, Lloyd availed himself of Dick Beusberg who came up from town to work for a week on the construction and other tasks that would free him to work fulltime on the bedroom. It was completed on August 25th: "Slept in the new room last night—it is lovely though still unfinished. . . Last night we had in nearly two dozen neighbors and had square dancing and games. They stayed until 1:00 AM, and I think everyone had a fine time."

It is surprising that the most striking part of the room gets no mention in the diary. The part of the room that faced the beloved view down the valley was right at the southwest corner, so rather than simply make the corner of the room there of interlocking logs, Lloyd had to make four corners. He built a three by three foot dormer-like extension that jutted out from the corner, and he fitted it with a tall gothic window that opened the view to those lucky enough to inhabit that room. Doli, again ready with her paints, painted around the frame of the window in gothic lettering: "To the Glory of God and in Loving Memory of David Rodney Shaw." It is of course called David's window. The alcove is a step above the floor, and curtains were installed on small hinged rods that could close out the light or open against the walls of the alcove. Generations of Lloyd and Dorothy's descendants have staged dramatic productions on that wee stage.

The diary entries for the summer of 1936 are brief, partly because events from previous years repeated themselves and partly because Lloyd was so busy. He had been named chairman of the Pikes Peak or Bust Celebration in Colorado Springs and thus wasn't free to move to the cabin until the end of June. After the event "the Central Committee of the Celebration came up to supper on July 3rd with their wives, and we had a lovely evening. They presented us with a beautiful set of hand-wrought fire irons."

The family had gotten in their garden earlier in the season, but "the season has been unusually dry until nearly the end of July. Then two solid weeks of rain filled everything to overflowing. . . the garden has done splendidly, but first the rabbits ate up our beans, then the chipmunks robbed us of our peas, and even the horses got in and ate the hearts out of the lettuce. But the growth has been wonderful even though we can only manage to get a very small share of the produce."

Work began immediately on Doli's room, the east bedroom. Fortunately Dorothy's nephew Bob Hermann came up from Denver and "helped as well as a 16-year-old boy can help. He proved very valuable moving gravel. . . helping with cement and laying the floor. Since July 30 I have plugged on alone." It is a given, of course, that Dorothy and Doli were helping all the way. Near the end of August Bob was able to come up again and "help me with the rafters, sheeting, roofing, etc.," and Doli was soon able to spend her first night in the room. Again Lloyd omitted a special part of this room in his diary account. Doli requested a bay window at the east end of her room. Whereas David's window had required the fitting of four corners instead of one, this detail would necessitate the building of four corners of fitted logs instead of a solid wall. But esthetics mattered and were worth the hours of extra work that they entailed. Since then generations of children have sat in that window seat.

Lloyd concludes his diary with these thoughts. "And it is beautiful! It is lovelier than we had dreamed. Again I feel, as the first entries in the diary record, that something outside us has helped and directed and achieved for us. And I feel a challenge—a responsibility—a charge to do something fine and beautiful for the world in this magic setting. Strange forces seem to hover behind us—we must find a way and build a path to beauty and to happiness that others can follow.

"Is it to be writing? We have been too busy to try that yet. Will it be crafts? We moved in a loom that we bought for Doli on her birthday—and our spinning wheel, and they have been hummingly busy all summer at their ancient and lovely crafts. I don't know what it is to be. Perhaps the ancient and most beautiful craft of simple living. Or perhaps to store up beauty and power to deliver later in some way down in the cities. But something beautiful and worthy must be done. This beautiful valley and this lovely cabin are a stage set for something that I pray we are big enough to play."

This valley and the dance may have been the two great wellsprings of beauty in Lloyd's life. Thus it is appropriate that they came together during the summers when he wrote *Cowboy Dances* and later *The Round Dance Book* at Coombe Corrie. In this way he did "store up beauty and power" and deliver them down in the cities—and give them to the entire nation.

As with everything he found and loved, he had to share it. Thus thousands of people have been guests of the Shaws (and their descendants) at Coombe Corrie. When he was conducting his huge summer classes, he insisted on bringing everyone to the cabin for an evening, including a catered picnic supper. When there were 200 registrants, he hosted half of them there one night and the other half another night. There seemed to be almost no limit to the number of people who could crowd into that living room and perch on the stairs leading up to the bedrooms.

The cabin and its lovely valleys are unspeakably precious to Doli's children, to their children, and now to their grandchildren. Two of her granddaughters chose to have their weddings there—of course with a picnic the day before so that all the attendees could explore the cabin, climb the big rock, and hike its valleys. The product of one of those marriages is, at this writing, ten years old. When his teacher in Brooklyn asked him to write about what made him happy, he wrote, "I am happy when I am in my cabin."

[The descriptions in this chapter are based on a diary kept by Lloyd Shaw during the construction of the cabin.]

THE WONDERFUL WESTERN YEAR: A Treatise on Education (Dorothy)

It was a sweet spring, the spring of 1933. The meadowlarks came back to shout alleluia all over the pasture. The willows burgeoned with pussies. Mary Elizabeth Gately found the first anemone squarely on the equinox and had her name in the paper. Mary Ann Elser put on a perfectly wonderful dance festival woven around one of Carl Sandburg's "Rutabaga Stories." The high school presented Frank Molar's "Swan" with their usual polish. The boys camped at the Great Sand Dunes, and the girls chopped firewood in a wet mountain valley. Homework doubled. A small and closely knit senior class kept happily busy with picnics for breakfast as the days grew steadily longer. Buttercups broke into waves of gold along the creek.

A fine year was drawing to an end—but not quite fine after all. Underneath ran a deep current of bewilderment, a sense of undefined betrayal, a foreboding of loss. There had never been defection within the faculty; bursts of temperament, yes, teachers who didn't understand and quietly removed themselves, and others who never would understand and were quietly removed with mutual good will. But a sense of rivalry, a jockeying for position, an uncomfortable awareness of unspoken disapproval tugged at the heart. This sort of thing was unknown at Cheyenne School.

It was our dearest teacher and closest friend whom we watched so anxiously. He was like a man caught in an undertow.

For a dozen or more years he had been disciple, colleague, and right-hand man, a competent and eager teacher, wonderful at outside activities, a warm and merry friend of faculty and students. What it was that closed his heart we never knew. Perhaps some long and severe attack of typhoid fever suffered some time before had caused a personality change. We held our peace and mourned for him. And then we became aware of division. Quietly, unconsciously at first, the faculty and, to a certain extent, the student body was being marshaled into two camps: his side and our side. About what we never knew.

Lloyd's undated resignation (he kept it in case anyone wanted it of him) still lay in its corner of the desk drawer, and the usual spring file of offers of new positions lay in another drawer. Our own daughter was being graduated with a happy little senior class. It seemed like a good time to date the resignation, for a fight is one thing, but conflict is another. Continuing conflict with no conclusion has no part in any good life. But to fight with people about something completely nebulous is to be in conflict in a situation where conflict has no place. There was a host of friends who had always measured success by size and who had always felt that Lloyd was wasting himself on this small, obscure school district. He knew that they were wrong, but for a moment the idea of division within the ranks of Cheyenne School was more than he could face. He was not the kind of man who could live in a cold war. The school board, more sensitive than we to murmurings in the community, had been urging him for months to let this man go, this good teacher, dear comrade, lost friend. But it was not until he actually confronted him in the office with clean words plainly spoken that Lloyd realized the danger to Cheyenne School that lay at the bottom of this man's confusion. He did not renew his contract nor that of two other dear and useful teachers, and he left his resignation undated and unsigned. The anguish that followed this decision lay like a chronic nausea upon the spirit, and when the news became public property, there were the usual recriminations, the taking of sides in dead earnest, and the heartbreaking bewilderment and resentment of the junior class, whose sponsor this man had been and whose affection he merited. There were parents whose anger has endured to this day, recalling weeping children coming home to tell the tale. We could only stand fast. It was impossible to explain to them and still leave this teacher as a happy memory for them to keep. How we yearned over them and loved them, who could not possibly be as bereft as we.

So the beautiful spring came to a close, and commencement came and summer. Cheyenne School still stood partially dismembered by the lie, and September would come and the school must be made to cohere again, to work and play joyously in unison and confidence. What could Lloyd do? If this seems like a tiny tempest in a very small teapot, do not see it so. This is education for the masses at the public school level. It is the education of the whole child, that catch phrase that is so stereotyped in modern educational jargon. Crises of this kind are not unusual, and children are congenital side-takers. Within the limitations of their information, there are merits in their choices that must not be downgraded but respected. They may not be able to understand us, but they are lost if they do not trust us. We must all try to be on the side of the kingdom of heaven if we possibly can although we dare not call it that in public. We must re-level our sights on our original goal.

For such a spiritual leap, Lloyd's vehicle was amazingly practical, physical, even earthy—it was a horse. A senior class that would be docile, courteous, and completely uncooperative might be even worse than an openly rebellious one. This incoming senior class had unusual qualities for leadership. Their attitude could make or break the school during this year and color attitudes for years to come. It was necessary for them to feel a solidarity of leadership in some completely extraneous activity that had nothing to do with what we had ever done traditionally before.

The answer lay across the highway from the school where some 200 acres of gracious pastureland swept in rolling hills and hollows clear to the Gold Camp Road. This land was part of the vast Stratton Estate and was generously loaned to the school for whatever activities fitted it until such time as it should eventually be divided into home sites. The loan included the right to pasture a suitable number of horses there. The youngsters had only the responsibility of the daily feeding of grain and attention to their horses. A sunny afternoon in spring would find a dozen to 20 youngsters roaming the wide acres with halter and oat bucket, seeking their free-faring mounts. From first grade to senior in high school, the student body was horse-mad.

August wound down into dwindling streams of gentians in high meadows, the school building smelled of fresh varnish, new textbooks accumulated in stacks for labeling, September came and with it an uneasiness. Perhaps this was not going to be a good year. Almost everyone in the school family felt it. The fresh wound still smarted. Registration was accomplished with its usual quiet good humor. The office gong rang as usual for the first high school auditorium assembly. The seniors came in and assumed the seats in front that they had coveted for 11 years and sat politely, with brightly polished chips glistening faintly on their shoulders. Lloyd walked down the aisle, stood to face them, greeted them, and made the necessary announcements concerning procedure for the coming days. He leaned against the piano. He grinned and started to talk.

"It's usual for us to have some kind of special activity for the fall, and I have an idea I think you might like. We've had an awfully good summer for grass, and the pasture's in fine shape. The Stratton Estate people think it will take care of more horses than we've had in the past couple of years, and I've been up to see Jack Gaylor at Green Mountain Falls, and he'll be glad to let us keep his whole dude string for the winter, just for their keep. This will mean that those of you who don't have horses of your own, and that's 95% of you, will have plenty of opportunities to ride. All you'll have to do is catch the horse.

"It seems to me we'll need a corral. I've been to talk with the Forest Service people, and they would be glad to arrange to go with some of you up the Rampart Range Road and mark lodge pole pine that you may cut. We could take the school truck and maybe borrow another one and go out and cut and trim the trees and load them and bring them down. And right out here at the end of Cresta Road we could build a big corral and a handsome rustic gate where the road runs into the pasture. I went to talk to Mr. Paulson at Tarryall Ranch the other day. He has the best string of rodeo stock in this part of the country outside of the big professional people— good lively critters that are well cared for. They'll be a challenge after a month's rest and cold nights. Mr. Paulson is willing to let us have them free of charge. It will be good publicity for him, and he says you fellows can herd them down from Tarryall. We'll truck your horses up, and Woody will go with you, and Paulson will send a couple of his men too. It's 60 miles, and you'll have to camp overnight at Divide. We'll drop off your sleeping bags for you.

"I don't see why we can't manage this perfectly well. It will be a great experience. We've got some good top hand material. John and Bill spent the summer on a ranch in Arizona and got a lot of pointers, and Chuck will be good too. After we've got the animals all down and Gaylor's string in and rested and the corral built, I suggest that we put on an honest-to-goodness, bang-up rodeo. Oh, yes, I've talked it over with the school board, and they're for it."

He talked for about 15 minutes, laying out his plan. The atmosphere in the sunny auditorium thawed. He didn't give them a chance to say a word until he'd told his whole story. The chips on the shoulders melted. You could almost hear the gears grate as the wheels went round: "Uncle Harry's got an old saddle out in his garage; I'll bet he'd let me have it." "I wonder if we'll have a queen." "Have I got the nerve to ride a bucking horse?"

Then it broke down into a free-for-all. Ideas shot up like rockets on the Fourth of July. Everybody had a dozen questions. They'd all been foreseen. All summer long, this school master had been building this outside curriculum to keep several hundred youngsters so busy that puzzles and animosities would be burned away as the young muscles hardened and grew lean.

It was a wonderful autumn. All the boys who wanted to went to cut lodge pole pines on a sunny Saturday with two foresters and some of the faculty men. They learned how to chop a tree and how to trim it and what to do with the slash. They learned how to load the slim poles on the trucks. They were so tired they were staggering by bedtime, but on Monday morning the beautiful stack of poles lay on the site of the corral just inside the pasture fence. Woody and Mr. Evans took over the supervision then and with Lloyd of course, whose hands had grown log-wise building his cabin, they drew a plan, and the boys measured and cut and fitted, and made a handsome corral. They were there the minute school was out every sunny September afternoon, working until twilight. Such a pounding and scraping as rang across the empty stretch of pasture! Finally the beautiful great pole gate off the highway with wide and easy swing. Finally the chutes built into the side of the corral. Mr. Paulson of the Tarryall ranch sent down three bucking horses and three steers to practice on, first with a surcingle, then with only a halter, and finally with a saddle. The weather held. It was one of those miraculous Colorado autumns when day follows golden day, soft, windless, frostless.

Everything went on as usual. The boys camped at Hoosier Pass and the girls at Spruce Creek Camp on the Tarryall River. There was folk dancing on Wednesday evening and play parties in the woods clearing, and there was always school—school came first. That was understood, but with long afternoons in the winey air and sound sleep at night, it was easy to concentrate during class hours. Homework wasn't too much of a problem, and always wherever you looked, you could see a row of horses with riders angling beautifully across the sunny hill and loping homeward across a burning sunset. The children were beautiful: the boys lean in their tight, clean jeans, brown and hard. The girls rode straight, usually bareback, like young centauresses. The corral rang with laughter, banter, busyness. It was a beautiful kind of busyness.

Newspaper reporters began to turn up. Clippings began to come from the *New York Times*, the *Chicago Tribune*, the *San Francisco Examiner,* and the *Christian Science Monitor.* A film crew came out from Universal Studios to take footage that would be shown nationwide in the newsreels that accompanied the feature films of the day. The superintendent began to be subjected to endless interviews. "Isn't what you're doing very dangerous?" "Oh, not nearly as dangerous as football," he would reply. There would be a few scratches and bruises but no permanently injured knees or shoulders. "Aristotle, the greatest of educators, sat on a corral fence and watched Alexander the Great tame a wild horse. I consider what we're doing just good education."

It *was* good education! It was another facet of the individual athletics that Lloyd felt so strongly about. It was a boy against a clean and not unfriendly animal. It was a girl scrambling alone across a sunny meadow, catching and haltering her horse, riding down the sunny afternoon, serene and confident, going home to a tub and supper and a chemistry assignment and an untroubled sleep. It was a young child hanging on a corral fence watching the big boys as he had watched them in the Christmas play and on the dance floor and hard-pressed at basketball, playing hard, cleanly, and with a surprising amount of courage.

It sounds costly. Actually it was part of the still-necessary depression program of inexpensive activity. Almost everything was donated and put together by the children. It was expected that any expense would be covered by proceeds from the rodeo and from the fall play.

The Gaylor string had arrived and were growing fat and perky. They were to be ridden for the asking. No one dressed up very much. Even the queen and her attendants wore plain shirts and well-worn leather chaps. Until the rodeo season, the student body treasury was paying for the hay and grain.

What did the parents think? Had they become used a little to the superintendent's surprising ways of keeping their children out of mischief? They were amazingly cooperative. There was always faculty supervision. The superintendent was having the time of his life, and everyone must have known it. Fortunately his was the only broken bone of the whole adventure: a cracked rib in a wrestle with an eager-eyed young calf. Just enough danger: that was the need. Young boys need danger. He knew that from his own youth. But clean danger, and not so much that the mind becomes callous.

Everybody was in it, from the littlest ones to the President of the School Board. The second and third grade boys and their mothers were buzzing with a sort of hilarious secret. The intermediate boys and their fathers were equally occupied in the basements and garages of their homes. Colonel Dwayne Hodgekinson, aged eight, and his drum and bugle corps were practicing furiously all over the place The merchants of the town were outdoing themselves in assembling a fine array of prizes. And Colonel Neal, head of the army remount service, and Ray Bell, the former national rodeo champion, agreed to be the judges. The weather, the blessed weather, held.

On the Saturday before the rodeo, the boys went to the U-Quarter-Circle Ranch in the Tarryall to bring down the fresh stock. Ten long-horned steers for bulldogging, an adequate number of bucking steers, and a string of frisky and unridden bucking horses. Bill and John, Chuck and Herb, Bud and Melvin—I can shut my eyes and see them in the frosty October morning, responsible and secretly elated, loose in the saddle, alert and proud, jogging down the Tarryall Road along the river, laced with ice along the banks, under the leafless branches of the alders, hugging the cliffs on the uphill side. A steer makes a break, and a boy dashes into the straw-brown meadow to cut him off with a little whoop and a swinging rope. Yesterday he was a city boy sitting in a classroom, conjugating a French verb. This morning he is a man alive, singing under the sun, the blood of a hundred wayfaring ancestors running hot under his denim jacket.

The critters ahead are no children's playfellows. They are veterans of the big rodeo circuits: wary, expert opponents in an old, old game. Country Butter is among them, a honey-colored horse trotting tranquilly enough in the herd, but an animal that top hands view with misgiving at any rodeo. "Dibs on him," says Bill with a grin. "He's mine next Saturday."

The Utes rode here, coming back from hunting antelope in South Park, saddleless, straight-legged. There are ghosts of pinto ponies nibbling the brown grass at the roadside. There's a great hawk hovering where a great hawk hovered a hundred years ago. There's a tuft-eared squirrel cursing from the safety of a spruce tree, and it is 30 October miles from the U-Quarter Circle Ranch to the Crescent Ranch, where there will be a corral and shelter for the night. Their past surrounds them. Their futures ride within them. The sun sets in rose ladders and on go the denim jackets. Good education? I think so. Inside the denim jackets ride a most imaginative businessman, an inventor, a very great test pilot, a nationally-known research chemist, and a governor of Colorado.

While the top hands were herding the bucking stock down the pass, a group of the less experienced boys were rounding up a herd of burros from a sheep ranch in South Park to be trucked down for the wild burro race. Wild they were! Strangers to rope or halter, with an unexpected breezy lawlessness that becomes plain stubbornness in a broken burro. Fresh as morning, they were finally delivered at the paddock by a very weary group of boys.

The lodge pole runners of the corral fence made the only grandstand. Someone was always sitting there watching practice rides in the afternoon. One day John turned up at the chute and said, "I'd like to try Mittens." Mittens was an ugly little black horse with a Roman nose and two white feet and a doubling-up bucking technique that was irresistible. Woody and the boys got Mittens into the chute and the bucking strap on, and John lowered himself cautiously, got a firm hold on the surcingle rope, made ready to shout, "Let 'er go," and suddenly slumped. He looked at Lloyd despairingly. "Pappy, I can't," he said.

Lloyd laughed and said, "That's all right, John. Nobody has to. It doesn't matter at all. Hop down." But it did matter.

"I'm awfully sorry," John said. "I just can't."

"We're just doing this for fun," Lloyd said. "It's not important, you know. And I wouldn't let you ride unless you felt perfectly confident, so forget it, and don't worry." And John went home.

The next afternoon he was back. "Saddle up Mittens," he called from the end of the corral.

Lloyd looked at him thoughtfully. "Sure you want to ride him, Johnny?"

"Yes, I'm sure."

"You're under no obligation, you know. Feel good about it?"

The answer came sharp. "I don't want to ride him. I *have* to ride him. I couldn't sleep all night."

The schoolmaster looked at him thoughtfully again. "Right you are. You have to ride him. Saddle him up, Woody."

Once again the bucking strap, the boy lowering himself cautiously onto the twitching back, the rope held fast in his left hand, the legs wrapped tight, hugging the belligerent barrel of horseflesh, a spare hand flung up in a gay gesture before joining the other to clutch the rope. "Let 'er go!" he cried! And out came

Mittens in a spasm of furious action to be ridden triumphantly to the whistle.

At supper Lloyd told me about it with shining eyes. "Courage," he said. "Courage deliberately built up over 24 hours is so much more valuable than foolhardiness right this minute."

There was a grace about it on that Saturday afternoon when the crowd began to assemble. It had style, but it was ours—it had the Cheyenne brand. Top hands from all over the country came to see what these children were up to, but they weren't allowed around the chute. They were just part of the curious crowd. At a quarter to two the school orchestra began to play, seated on folding chairs on the packed dirt just outside the corral fence. There were only a dozen or so of them left. The rest were all in the rodeo. But they tootled and banged and sawed stoutly.

At two o'clock the parade entered the arena to cheers and wild applause. Beloved Betty Jean, the queen, on Lady, stepping proudly while the Cheyenne flag tickled her flank, led the procession, followed by her attendants, Jane Gray and Jean Sinclair. Then came the saddle bronco riders, the bare back riders, the steer riders, and behind them smaller children on bicycles with wooden horse heads fastened to their front fenders. Behind them came a herd of little children on hobby horses.

It was a wonderful show. One after another, the events unfolded, some producing cheers and excitement, others producing hilarity, as when it was announced that Frank Perkins, a member of the Board of Education, would ride a steer, and a small calf with a doll tied to its back was released from the chute. There were certainly some bruises but no injuries. For the girls there was a competition in graceful bareback riding and a race in which each one had to ride bareback across the arena, saddle her horse, and then ride back. The small boys rode and roped calves and also competed in a hobby horse race. The girls of the junior high did a good business selling refreshments from a teepee pitched on the grounds. The grand finale was the wild burro race in which the contestants first had to catch their mounts and then ride them around the arena.

At the end of the long, golden afternoon, the crowd dispersed, and the children returned to their homes, dusty but inwardly cleansed and proud, ready for another wonderful school year.

IT WILL FLAME OUT (Dorothy)

If Lloyd Shaw were administering a small school system today, he would smile tolerantly when confronted with the "prayer decision" of the United States Supreme Court, dismiss it with the conclusion that it was a matter of semantics and remind any who listened that it was not concerned with the main issue—the relation of humans to their god. He might quote Gerard Manley Hopkins:

> *The world is charged with the grandeur of God;*
> *It will flame out like shining from shook foil!*

For the young, he saw this God with whose grandeur the world is charged as the one that could and should be approached in their behalf. There are no creeds and no dogmas in the way of this aspect of God. But He is very immediate. He can be seen and heard and, in a limited way, apprehended by the innocent young. They are, by nature of their innocence, untroubled by the terrors of infinity.

His duties as an educator were clear in his mind. The academic obligation was there, first but not foremost, to be met with the highest possible standard of excellence. That was relatively simple. It called for judgment. But above and beyond this academic preparation for whatever career life might offer was the need to prepare for what life was sure to offer—the need to live in the world, the world full of people, the world that was charged with the grandeur of God. The two things usually went together, but there were chances, varying with one's personal good fortune in the matter, of encountering the grand world, all alone—empty. He felt almost fanatical about his duty as a teacher to use whatever was at hand to bring these children and the grandeur of the world together. He had much at hand.

Once, on a spring dance trip to New York, Lloyd's first-day course in the city of New York ended with the usual exhibit— riding the Staten Island Ferry past the Stature of Liberty to the Staten Island Terminal, then straight back onto the boat again and back into New York with the time carefully chosen for the sunset to glow on the towering town and for the fairy-tale lights to start coming on in all the castellated skyline. On this particular trip there was another group of school children in the ferry boat: fifth and sixth graders from the lower east side, scrubbed and shining, awed into silence, listening respectfully to the explanations of their teachers. There was a horde of them, and their behavior was admirable. Our older children also listened respectfully to their teacher and what he had to say about the Statue of Liberty and the liberty for which it stood, what he had to explain about the arrangement and history of New York harbor, what he had to tell them about why they were coming into New York by sunset and twilight. But it was the little tenement dwellers from the lower east side who made—and stole—the show on this particular occasion.

As the sunset colored the miraculous skyline, and the water grew very still and luminous, we all gathered at the rail of the ferry boat, quiet—big children from Colorado and the little children from the lower east side of New York City—thinking long thoughts perhaps? Suddenly, and apparently quite spontaneously (we saw no evidence of teachers setting it off) the little tenement children began to sing! A few voices at first, then more—reedy little voices accustomed to singing:

Oh, beautiful for spacious skies,
For amber waves of grain
For purple mountain majesties
Above the fruited plain
America! America! . . .

By that time the big children from Colorado had joined in as well as their teachers, and by that time everyone was weeping, that good kind of weeping that we have so rarely—just quiet tears streaming unwiped down happy faces. The song rose to a glorious crescendo at the end—

America! America!
God shed His grace on thee,
And crown thy good
With brotherhood
From sea to shining sea!"

The big children from Colorado gathered around their teacher. They were shaken. They, after all had grown up at the foot of Pikes Peak, the mountain from which Katharine Lee Bates had viewed the fruited plain and the purple mountain majesties and been inspired to write her poem in 1893.

"Pappy," one said, astonished, "they knew all the words!"

"But they can't know what they mean," said another. "They have never seen amber waves of grain or purple mountain majestics, have they?"

"They have never even seen New York," Lloyd said. He had been talking to their teachers. "Most of them have never been more than three blocks away from the tenement in which they were born. This is a program of Mayor LaGuardia's. They go in groups like this on various tours as the guests of the City of New York. Of course, this is the favorite and most important one."

"But, Pappy, they don't *have* any of it! They sing those words, but *we* are the ones who *have* it!"

"Oh, I don't know about that," he said. "You'll find plenty of prints of pilgrim feet around here, beating a thoroughfare for freedom, and you'll find a fair share of heroes, and just for a few minutes, at sunset, they have an alabaster city, gleaming undimmed by human tears, until you get close enough to see them."

"But *we* have the purple mountain majesties! And there's no way we can share them!"

"Isn't there? I wonder. Let's work a little harder at soaking them up ourselves, shall we?"

Soaking it up! By the process of immersion, just a quiet, untalked-about baptism in the grandeur with which the world is charged, under the disguise of camping or hiking or riding a horse along a dim trail.

It is May, any May of any year. The school is already an unsteady flutter of plans: plans to give exams and plans to pass them; plans for the Junior Prom and plans for the Senior Play; plans for the spring camping trips.

The gong rings on the speaker system. "Will the boys who are interested in the spring camping trip meet me in the auditorium at 12:45." Practically the whole male population of the high school is there. They can't all go, of course. Precedence goes to upper classmen, but a few sophomores whose attitudes have been especially good have always had a chance to go. There must always be a backlog of experienced campers to help along the new ones. This is a thing that rolls from year to year and season to season. The possible places are discussed, and a happy consensus lights up: Twin Lakes. It is not going to be quite mid-May by the coming weekend; there is deep snow in the Sawatch mountains, deep snow on Independence Pass above 12,000 feet. The nights will be cold at Twin Lakes and the water frozen at the lake's edge in the morning. They will need plenty of bedding in their improvised bedrolls and plenty of warm clothing. Excited

220

beginners have a hundred questions about all this. What about our grub? How do we go? How do we double up in the tents? On and on. It is made clear that there are tents enough for all. The student body owns a collection of umbrella tents; any private ones are a welcome addition. Four boys to a tent, and they may organize themselves, but don't put all the greenhorns together. Each tent group to plan, bring, and cook their own food, four boys to a group; a discussion of things that are good to bring and the way to cook in the hot ashes under a going fire. (They will make some dreadful blunders on the coming weekend, but the next trip will find them old hands.) They will need a hand axe and a good knife. "And this time let's take our skis! Perhaps we can drive part way up the Pass and ski back down to where the snow leaves off!" That's Pappy talking, and he is answered by a cheer.

It is soft spring on Saturday morning just at sunrise. It is even a little fragrant with small promises, for the lilacs are coming out. Let us suppose that this is a May morning a longish time ago, before we had the final Flexible bus, and the little old yellow bus that we got second-hand from a school on the Western Slope still has to do. (In all the years of Lloyd Shaw's Cheyenne School, the school administration never owned a bus. All the buses they acquired belonged to the student body, purchased by the students themselves with the money they earned or begged or borrowed.) The little yellow bus is lined up, jauntily enough, considering what is going to be asked of it, as well as the administration's little Chevrolet maintenance truck and the cars of several faculty members. The incredible load is gradually and quite expertly stowed in and on top of these vehicles. It is the ultimate honor, reserved for seniors, to ride on top of the bus or wind-blown on top of the great load in the truck. Freshmen, if any, are likely to end up in relative comfort in the teacher's car. Woody will be driving the bus; that is one of his jobs. And Pappy himself, or Pop Evans, may be handling the truck. Or perhaps Pappy will be sitting backwards in the front seat of the bus, explaining the countryside and stopping the whole caravan at intervals to pop out and tell them things he feels they ought to know: "this is a noble stand of narrow-leafed cottonwood; smell the varnishy odor of the new buds. Or, "Right there along the road is a marmot, a kind of ground hog." Or, "there used to be a bridge here for the narrow-gauge railroad. The trains kept running into cars on the highway."

It is mid-morning by the time they pull up at the top of Wilkerson Pass. "Oh, beautiful for spacious skies. . . for purple mountain majesties. . ." Under a sky like a columbine, the great South Park spreads out below, and beyond it the range rises, purple paling into blue, and blue exploding into alabaster where the great snows lie on the summits. "That's a herd of antelope, I think," says Pappy. "Watch for them when we get down into South Park." The spring run-off has not started yet; the lakes are ice-covered; there is the slightest greening along the grass roots.

The first leaf has not yet broken the buds of the aspens at the Twin Lakes Campground, but the regal purple catkins hang like long tassels and the whole grove is fragrant. The campground is clean and deserted—probably they are the first ones in. They unload like streaks, hurrying to get settled and eat a sandwich and head for the pass, for the days are still short at the evening end. Off the bus top come the skis—such skis! These boys are still almost the only skiers in the Pikes Peak area. They discovered it, along with Pappy, and they helped him put on the first tournament at Glen Cove on the Peak. For the most part, they and their fathers have made their own skis—no metal edges, no laminated structure. "My Dad made our skis," one told me. "He bent the wood in hot water in Mom's washer." They still ski the way Thor Groswold taught them when he came over from Norway. They still do a telemark turn and a Christiania, and they use the kind of bindings Lt. Albizzi of the Italian Alpine Ski Corps of World War I taught Pappy to make: an intricate arrangement of leather thongs that permit a ski to tear off from the foot without breaking the leg, the ski, or the binding. At this moment the home-made skis and the few expensive commercial ones are gleaming with fresh paraffin.

The willing little yellow bus is stacked high with skis and boys, and the truck has a substantial load too. Those who do have skis have already organized a hike with two of the faculty men. "Hey, Bill! Be sure you get the spuds started!" calls back one of the skiers. Off they go, having remembered their shovels at the last minute. The thick stand of aspen along the valley floor widens into spruce forest, thins, and opens into a great bowl rimmed with the highest mountains in Colorado. To their right Elbert and Massive lift, glistening with that spring shining that comes to snow that has thawed and refrozen many times. To their left, the pure white pyramid of La Plata Peak rises into a cloudless sky. Clustering around these giants, a hundred lesser mountains, all white, all beautiful. "The world is charged with the grandeur of God. . ." Do they talk about it? Certainly not. They are simply being immersed in it. They talk about everything and nothing until they are suddenly too busy to talk with the first drift across the road, which had been plowed to this point. The vehicles charge into the drift and back up until they break through and the pushers hop back on. Farther along they have to shovel. The trees are left behind and the wind begins to blow off the snow cornices. The going gets tougher. They are out on foot all the time now, pushing, shoveling, running ahead. No use putting on the skis; the road goes straight up. They get the little bus and the truck turned around a half mile short of the summit and do the last untouched stretch of snow on foot, wallowing and laughing and gasping for breath. The Colorado Mountain Club register on the summit stands clear of the snow in its metal cylinder on it long post. They all sign it happily dating the entry and announcing that on that date they opened Independence Pass for the season. The notation on the summit says "Elevation 12,095 feet."

Now they can go down! To drop 3000 feet, flying along those great crevasses, opening out onto those wide white meadows—no tows, no devices, just skiing, from the top of a mountain pass to the spring world below—"We are the ones who have it!" Do not bother to talk about it, young ones; do not even take time to think about it. Feel the wind stinging your cheeks and your feet stiffening in your inadequate boots, and your heart racing with pure joy. But somewhere, deep in some secret repository, make a note of it—where you have been and Whom you met there.

Their schoolmaster has gone with them, all the way. He follows them now, on his good skis, bringing up the rear as always to make sure that everyone is safe. He is probably happier than those who are 17. He has been 17 and that is long since done. He knows who he is, and a little of who they are, and very certainly what he wants for them. The snow isn't very good for skiing this late in the year. There is some new powder in the shaded places, but most of it is either mushy or icy. So he goes a little cautiously, all but tasting his joy in it, momentarily alone.

By the time they had flown down to the last of the snow, loaded into the waiting vehicles, and reached the camp ground, the fires were burning, twilight was deepening, and the magical day slid into the past tense. What good camp keepers boys can be! A huge potato wrapped in aluminum foil fished out of the hot ashes and crying for butter, a steak slapped casually onto a bit of a grill and coming off crusted and juicy, a jar of mother's peaches opened and waiting with a tin saucer and a big spoon alongside, while a can of tomatoes simmers in a corner of the fire. And half a loaf of bread apiece with butter and jam. How quickly they clear things away and wash the dishes in the edge of the lake and stow their supplies safely out of reach of rats and porcupines.

Somebody chuckled. Somebody else threw another log on the fire. Ice was forming in a water bucket nearby. Lloyd told them stories of his solo climbs in the mountains and of the time he may have encountered an axe murderer on Pikes Peak.

"Golly, this is great," Chuck muttered. "Wish we could come back again next week."

224

"Can't do that," said big Shelly Mac. "Have to let the girls have their turn. Anyway, you shouldn't worry. It's only about five months to the fall trip, and I'll bet you go to the Sand Dunes. And you'll be there and I won't."

"And we won't," whispered Soapy. He was lying flat on his back, looking up into such a majesty of stars as he had never seen before, jewel-bright and unbelievably near. "Oh, beautiful for spacious skies. . ." and someone else picked up the tenor part.

"What about the girls?" asked the lady who was writing her master's thesis on this experiment in an extra-curricular outdoor program. "Evidently they went separately. Isn't that surprising where there seems to have been such a good relationship between the boys and girls? Why didn't they camp together?"

The girls went the next weekend and to the same place. But girls are different. It would have served no good purpose to try to combine these two happy occasions. The boys' camp was no Boy Scout affair; it was a man's camp—grueling physically and challenging spiritually. After his program of individual athletics had really gotten into gear, Lloyd had a school full of well-rounded young athletes. They had unusual stamina, and they regarded their camping trips as great masculine adventures. Girls will wade a spring torrent with all their clothes on and cook dinner in their pajamas. And the girls had not had the opportunity to become such expert skiers, although they would in following years when skis became more available commercially. The hike to the summit of Independence Pass was grueling in the deep snow, and the ski down was taxing for a man's strength. The boys respected the girls for all the things they could do well. Female chaperones would have been necessary too, and this would have been a frightful violation of masculine dignity. And then, there was the obligation not to lead them into temptation. After all, the objective was always to make them forget each other as creatures of the opposite sex.

The girls hiked over miles of hills and valleys and went down the snow slides on the seat of their breeches. They lay in the sun and chattered. They cut mountains of wood for their fires— some of them were really good with an axe. And they dreamed dreams. They always brought too much stuff, and something usually happened to some of it, and they screamed with laughter. Not long ago I encountered a suave and charming woman who began to reminisce at once about Cheyenne School. "The camping trips!" she said. "They were the most wonderful things. I shall treasure them all my life! Did you ever know about the time Pappy brought the pancake syrup? He had it stowed in the very middle of his sleeping bag so it wouldn't get broken, and he showed us the pancake flour he had brought to go with it and made our mouths water with his description of what they were going to be like in the morning. But, when he got ready to go to bed, he found the syrup had leaked and his sleeping bag was full of it. You can't imagine how we laughed. We thought it was the funniest thing that had ever happened. It still seems funny to me."

The faculty cooperation was a lovely thing. The girls really needed the men teachers, and they came and brought their wives along. And some of the women teachers became real camping troupers. Everyone grew. They grew the way things grow in high, far places where the ultraviolet light is potent and the nights are cold.

The lady who was writing her Master's thesis asked a strange question. She wanted to know what sort of a questionnaire the kids filled out after the trips were over. "You know, to evaluate the experience educationally."

"Evaluate?" I said. "You mean to fill in a lot of blanks indicating what was good and what was bad about it and why? And how it contributed to your progress? And whether it was a profitable experience? Answer yes or no?"

How could you evaluate it if you were 17 and it was magic? The next fall the boys did go to the Sand Dunes—not big

226

Shelly Mac and Soapy and some of the others. They could begin evaluating. They had graduated, leaving gaps for sophomores to fill.

You go to the Great Sand Dunes on the weekend when the harvest moon is full. This time the little caravan headed south through Pueblo and Walsenberg and over La Veta Pass. It was a little step ladder of a road then, angling back and forth up a golden hill. Pure gold—acres and miles of it—golden aspens, undiluted, one of the greatest displays of autumn color in the west. Web worms have taken the trees since then, and the golden robe is thinner, but it still lies like something around a king's shoulders, as you head up from the little town of La Veta. The campers came down in the blazing September sun into the San Luis Valley, whose gate post is Mount Blanca, the final and superlative peak of the great Sangre de Cristo range, lifting on that morning a summit pristine with the first snow of the year, a summit only a few feet lower than Mount Elbert, the highest mountain in Colorado.

Pappy used to tell them how the mountain ranges of Colorado were a little like a very crooked ladder, with uprights on each side and the east-west ranges making the rungs. And in between the rungs the mountain parks, fertile, relatively flat, and beautiful land. Farthest south of these parks is the San Luis Valley, which was once a sea. Even now it is flat as a sea and as dry as a desert. Its waters are underground, and great artesian wells go deep and bring up leaping water for vast miles of hay meadows and cattle range and farms. Just where the ancient sea would have broken against the Sangre de Cristo Mountains, just where a great river plunges off of the slopes of mighty Blanca and loses itself in the earth, the dunes lie like memories of seacoasts— 35,000 acres of pure, fine sand totally devoid of vegetation, always in motion, always blowing from hill to hill, moving like waves against the great sea wall of Mount Blanca. They are among the most beautiful things in nature, and the Great Sand Dunes of Colorado are among the finest in the world.

It is only a little way from US 160 to the edge of the Dunes and a modest government installation, for the Great Sand Dunes are a national monument. The installation is closed by late September, but Pappy knows where there are suitable camping places with meager water and a few straggly cottonwoods at the edge of the sand. They have to find a bit of solid earth—you can't peg a tent down in a sand dune.

They pitch their tents and set out to explore. Every little pointed hill turns up a story in this place. There are tales of fences built on top of fences, of a whole flock of sheep and their herder buried under mighty dunes when a great wind moved them from one place to another, of lost children, wild horses that have grown snow-shoe feet to accommodate themselves to wandering on this unquiet sand. Tracks do not stay, but the campers are determined to find one of these latter creatures, tracks or not. Zebulon Pike came upon this place in January of 1807 and did not linger, but men have lingered. In the little museum there are some points that are typical of Folsom man, cut in his particular way from flint.

Dinner is an adventure. "Mom," said Chuck when he got home, "there was even sand inside the eggs when we opened them!" The food is good, but every bite grits. And then there is the campfire and the talk. There are plenty of real ghost stories for this place, and Pappy does know them. "Stay together," he warned them. "Don't go out on the dunes in groups of less than three, and if you feel lost, holler!" The whole night grows eerie. The full moon has risen and stands high, and the air is as soft as milk. The wind has died. It is completely breathless.

"And then," he told me after they came home, "something happened. It never did before and it never will again. It was absolutely wonderful."

"What?"

"I'm not sure I know. They were transfigured or something. The first thing I knew they were all on the dunes in that moonlight. They had taken off everything but their shorts, and they were running barefoot, playing a fancy kind of hide and seek. They had divided themselves into little bands, and they were playing against each other—and they never made a sound. One group would be huddled in the lee of a dune, absolutely silent, and another group would suddenly appear over the top of a dune like ghosts with their arms held up. They pounced and rolled, and you could hear some whispered snickers, but they weren't going to let the other groups know where they were, so they were quiet. It was weird—half-naked in that great moonlight—they looked like beings from another world, or like Folsom men, perhaps. There wasn't anything to it—there really isn't anything to tell. I don't know why it made such an impression on me.

"And by the way, while we were cooking supper, we had a great sunset—one of those all-over-the-sky ones. It was an extra good camping trip."

What if they had all been given questionnaires on Monday morning on which to "evaluate" their experience! What would a student have said, I wonder. "We learned quite a lot of history and geology about that part of Colorado, and we played hide and seek on the dunes." And he would take out that part about hide and seek because it sounded silly and not very educational, and he would end up by leaving in just the history and geology. Unless he was a poet—we had a few. He would also leave out how he had learned to make an efficient little cook stove out of a two-pound coffee can. And he wouldn't mention the all-over-the-sky sunset, not on a questionnaire!

To his father, waiting at the school to pick him up, he would say, "Gee, Dad, we had a swell time!" To his son, he will say, "There's a full moon this weekend. Let's take the tent and go over to the Great Sand Dunes!" To his grandson, he may say, "Once upon a time when I was 17 - - -" And he won't know how to tell it because he will have arrived at evaluation, and he will realize that his whole youth was shot through with a very special magic—like being lifted up out of the lower east side and plunked down on the Staten Island Ferry at sunset.

The lady who was writing her Master's thesis said, "I'm sorry. I think you were perfectly right not to do it, but I don't think my college is going to accept all of this as being a genuine educational project if I can't get something like evaluation questionnaires to support it."

BACCALAUREATE (Dorothy)

The year was 1938, and it was June. The day was Sunday, and the hour was five o'clock in the afternoon. It was almost summer; the sense of it shimmered in the late afternoon light, and in the gentle coolness of the auditorium where closed radiators were quiet at last. The blue velvet curtain was drawn on the stage, and against it flickered a huge bowl of great red peonies from Mr. Taylor's garden. There were some plain candles in two candelabra, a table for the superintendent's book and papers, and, for the remainder of the setting, there was quiet. It was an easy quiet—grave rather than solemn. Each year on the Sunday before commencement, the high school came together once more to re-enact the little vesper service that had once been a weekly feature of the weeks of springtime, to sing their favorite hymns, to read together their favorite psalms, and to listen to their superintendent have his last fling at saying what he thought about their lives—theirs and his.

Parents and teachers and students came quietly and sat quietly, listening to Evelyn playing "Jesu, Joy of Man's Desiring" on the new Hammond organ. She was weaving a little spell of her own that modulated into another mood as the seniors entered and filed into their usual places in the front rows. They were astonishing, especially the girls, who had completely grown up since yesterday, so chic and smart in their new suits, their pretty hats, their high- heeled pumps, their white gloves. They had even

231

done some sort of magic to the sunburns from last week's camping trip. They all looked ready to take on the world. Gravely ready.

Behind them came Pappy, walking briskly to the little table. He had to tell them just once more, for the last time and forever—he had to tell them what he thought, what he had discovered. Whether they ever used it or not, he had to give them his map. He wouldn't have dreamed of letting anyone else make this sermon to them. What clergyman in the area could possibly know, looking into their transparent faces, exactly to whom he was talking?

They rose and sang the first hymn together; it was always the same: "Now the Day Is Over," and then they said the Lord's Prayer, and then they sang "Abide with Me." They loved the hymns for the end of the day, for they have the qualities of lullabies for children grown so tall that they must sing their own. They read together their school psalm, "I will lift up mine eyes unto the hills. From whence cometh my help? My help cometh from the Lord who hath made heaven and earth . . . " This was part of the map; some of them did not dream how often they would reach for it. The Lord is thy keeper, the Lord is thy defense upon thy right hand . . . the Lord shall preserve thy going out and thy coming in, from this time forth, for evermore." They were indeed "going out" from this first cradle of their adulthood; they were as transparent as dewdrops.

They scarcely needed the hymnals. The next one was the "Crusaders' Hymn" and they could sing that with a soprano descant. They sang it on camping trips and riding in the bus coming home from Denver late at night after a basketball game. They sang it now:

Fair are the meadows,
Fairer still the woodlands,
Robed in the blooming garb of spring . . .

And the clear voices somehow put the unruly young persons into clean white habits cut from the fabric of their own best hours.

They folded their hands in their laps as Pappy stood up. Always in classes, it had to be by indirection. Now he could say it plain, and if there were some who were rejoicing that he would be saying it to them for the last time, it is likely that they were the ones who would be astonished to find it coming back to them at an unlikely time and place. He arranged his notes, looked at them hard, and talked.

"Another graduating class, and what am I to say to them: Not the same things that I said to my first class here at Cheyenne Mountain School 21 years ago, for I am not the same man and you are not the same boys and girls. I must simply tell you what I think after those 21 years of watching children grow from five-year-old kindergartners to 18-year-old seniors only to walk out of that door and away from us forever. And it is not exactly *thinking* I shall talk to you about.

"We are on a vast plain, darkling. We are ringed by mighty mountains, blue, dark and forbidding. Somehow, we must find our way from here. No individual understands or has ever understood life, but we must somehow find our way from here. And my instinct is all that I am willing to trust—my spirit's reaching. Like a compass needle, it has been quivering and returning to one pass through those dark mountains. I feel that it is trying to point me to the way of life. As independent of reason as those dark statements of the master, as logically contradictory, it whispers: 'here is the truth.'

"There could not possibly be anything original in what I have to say to you. Who am I to think new thoughts? It has all been written and said many times before. Nevertheless, this is my own, and I cannot tell you where I found it. It may be printed, but I do not know the book.

"What we read and what we hear means nothing to us until we make it a part of our own thinking. What we think is of little

233

moment until we make it a deep part of our own feeling. There is a great danger here, for we know what dark feelings of anger and pride and jealousy can possess us, and how these feelings can rule our very lives. But feelings do rule us—in spite of the danger. We can only try to keep these feelings high and beautiful.

"So it is not what I have read or heard or even thought that I would speak of to you. It is what I have been *feeling* with increasing intensity all year, a feeling that a certain simple and very homely truth may be the only pass through which we can cross over the dark mountains that enclose us. I feel at times it may be the very secret of life.

"And it is particularly significant to you because you are now finishing the epoch of your childhood. Now the great year has arrived and you are going off to college to live your own life, to think for yourself, be your own master; you are leaving home. You are spreading your own wings to fly into the far blue of your dreams. Others may have trouble, others may meet failure, but you, being you, will sail through to your own rosy harbor. Do you member, Mrs. Jones, when you were trying to disillusion a certain history class of boys with the nature of war, you showed them a book of dreadful war pictures, with mutilated bodies blown to bits? And their attitude was, 'how fascinating. We'd like to see that! The other fellows might be blown to bits but we'd be lucky. We'd take our chance.' Some of you will even approach marriage with eyes as blind as this, for youth is wildly confident; but remember, each of you is the other fellow's 'other fellow.'

"And so you will have luck and success, and this will be added to you, and that will be added to you. You will grow by accretion, layer after layer of luck and success until you are the person you dream of being.

"And I hope you do have luck, and I hope that much will be added to you. But here is my secret conviction; here is my compass needle; here is the point of all I want to say. I don't believe it makes much difference whether you have luck or not. I don't believe it makes much difference whether or not anything much is added to you from the *outside. Only what happens within you really matters!* Your chance of happiness and success in life, like the Kingdom of God, is within you.

"Not only the people about you but also your own dreams and urges will tell you: lo, here! Lo, there! And they will set you scurrying after success here, there, and everywhere. And all the time, the only answer lies written within yourself. The Kingdom of Heaven is within you, and that is all that is worth having in the kingdoms of the world.

"Oh, but I hear you mutter, 'Nonsense! If I had the right chance, the right job, the right opportunity, the money, the friend, the perfect husband or wife—if I had this—or if I had that, I would be successful and happy.' And it sounds quite reasonable. And my compass needle swings around and says, 'No! If you can't be happy and successful without those things, you could never be happy with them.' It all lies within your own, very self.

"Luck! Do you remember that article I reviewed for you a few weeks ago called 'There is no such thing as luck,' with all its statistics about unlucky persons whose bad luck went straight back to some uncorrected flaw in themselves. It seems unreasonable to say there is no such thing as luck, and yet I have walked around and around that idea and I am increasingly impressed by it. Of course, we are at times unfortunate, but in that long, long turning of 'fortune's wheel' that Shakespeare so believed in, we are as often on the top as on the bottom, and what is more important probably doesn't make as much difference as you think. We lose perspective.

"You may call it luck, bad luck, if you choose, but you will certainly be called upon to endure personal sorrow. You may lose a child as we lost our little boy, and someone will come, very simply to comfort you, completely omitting to tell you that he has lost more than you ever possessed, and that he has suffered more than you have imagined possible. And he will not point out that

235

his own head is lifted above disasters like the summit of a mountain above the lowland clouds, in the pure air of eternity, where there is nothing but the abiding peace of God. You will notice this yourself. And you can't possibly say that luck has anything to do with it, or any other external thing. Believing in luck will undo any person. Luck is the most fatal and dangerous alibi in the world.

"There was a wealthy young man, athletic, active, dynamic, and personable, building a promising career in public life— suddenly stricken with infantile paralysis, his career ruined, crippled for life. 'What rotten luck,' you might say, although up until that moment everything he had had been good. Fighting it through at the Warm Springs Sanitarium, he had to turn to the life within him, and he found a well of power that has made his career. Strong men are broken in the presidency. The strain of being torn by a thousand conflicting and selfish interests leaves them worn and weary. And yet this man, taking office in these most trying years, years of such conflict as the world has not known before, looks more radiant and healthy today than he did four years ago.

"Was this bad luck—or good? I don't care about your politics; right or wrong, he found something at Warm Springs, where most men would have given up. He found the power that was within him. And, that power has given him, walking painfully with braces, a spirit that untroubled men never find.

"But happiness is more important to you right now than power or success. Be careful where you look for it. It doesn't necessarily live in big houses with swimming pools. It is just as likely to be in a little room out at Sunnyrest Sanitarium. It comes entirely from within. It is in the little house of your heart; and I am asking you to remember Maeterlinck's play that I read to you last Christmas where the blue bird for which the children hunted so far was in the cage in their own little house all along.

"But like a pack of hounds that have lost the scent, we all go yelping down the trail after things. Things, things, things to make us happy. Fifty million radio listeners, including you and me, counting on that car that Camay or Ivory or Old Gold promised us, with a few thousand gallons of gasoline thrown in. But a lot of sensible people, and happier people too, went out and worked hard and bought a new car and paid for the gasoline themselves and are having a wonderful time while we wait around for our lucky present.

"No, my compass needle points. My deepest instinct is that happiness and success and power and all the matters in life must come from within yourself. And where you go or what you do makes little difference. It only matters what you are.

"How discouraging! This world of rosy dreams that you are about to enter is of little importance, if I am right. And I seem to be trying to turn you right back to that same old self you have lived with all your life. (And you will never escape that self, try as you will.) You can hardly believe that you are not going any place that matters much, that it is the same old you after all.

"Discouraging? No! The greatest miracle in the world is you. *You* are a journey and a habitation. The devices of modern invention are crude child's toys compared to you. All the mighty thoughts that any person has ever thought, your brain can reach to. All the beautiful poems and paintings and music of the world your spirit can respond to. What others have been is not impossible to you—the trained body of the man on the flying trapeze or the dancer in the Russian Ballet could be your body. Limitless in possibility you stand, with a mind that can reach beyond the farthermost star, with a body that can dare and do impossible things, and with a spirit that can stand alongside your favorite hero—humbly equal.

"You are miracles. Your teachers and I have been watching you with tenderness and alarm. And I would turn you away from the false promises of the world—from the radio advertiser trying to tease you from your normal lives with false promises of shining cars and thousands of gallons of gas to carry you to hundreds of places that are blazing with lights and are utterly empty. I would turn you to that endless world within yourself. There lies your only chance of success and power and happiness.

"The kingdom of heaven is within you. That you may enter into the kingdom is my prayer.

"Let us stand," he said then, "and sing hymn number 120: 'Dear Lord and Father of mankind, forgive our foolish ways.'" He turned the pages, "The words of this hymn were written by John Greenleaf Whittier, a somewhat discredited country school teacher who never went anywhere or accomplished much of anything. I wish you'd listen to them as you sing them:"

> *Take from our souls the strain and stress*
> *And let our ordered lives confess*
> *The beauty of thy peace.*

What a strange way for a school master to talk to graduating seniors! Not—you can go out and lick the world, but you can go *in* and lick the world. A map, roadless, with a place named the Kingdom of Heaven written on it in invisible ink! And a little compass, stubbornly pointing right through oneself to find the North Star. Of course the one who looked most likely picked up the map and rolled it nicely and tied it to his knapsack and stuck the little compass confidently into the packet of his hiking shirt. Possibly he lost it not long afterward and forgot all about it—and the map too. And possibly some unlikely one came along and recognized it and picked it up with a happy exclamation, "Why, that's Pappy's old map! And here's his little old compass— wonder if it's any good," and followed them straight into the kingdom that had been within him all along. Possibly.

I've wondered why he wrote it down. He never made full notes, just little reminders on 3 X 5 cards. And of course his discourse dashed away from this little text on a dozen delightful digressions and illustrations. But this was so terribly important that he wrote it down and filed it for someone, for me, to find. And I've wondered what they said back to him in their minds—those who listened.

We sang the school hymn at the end. The ghost of Kenneth Hartley came and sat on the organ bench beside Evelyn and played the music he had written for us. The words were ours too. The school hymn was not like any of our other songs—we sang it only once a year.

Beneath thine eyes the mountains stand,
All clustered in thy keeping.
Their bright cascades on every hand
For thy delight are leaping.
Unto thy praise the spruces sing
And underneath thy brooding wing
The little lakes are sleeping.

God, give thy children eyes to see
Thy beauty and the splendor,
And let us, like the mountains, be
Serene and strong and tender;
So when life calls us to the fight,
May each go forth, with heart a-light,
Forever thy defender.

"The Lord bless us and keep us . . . "

The sun was low and the smell of the lilacs came strong. High heels and pretty hats and clean white gloves; new suits and gift neckties—they all trooped home to supper.

MOVING BEYOND COLORADO (Lloyd)

As we kept dancing over the state, I couldn't help commenting now and then that we would soon get invitations from all around the nation. The kids just laughed at me. But I had a firm feeling that we were soon to start. I didn't know just how it was to come about, but I had a strange hunch that we would soon be dancing from coast to coast. We had danced for all the universities and colleges in the state, we had danced for high school after high school, and the bigger they were, the more certain we were to get an invitation from them. We danced for chambers of commerce and for luncheon clubs. We danced for conventions until it seemed to me that everyone had had a chance to see us.

And we didn't let the trips turn our heads. In fact we found that in order to maintain good relations with the rest of the school, it was necessary for us to treat the trips as if we hadn't made them. We just happened to go, without saying much about it. The school was a very busy school. We had a thousand other things we could do, so there was something that every student could fit into. We had trips to the cabin, we had a rodeo, we had a large pasture of horses up above the school, we bought a glider, which we tried to fly, we had our plays, and we had a thousand other things besides. But into a very important and little spoken-of part of the school had grown our interest in the dances. These we were letting develop as they would as long as we kept them the truest we could to the originals from which they sprang.

240

And on Wednesday nights we continued to have our big dance for everyone. The team was no special part. We all danced for joy, and practically everyone came out for these dances. All we did was folk dance and square dance and do it as it had always been done in a community. We danced for fun, and we all had a wonderful time. The team had graciously learned to take their part in it as part of the mass of dancers, dancing purely for joy. And joy was the secret of these precious evenings!

The first out-of-state invitation to dance came in 1933 from Santa Fe, New Mexico. They wanted us to dance for their annual festival called La Fiesta de los Conquistadores at the end of August. I decided to try the dancers out on this out-of-state and out-of-school-year trip. So late in August we rolled down to Santa Fe in our bus, taking mostly people who had graduated from our school, and we had a particularly good time. We got caught in a terrible thunderstorm on the way down with great lakes in the low parts of the road, but we attacked the pools singing, "We're all going down to Santa Fe to join the big fiesta," and we got through. We danced in the central plaza of Santa Fe, the little park that marks the end of the Santa Fe Trail. The southwestern architecture, food, and people and the native people selling their wares in the veranda of the Governors' Palace made a strong impression on our kids.

The little bandstand in the center of the plaza would hold barely one square, and we would have to crowd the piano into the corner as well. We danced there repeatedly to crowds standing in the park watching our youngsters with great enthusiasm. We also danced in the ancient and elegant La Fonda Hotel. (I took them to dinner there one evening in spite of the price, which floored me.) We were housed in the beautiful southwestern home of Mr. Means, the architect who designed the Fine Arts Center in Colorado Springs. We were also invited to the home of the great poet, Witter Byner. I loved the man every time I met him. But I was warned by the good people of Santa Fe how free he was in his

241

moral viewpoints. But I knew my kids very well, and I knew him slightly, and I knew he would treat them with every consideration and with the charm of a great man. He was charming indeed, and the youngsters were very sorry when they had to go to another engagement. His home was fabulous, and he treated them fabulously.

It was a rare trip, a rare experience. But I wondered if it was necessary to limit it to alumni. They were fine, but some of them had been away from me long enough that I expected in a little while they would look indulgently at me, having sized me up, and go off and do as they pleased. I wasn't completely satisfied that an alumni trip was the best sort of trip after all.

The next spring our daughter Doli wrote me from Scripps College in California, saying that they would like to have me bring a set of my dancers out there. She and another girl would fit into the group, so I would need to bring only two girls and four boys. So we went out on our next spring vacation. One of the boys, Bud Udick, took his car and three other boys. "Teach" Johnson, our pianist, rode out with her husband, and Mrs. Shaw and I took the two extra girls. We had a perfectly delightful time.

Scripps College received us graciously. It is a rare and beautiful college, and we did our very best for them. One day we rode the few miles west to Los Angeles, where we had accepted an invitation to dance for one of the Los Angeles high schools down by the coast. We made a real hit with them, to their complete surprise, and we rushed on trying to crowd enough to fill months into one afternoon. We had a fine time and enjoyed ourselves immensely.

Just above Scripps College was Padua Hills, an exclusive restaurant where people rode out from Los Angeles and from all over California to dine and to enjoy a Mexican Theater where a cast of young Mexican performers put on marvelous plays in the old tradition. There were also shops and lovely buildings, giving the play a charm all its own. The proprietress, who had seen our performance at Scripps College, insisted on our coming up as their guests, having a meal with them, and meeting their young Mexican staff, and perhaps dancing with them. Of course we went.

When we arrived, they took us into the theater where the cast was practicing their play for the coming week. But they broke it off quickly, and Mrs. Garner introduced us and asked us to dance for them. They were very talented, and we were intimidated, but we did our best. And it was not long until they were dancing with us, and we were all having a wonderful time. Then they took us to dinner where they sat down at the tables with us. We connected immediately. After dinner we all joined in dancing again. We all became filled with undiluted joy. It was contagious. But Mrs. Garner had to steal a few of them away to help take care of her crowd of diners, and the rest of us danced a few more dances. Then Mrs. Garner announced as sweetly as she could that they would have to go now and get ready for their parts in the play. They didn't want to perform that night. Some of them actually cried! But there was nothing that they could do since people from all over the state had bought tickets to their play that night, and we ourselves were due soon down at Scripps. We were to teach the California people as many of our dances as they wanted to learn. Then after a short rest in bed, we would have to hit the road back to Colorado.

So we reluctantly left this perfect evening. And we taught our crowd until they were getting tired. I had announced the last dance of the evening, and we had taken our partners and begun dancing with them when the whole cast from Padua Hills came bursting in upon us! They had finished their play. Without taking time to remove their make-up, they had hurried in their gorgeous Mexican costumes, and my youngsters broke into applause.

We finished our dance and said good night to our guests. We told them that our friends from Padua Hills had come and we were going to dance a few dances with them. Any of them who wanted to could remain and watch for a while, but our whole attention would from that moment be given to our friends from Padua Hills.

The crowd stayed a long while. Cheyenners would take Padua Hillers for partners as far as they were able while the remaining Padua Hillers danced together with delight. We changed partners every dance. We would teach them one of our favorites, and they would teach us one of their ancient dances. What a wonderful time we had! One of their ancient dances that became a favorite with every group of Cheyenners that ever danced thereafter was called Matlanchines. A simple step to the beat of a tom-tom had every dancer struggling to hold back tears by the end of the dance. We have seen native groups do it fast, so we could hardly recognize it. But the slow, soul-searching beat of this magic dance carried us on beyond the stars. It is unbelievable to a true dancer!

The music, as I remember it, had a 4/4 rhythm with a strong accent on the first note of each measure. It was an ancient native tune, and as our pianist played, its simple appeal caught something in the back of your throat and sort of choked it. The dancers with their arms folded in front of their chests marched with a certain indescribably majestic mien.

We danced with our friends from Padua Hills until two or three in the morning. Then there was a deeply felt farewell and back to our cottage camp for a couple of hours of sleep before starting on the long road back to Colorado. When I later tried to teach their dance to my youngsters, finally one would catch it, and the others would gradually imitate him or her, and soon all of them had passed across the immeasurable distance to the magic of this simple step. The step was a perfectly flat-footed step forward on the accented step and then a catch step with the other foot, perfectly in a straight line just lifting the heel a little bit and then down to the full step with this same foot and the slight magic lifting of the other heel following it. There are a thousand ways you can try it, as our ancient ancestors did, but at last you may possibly catch just the step that carries you miraculously on the pathway to the gods. That is it! It is a step like a fluttering heart.

Down opposite sides of the hall the men and women march in single file. They meet at the far end of the hall, and without expression, without a gesture, march down the hall side by side. Then they turn into a large double circle with the men on the outside. When they complete this circle and the music changes, the men turn back while the women continue forward; another change of the music and they change their directions; another turn and the men all grasp hands as they continue marching in one direction while the women grasp hands in a large circle as they keep stepping out the magic steps in the other direction. Every eight or sixteen bars there is a subtle change in the music, and each change is met by a simple modification of the dance. The men throw their grasped hands over the women's heads, and at a later change in the music, they stoop and take hands again below the women's joined hands.

Everyone is crying now or fighting to hold back their tears! Don't ask me why! I simply do not know. But this simple step, this magic music, and the very simple and dignified formations of the dance command your tears. The matter has gone beyond all speaking—it is beyond all knowing by our sophisticated modern minds. And when the dancers at last join hands in couples, still almost stiff in their mien, still so dignified because they are really dancing in the presence of the very gods, they march from the hall in a long double line. And if you do not brush your tears away and clear your nose, there is simply something the matter with you. You have missed one of the eternal things for which we are here.

Dr. Alexander, a great professor at Scripps College, who knew much more about life than most men I have ever met, pointed out one of the dancers to me, a brilliant looking girl of such incomparable beauty and dignity that was simply indescribable, with a reddish tinge to her hair and an untouchable way of carrying herself, something quite beyond this world, and he said, "She is almost pure Aztec! She has something that the others can never get!" But so many of them had something that this world has forgotten, but worth far, far more to all of us than the things that are pointed out to us daily as being of greatest worth.

The California trip was a purely delightful experience, but I got to wondering if I couldn't handle a group of undergraduate students as well. So in 1939 when I got an invitation to bring my group to Washington DC to dance in the National Folk Festival, I decided to go. It would be a spring trip, and it seemed easy to me to arrange our spring vacation to use up most of the time we would be on the road. I had had other nibbles and other invitations, and I decided we could make our expenses—we could afford it.

One difficulty was our school bus, which we had used for nearly ten years. It was a dandy bus, but it would be a little small for our trip. It allowed very little space for baggage. We decidedly needed a little more room. So I got in touch with the agent in Salt Lake City, who had sold us our first bus and who specialized in handling buses both new and used.

We picked a good bus, a new one this time. We offered our old bus for sale, and nothing happened. We would have to go into debt to handle the cash difference in prices if we couldn't trade in the old bus. It is always so easy to sell a bus when you talk to an agent in your office, but it is always so hard when you have to go out and look for a buyer. We almost became stuck! At that time one of the mothers who had a daughter in my school phoned me about the bus. She said she would be glad to pay the cash difference if I could sell the old bus, but she didn't want her name mentioned in connection with the gift. But I wonder, now that she has left this life, if I would be doing wrong in mentioning that it was Mrs. F.M.P. Taylor, whose generous gifts had so helped our beautiful city, who made the proposition to me. In any case, I sold the old bus and soon had the new bus delivered to us.

We got it just in time, and I recall Mrs. Taylor driving out by the school and waving to me as we started out on our first trip for undergraduates beyond the state. I couldn't say anything to my pupils and be fair to her. But in my heart I blessed her for her generosity and her faith in us.

THE FIRST UNDERGRADUATE TRIP
(Lloyd)

At last the morning arrived when we were to start on our big trip. The youngsters who were going had so many things to get ready that they were more or less excused from the first class, and there were enough others that wanted to help them that we finally gave up, in trying to check the school too closely. At the hour we had announced for the departure we had, frankly, to turn all of them in the high school loose to see us off. Many of them just crowded the windows on that side of the building and waved us goodbye, but many of them were down in the school yard clustering around the bus and making it a real send off.

We had taken enough trips all over the state to know pretty well what we would need on a trip, and we had learned to pack the bus neatly. The longer cross-country trip required a little more baggage and a little more careful packing, but we never had much trouble with this. We had already learned that we couldn't let each student choose just any sort or size of suitcase. Some of them had gotten the idea of real world travelers, and they thought and planned very carefully to make the very least take care of their needs on a very long trip. Each student could have a small suitcase with toiletries and travel clothing, which would be placed on the overhead racks inside the bus for easy access.

In the same way, we had divided the space on the luggage rack on top of the bus. The costume trunks were foot lockers that

248

fit exactly into the available space. Two girls or three boys were assigned to a costume trunk, and the girls had a pretty hard time of it, packing their skirts with yards and yards of frills. But they became expert packers, and I would sometimes see them with enough skirts to fill three trunks, laying them closely together and packing them in and then forcing the lid down carefully. One of them would stand on the lid and jump and stamp, while the other got the last frill inside and latched it closed. The boys, God bless them, were mostly sloppier packers, but at that, you would be surprised at their neatness.

Then there were the private suitcases, again with maximum dimensions permitted and one suitcase for two people. When all the suitcases and costume cases had been stowed on the top of the bus, the hoops that the girls would wear for hoop skirt numbers would be laid on top, and then it all would be covered with a large, specially sized green tarpaulin, which was carefully strapped into place. There would be the inevitable late arrival whose luggage was quickly added, and then everyone would get in the bus.

The yard would be crowded with cars and school kids and some of the parents who had driven down to see us off. The last parental kisses would be given, and I would finally get everyone on the bus and the door closed. With a great shout of farewells we would be off.

I always had a great choking in my throat for the great crowd that we left behind. Many of them were younger dancers that would soon be old enough and experienced enough to take trips with us, and they were at ease. Many of the parents, inexperienced in sending their child off on a big trip, showing infinite love and infinite worry, had that look in their eyes: can we trust you? Do you understand how precious my child is? The youngsters who had not given enough time to the dancing practice to deserve the trip were jolly and cordial, full of the best wishes in the world! And then there were those few fine youngsters who had danced with such enthusiasm, who knew their dances well enough to make the trip but who, because of some trick of body size or confirmation, had been left out. They broke my heart! And now and then there was the one who knew all the dances well but whose personality would never have fit into the exigencies of a trip, who everyone knew just somehow couldn't go, of whom no one had spoken

to me, but about whom I also knew all too well—and I choked back a tear as I wondered what such a one was thinking.

And hanging out of a window here and there were individual faces that haunted me. I knew that they could be beautiful dancers if only they wanted to, if only they dared to try. But something held them back, something that I could not reach, and just for a moment I thought I caught a flavor, a depth, a distance in their eyes that spoke volumes to me of their confusion and wondering and refusal to try.

We had encouraged the kids and all their parents not to follow the bus when we started. We were soon heading for a great adventure! Everyone was very excited at first, moving around the bus, getting settled in, putting away this thing or that thing that they still held in their hands. They were all fairly buzzing with excitement at the starting of the trip.

It became a habit with me to sit in the front aisle seat where I could watch anyone get in or out, could answer any questions the driver might have, and could more or less control the bus. Soon I got in the habit of sitting up on the arm of this seat facing back down the aisle, and talking to the students whenever I had anything that I wanted them to think about or to know.

We had hardly left Colorado Springs until I had talked over with them their duties to the school, their duties to each other on such a trip, and their duties to keep their eyes open and their minds alert for every new experience that might come into their ken. Eager, fine groups of youngsters seemed to appreciate this very much and would often call out to me when we were riding through a barren bit of land, "Pappy, talk to us!" And I would talk! As we watched the red sun creep down the western Kansas sky, I quite naturally fell to telling them about the early days of Kansas and the pioneers pushing on after that same sun until they found the spot in which to build their homes and plow their fields. We pushed down through Oklahoma and did our first show at the University of Oklahoma. Then it was down to Little Rock where we spent the night. I remember quite a few of them getting up early to see the new birds that they had heard and to glory in the gorgeous dogwood blossoms, something they'd never seen before.

We rolled on through Tennessee, and I remember their great interest in Jackson's Hermitage there. And then into the Shenandoah Valley, beautiful in its fresh leaves and new blossoms of spring. I told them long stories of the Civil War and of desperate men marching back and forth through that frightening land.

Then Washington, D.C.! We checked into the Federal Tourist Court and then went immediately to the Lincoln Memorial. Somehow it is the best of Washington to me as we stood on its wide steps looking up past the long reflecting basins as they took on the first colors of the sunset. And beyond lay the tall shaft of the Washington Monument and farther still the abiding power and beauty of the Capitol Building itself. The youngsters were deeply impressed, and when we stepped inside the memorial and looked up at the great statue of Lincoln, I softly read his immortal words of the Gettysburg Address. I think we all had tears in our eyes, tears of bravery, tears of uplift, tears of aspiration.

Since it was spring break and it was the only tourist court (nowadays called a motel) within the city limits, dozens of schools had brought their senior classes to stay at the Federal Tourist Court. Most of the students had not yet learned to travel and were in the charge of people who had not yet learned to control them. More shocking was that children from some of more remote schools in the south were unfamiliar even with toilet paper. On the floor of the toilets were the corn cobs that they had actually

251

brought with them to use. Some of these kids were drinking much more than they could hold and throwing up in the toilets, those that got that far. Our girls reported much the same conditions in their restroom, so finally we found some fairly large restrooms in the administration building and were happy to walk the greater distance to use them.

Before we left, I went to the manager to lodge a friendly protest. Tired and desperate, he reached for a pile of outgoing correspondence. The first letter to a school board in a nearby state told of the damage done to his camp by the students from that school—beds broken, mattresses and pillows deliberately ripped and their contents spewed about the room, pictures smashed, and plastered walls kicked in. The bill for the damage came to hundreds of dollars, and this was in 1939. "Hundreds of such letters I have to write at this time of year! he said. "And you look fine to me, but don't be surprised if you get such a letter from me after I check up on your kids." I even wondered a bit if my kids were fooling me, but they were not.

At the National Folk Festival, held in Constitution Hall, we were scheduled for an afternoon and evening performance for two or three days. We arrived and dressed and were ready for our first performance in plenty of time. I moved them up back stage at the time we were scheduled to perform so as to have them all ready for their entrance. We waited and waited. At last I went to the corner of the stage to ask Sarah Gertrude Knott, who was in charge of the program, just when we were to appear. Things were very tense. At last I saw Miss Knott and started to speak to her, but she whirled away and said someone else would take care of me. Following her was the "someone else"—a very nice lady who explained that Miss Knott got very high strung at a program, that no one was to speak to her, and that they would get us on the program just as soon as they were able. I indicated that there was a limit to how long we would stay.

But I went back and we waited and waited. At long last they introduced us, and we rushed out onto the stage with our whoops and hollers. We soon had the whole audience with us, and we received an enthusiastic reception. They called us back for an encore, which was against the rules, but it seemed to me we would save them time by answering their call, so we went in for one short number. The audience applauded and applauded, but I directed the youngsters to go down stairs and get dressed. I had half a feeling that Miss Knott wanted us to go on again.

After the show I did find her, and she was a little calmer by then. I asked her what time we should appear for our program that evening. She couldn't tell me for sure. "Give me the approximate time," I asked. "Very good," I said, "we shall be there then, all ready to go on. We shall wait for exactly thirty minutes. If we are not called by that time, we shall leave the auditorium. We have so much to do here in Washington that we can't give more time than that to waiting."

"It might be 50 minutes or an hour," she said.

"That is perfectly all right with me," I explained. "We just want you to know that we won't be available after half an hour has passed."

Well, we always came on within our half hour thereafter, and we had a wonderful time. They gave us more time for our program, and we made a lot of important and valuable friends. It was a gorgeous experience, and we enjoyed every minute of it.

But we had all of Washington to see in these few days: the Capitol Building, the Washington Monument, the Corcoran Gallery, the Smithsonian Institution, and the smaller jewel-like things that you could find such as the printing office where all our money is printed. There were famous restaurants to eat at, great cathedrals to feast our souls at, and cemeteries with important bits of sculpture. We went over the river to Arlington and down the river to Mount Vernon. We could have stayed there for a week, we loved it so, but we had to move on. At last we were packed and ready to go when a delegation came to me to say, "Pappy, we want to go back to the Lincoln Memorial for just a minute. We want to say goodbye to it." And we went. They walked quietly in twos and threes around the portico looking at the places they had hurriedly visited. They wandered within the memorial itself and stood and dreamed as they read the immortal words written there. They looked quietly up at the statue of Lincoln, and all of them had thoughts rising within their hearts that they had no words to express. For a moment they saw into the future of our great America!

Then they said, "Let's go." And we were off through the crowded streets of Washington and on to the Naval Academy at Annapolis for a short stop. Then back to the bus and on to New York.

On the way up "Moppy" Smith came up to me and wistfully asked the person sitting next to me if she might sit there for a few minutes. She said that she had had a silly idea, but it kept growing and growing in her. She said that we had started from home more than a mile above sea level, and coming across the country we had constantly gotten lower in elevation. We were down to within a few feet of sea level now. And it seemed to her that the farther east we came, the more and more crowded the cities became, the greater crowds we met wherever we turned, and the more crowded together the towns became. "It's as though we were all spread out even over our country, she said, "and then the West rose up with its mountains until it stood a mile higher than the rest of the land, and all the people began to slip downhill, until at last we found them all crowded together at the lower edge. It is a great land," she mused, "and now most of the people are crowded together on the eastern edge."

"Is that silly?" she asked.

"No, Moppy," I answered, "it isn't. You had a very interesting analogy, and that is the way I love to have you think!"

We had no engagement in New York City, but we wanted our kids to have a chance to experience the greatness of this big city. We stayed at a guest building at Columbia University. One of our girls was getting quite a cold, and Mrs. Shaw made her comfortable in bed in her room where she decided to stay for the day.

The rest of us took a subway down to the theater district. I took them upstairs from the subway there and let them get their first feeling of New York and its size. But we didn't have them all, I found, when we got up to Broadway. One boy was missing. I had told them so carefully to stay near me at all times and to rush, absolutely push when it was time to get off the subway. If they waited in their seat until the train stopped and then started for the door, they would find the subway racing on. Some of them were quite leisurely, but they had made it. They had all made it but one.

The fascination of New York had gripped them all. Here we were in one of the busiest centers in the world, and they were amazed. So many things to see, so many things to exclaim to each other about. And I stood wondering what to do about Sammy. He was a big lad and he was resourceful, but this was a very big city, and I didn't know how to find him.

As I stood there wondering, I saw him running up the sidewalk. I hailed him, and he rushed to me as if I were the end of his world. It seems that he had broken my rule and had gone up the train exploring. He had found the motorman at the head of the train and stood watching him in his little compartment. We had stopped, he had seen a sign read "Times Square," and realized that this was where we were getting off. He turned and rushed back down the subway and reached the door just a second after the train had started up again.

At the next station he had jumped off in a hurry, rushed up to the street, asked a policeman the way to Times Square, and had run back with all his might. He was completely out of breath, but he had found us. And from that minute on he never let me get out of his sight again. Sammy was always to be found standing closest to me.

We walked over to Fifth Avenue and waited for a double decker bus with the top story open to the sky. At last one came along, and they were all New Yorkers now. Sammy's experience was enough for all of them. The top deck was not crowded and they all found seats. The crowds of people overwhelmed them. The buildings towering to the sky baffled them. Everywhere they glanced there was a new wonder. At last we came to the Empire State Building, and I made them all get off. I bought tickets for the tower and we started up. Such speed made them catch their breath. They were astonished when they reached the top and found they still had to wait for another elevator to go up the tower.

But at last we reached the top, and they marveled again. A perfectly clear day and all of New York and the areas beyond spread out to each horizon. There were ocean-going vessels tied up at the docks and some of them out in the stream heading for Europe. Then the great harbor and the Statue of Liberty and the islands and Coney Island, of which they had heard so much. The two rivers that sweep together at the point of Manhattan at the Battery, and the bridges to cross them. The mass of towers and buildings all about them on the narrow rock of Manhattan. And the huge expanse of Central Park, and beyond that miles and miles of streets and houses and utter immensity.

We let them stay for an hour looking through the telescope, studying the countryside around them, looking out to see or peering down at the tiny figures below. From there we went to Pennsylvania Station. There they rode the escalators, then out the side door and onto an elevated train. On the corner we found an automat, and it was lunchtime. In the hall full of tables, they crowded by twos and threes into the empty places at each table. The noise and the confusion nearly drove some of them crazy, but some of them gloried in it.

Next we took an elevated train to the Battery. Along the way we could see in the windows of tenement houses where the inhabitants were oblivious to the trains that passed all day long. We got off at Battery Park and headed for the ferries. Once on board the ferry, I told the young people to scatter and make themselves at home, to wander over the three decks at will. The kids scattered. On the return trip, two kids were missing. They had stopped to watch the jam of traffic in front of the ferry building and rushed onto the ferry just as the gates were being closed by the laughing attendants. I preached them a little sermon: If you travel with a party, you have to stay with the party. If you go off on little excursions of your own, we'll leave you to work your way all the way back to Colorado!

As we rode back on the ferry, the first lights of evening were coming on in the skyscrapers. The youngsters were enchanted. The sky was beginning to show the colors of sunset, and the magic was upon us. At last we called it an evening and returned to our quarters at Columbia University where we went up to check on Bookie and found that she was much worse. Her temperature was rising and she had a case of pneumonia. We took her immediately to a nearby hospital. Soon we were told that she had a very high fever and they doubted that they could save her life. But they said there was a new sulpha drug on the market that people were not yet familiar with but that they were willing to try it if they had a parent's permission. They wanted her mother to come to New York. So we phoned her parents, got their permission, and were told that Mrs. Smith would leave for New York on the very next plane. The effects of the drug were positively marvelous, and the fever began to go down. Mrs. Smith arrived, and Dorothy stayed in New York while the rest of the team and I made our way to Bennington, Vermont, Dorothy following by train the next day.

In Bennington we were welcomed cordially; indeed we were feted and made to feel very important. What a gorgeous time we had! After our program concluded before an eager crowd, we invited them to dance with us. And out onto the floor came these dancers, some of the best dancers in the country from the Bennington School of the Dance and the young men they had chosen for their partners, good dancers all. They knew very little about square dancing, but they learned quickly, and their love of this new "old form" was touching and inspiring. I remember distinctly that the girls wore shoes at this dance. I had been there alone some years before, and the dancing girls all came out to dance in their bare feet, as that was the way they did their dancing in the Bennington School under Martha Hill. But a few minutes of our dancing with the boys whose feet were clad in boots caused them to put on shoes.

Another memory that still stands out in my mind is how these expert dancers who were used to covering the whole floor in the dancing had to learn to stay in sets, dance in sets in a fixed position on the floor, each person working in a ten foot square. At first when I would call "promenade home," they would end up almost anywhere. But soon they got the idea, and all went to their home spot on the floor. They loved it once they had gotten the idea.

Another memory is the orchestra that they furnished us. Our "Teach" played the piano and provided the rhythm and the tune that we wanted, but on the faculty of the school of dance they had all sorts of professional musicians. One at a time they would get their instruments out and play with us until at last we had a great laughing, eager orchestra. They were terrific!

I recall that a few years before I had visited Bennington alone and had conducted a square dance at the end of my talk and had such an orchestra as this develop. At this time I wanted to drive over the mountain and meet Ralph Page, the authority on New England contra dance and the old quadrilles. Ralph was calling a dance, and some of the faculty volunteered to drive me over the mountain to attend his dance. Ralph has been a very good friend of mine ever since. I recall that he told me that the building where they danced had a spring floor. Wagon springs had been so arranged under the main girders that the whole floor was a little bit alive to every step. It was a wonderful floor, and according to Ralph, it had had a dance held on it every Saturday night since before the Revolution.

I recall that we had a young man with us who had played a clarinet beautifully at the dance the night before. He had brought his clarinet along and asked me to see if I could arrange for him to sit in with the orchestra. I spoke to Ralph, but he was doubtful. I spoke to the members of the orchestra, and they explained that they never let anyone sit in with them. But I insisted that he was very good and I promised that he wouldn't bother them. He had joined me by then and promised that he would play softly until he got the feel of the music. They explained that unless he had been brought up to that kind of music, he was bound to fail. And he told them that he had been brought up to it, more or less, as a small boy out in Utah where he used to be allowed to sit in with dance orchestras playing this sort of music. Reluctantly they decided to let him try it, and then I saw them get together in a hurried conference a pick a tune in an unusual key that they were sure would throw him.

They started and he didn't fall. He went on with them, looping and turning, and adding the most delightful harmonies to their music. In just a little while I would see one of them stop aghast and stare at him as he swooped on, playing unwritten music that would thrill an angel. It was beautiful! At the end of the piece they simply surrounded him, engulfing him with their praise and their wonder. They invited him to join them permanently. One of them even wanted to take lessons from him. He just smiled and played on with them and the angels for the rest of the evening.

As we were driving home, I found out that only the week before he had run down to New York to play in a small orchestra of a few players from the New York Philharmonic, in a composition he had just finished writing for a Sunday afternoon meeting of music lovers. This was my first direct experience with a real musician. And I have no doubt it affected me. I have always found since then that the best old time music is always played by the best musician, who has a real feeling for the folk, instead of a so-called "champion" who plays his fiddle in two or three easy keys and has the feeling, but not the experience, to touch the greatest heights.

But back to our Bennington engagement. Mrs. Shaw had returned late from New York where she had at last found Bookie well enough to leave in the care of her mother. She entered the hall where we were giving our program just before the intermission, and was immediately called to the dressing room to see Mary Ellen, one of my best dancers, who had complained a little of a growing pain in her ear. I tried to get her to drop out of the program that evening, but she wouldn't hear of it. She was going to dance. Late in the evening when we were dancing at the after-party, something evidently broke in her ear. She was very frightened, so I sent her back to her room with a couple of the girls to take care of her, and I had Miss Hill send a good doctor to come to check up on her. This young doctor reported to me that she had an infected ear, but that it had broken, and the infection was running out, which was desired. There was nothing to do for her now but take care of her until she was well enough to dance again.

"But," cried Mary Ellen, "we have only one substitute girl, and Bookie is sick in a hospital in New York, so I have to dance!"

"No, you don't, Mary Ellen. Just forget about it all!" exclaimed Mrs. Shaw

But Mary Ellen insisted, and the young doctor said, "I don't think it will hurt you since you are so determined to go on. So take her back to the performance and let her dance only when she is absolutely needed. Then take her back to her room and put heat on the ear and take care of her for a few days."

So Mrs. Shaw brought her back and let her dance the few remaining numbers in which eight couples were absolutely necessary. Then they took her back to her room, bought a hot water bottle for her, and put her to bed, while the rest of us danced on for quite a while with our new dancing enthusiasts at the after-party.

The next morning we rigged up a little stretcher that we carried in the bus, suspending it down the aisle between the seats, and carried her along with us, which she insisted on our doing. We didn't have another engagement for a couple of nights, and she asserted that she would be completely well and that we could not prevent her from dancing again. In fact, she had barely lain in the aisle on her stretcher for a full day before she wanted to get up and ride with the rest of us.

See the appendix for a list of the locations where the Cheyenne Mountain Dancers performed from 1937 to 1948.

On several subsequent trips to New York City, the Shaws and the Cheyenne Mountain Dancers were the guests of Lowell Thomas, a friend of Lloyd's from the mining town of Victor, CO. Thomas, a well-known journalist and writer, followed T. E. Lawrence in Palestine during WW I and is credited with giving him the title, "Lawrence of Arabia."

Thomas later wrote, "Lloyd Shaw and his Colorado square dance group made quite a sensation when they invaded New York. I arranged for them to appear at the Ballroom of the Plaza Hotel, the Rainbow Room atop the tall RCA Building, and at the Radio City Music Hall. Wherever they performed they were a smash hit, like a pleasant breeze right out of the Rockies. Only a genius like Lloyd Shaw could have accomplished this with a group of amateurs.

The Lloyd Shaws were with us on Quaker Hill for a summer and they had everybody in our part of New York State doing their square dances. He was a man of imagination and magnetic personality who inspired everyone with whom he came in contact."

THE FIRST TRIP TO SAN FRANCISCO 1939 (Lloyd)

Word that we might be available for a show began to spread very soon. Square dancing had not really started in the United States in this period. It had been more than a generation since it occupied a major interest in our country. But it was beginning to show a healthy flurry of renewed curiosity, and groups all over the country were beginning to be active in again reviving it. And they wanted us to come and light the spark. I began answering an ever-increasing stack of letters. I soon had to decide definitely whether we would travel any more or not. To make it at all possible and practicable for us, we figured that we would have to charge about $200 for a show, or if several shows came rather close together, we might be able to reduce the price for some of them. In the case of a really worthy group, we might be able to get by for $150. Of course we must remember that prices have changed vastly since the time when we took those trips.

Our bus had already been paid for. We had to pay only for gasoline and oil and any repair to keep the bus in good running order. Then we would have to pay the expenses of putting the kids up at a good cottage camp or hotel, and the expense of feeding them. Then too, I wanted enough to be left over to be able to pay their admissions to certain events, museums, or shows that I thought we should all take in. The adults in the party were of course treated just as though they were pupils so far as the expenses were concerned. We paid none of them any sort of special salary as they were all members of the school staff and were having a joyous vacation. That was all. Anything else was a personal expense.

I definitely planned that we should take a spring trip again, but when invitations began showing up for a fall trip as well, I began to be tempted. At last there came an invitation from the University of California at Berkeley in 1939 to come out and put on an exhibition for them, and then for several days to teach a class in square dancing, with my youngsters taking their class members for partners as far as possible.

When we started on this trip, as we left the school in our bus, I noticed a couple of carloads of our kids cavorting around us and waving their frantic goodbyes. They followed us a good many miles, lagging behind every now and then and suddenly speeding up with a great shout and passing us again, everyone screaming wildly. I didn't like it! Out of such little incidents are the biggest accidents born when the drivers of cars begin showing off. But I managed to hold my tongue, and after a while they turned back. I waited, of course, until we returned to the school, to talk to these drivers and to talk very briefly to the school auditorium and explain why I would have to make a rule against any such behavior on future trips. I am happy to say that this was the last time that anyone from the school tried to follow us when we departed.

We headed north to Denver, then to Laramie, Medicine Bow, Rawlings, and over the range to Salt Lake City. Here we circled the capitol building for them and let them wander briefly on the busy streets of this city, more or less dominated by the Mormon Church, with little bee-hive signs on most of the windows and the initials of the efficient Mormon organizations displayed everywhere. We went into the Tabernacle grounds where I let them look at this incredible building with its uncanny acoustics, a whisper from the stage being heard in the farthest seats. We looked at the Sea Gull Monument, where a startled man with a group of women stands gazing into the sky. I told of the westward immigration of the Mormons with their push carts and wagons, looking for a possible settlement. After they had their first crops planted, a horde of katydids descended on the fields ready to consume every plant. The Mormons believe that their prayers brought a vast flock of sea gulls, which fell upon the fields and saved the crops. Since this event the insects have been called Mormon crickets, and they still plague this region of the country from time to time.

But we soon had to push on, out beyond the Great Salt Lake, over the desolate Salt Flats, over the barren mountains of western Utah, and at last to the gambling town of Elko, Nevada. I let them prowl in a gambling hall adjoining a restaurant with its scores of slot machines and gambling table after gambling table. All the change we received in this town was in coins—dimes, quarters, half dollars, and silver dollars—the better to equip us to play the machines.

As soon as we left Elko, the youngsters had a fine time regaling each other with their experiences in the gambling hall. They had had a wonderful time, and their eyes were as big as saucers! They compared notes, they laughed, and then they quieted down to the scenery of eastern Nevada. In Salt Lake I had picked up a leaflet comparing the vital statistics of Nevada and Utah. Impressed on reading it, I quietly took my place on the arm of my seat, my preaching throne, and talked to them about it. The two chief cities were Reno and Las Vegas, great lush gambling centers just over the mountains from the two largest cities in California, San Francisco and Los Angeles. Gambling was the main industry of the state, but their divorce laws were so lenient that the two cities had hundreds of people waiting out the short term of residency to be eligible for a divorce decree. Even easier were the rules for getting married, where all that was needed was a willing partner and a wedding chapel. Very convenient. But other statistics of the state were not so heartening: the highest per capita rate of automobile accidents and deaths, and also murders and suicides. Utah, in contrast, had very low rates of murder and traffic fatalities and the lowest suicide rate in the country. There are some details concerning any religion about which it seems to me that an intelligent person might raise questions, but the great question is how the religion works.

We rolled on through Nevada. One needs a sort of cosmic, godlike viewpoint to appreciate its great barrenness, and to see the ultimate beauty of it all. A gorgeous sunset, for instance, will do wonders for you, but to simply ride through the barren miles and feel their tremendous beauty is a matter of growing up.

Then we came to Reno where gambling halls appeared to be the chief business. All of them seemed more or less alike, except for the garishness of their advertising. We took it all in and soon had had enough. A wholesome bunch of youngsters soon tires of it, and we were on our way.

As we approached the pass, we came to the place where Donner and his ill-fated party spent their desperate winter. Caught in the heavy snows, with all their food exhausted, this pioneer party made their camp. There was no Reno then in that completely unsettled waste to which they could return to get supplies. They tried to hunt, but the woods were exceptionally clear of game at that time. At last, marooned in the deep snow, getting shorter and shorter of food, they camped there until at last most of them died and some of the survivors had to eat the bodies of their former friends to keep alive. It is a tragic, desperate, and repulsive tale, but it is part of the history of the West. Some of the kids' eyes were staring fixedly out of the window, and I knew they were reliving that desperate winter and wondering just what they would have done.

But we soon ran up the pass and down the other side in these late fall days. On this mountain highway we passed ski areas with their magnificent hotels and their inviting runs. The kids could hardly believe the temperate conditions. Here were luxurious flowers blooming all around and, to them, a wealth of almost tropical vegetation on every hand. They were completely captivated. Autumn had regularly come and passed for them back home, and here miraculously were flowers in abundance and fruit and growing things. We spent the night in Auburn, and I think that many of the kids thought they would be willing to spend the rest of their lives right there. But we still had things to see!

The next morning we rolled down through the groves of orange trees, still in that glorious stage of ripe oranges and green oranges on the same tree, with a few white blossoms giving promise of more fruit in the future. Then there were orchards of all kinds, each of them heavy with their ripened fruit. There were also vineyards, with full bunches of grapes, and pickers busy harvesting them, and big trucks, many of them with even larger trailers, were simply loaded with grapes, some of them hanging carelessly over the sides, as they rolled on to the nearby wineries.

It was an entirely different world the kids were seeing, and they were fascinated. "Look, look," they cried, pointing out a newly-made discovery. And bordering the road for a while or a distant lane were the fascinating lines of wind-blown eucalyptus trees with their long shaggy bark, their lovely long leaves, and the little touches of blue on their terminal foliage. We were in an utterly new world! We rolled past Sacramento and then again out over the lush and growing countryside. Then we would catch glimpses of San Francisco Bay. Finally we pulled into Richmond. We were getting close to Berkeley.

So we chose a cottage camp that appealed to us and found that, being off-season, we could get good rates, so we settled in there as our headquarters. We had a view of the bay and also a railroad track behind the cottages, but such a noise as a train can make wouldn't disturb a group of healthy young people who, when they were tired, were definitely tired, and who when they slept, slept. In fact, we liked this "quiet" camp so much that for several years I brought groups of students back there when we visited Berkeley. It was our San Francisco home.

What a general fuss of arrangements and scurrying around there was whenever we made a two-or three-night stay at a camp. It started in all confusion and ended with everyone miraculously and happily settled in place. While they were getting moved in, I phoned Lucille Czarnowski of the University School of the Dance, and soon she and a couple of her teachers were there to welcome us. They explained all the details of our program to us and answered all our questions. Our first show would be the next evening, and from then on we would teach special classes for a couple of hours, in the afternoon or evening. The rest of the time was ours. They told us how to reach the places where we would dance, and everything was soon set. They made us feel very welcome! We had driven hard all day, and, after a little local exploration, we hit our beds and took the much-needed rest that was coming to us.

The next morning quite early we started out. Since this was the first trip west for most of them, I decided that we should cross the bay by the old standard ferry that was still running in spite of the recent completion of the bridge. So we rolled down to the harbor and were soon on the deck of the ferry. We turned the kids loose on the big boat to wander upstairs and downstairs, with instructions to be back in our bus before we reached the other side. Some of them were fascinated by the loading of the cars. A huge barge of railroad cars had just started across ahead of us. Many freighters from different countries rode at anchor in the bay. And in the distance, in a half haze, the looming city of San Francisco, rising from the misty bay.

But in another moment we were off! A bell sounded, and we pushed out from the slip and started to work our sure way across the bay. We moved close by huge anchored freighters, from which a hand or two was raised in greeting as we passed. Tugs still criss-crossed ahead of us while up on the new bridge tiny cars darted continuously through its great super structure on their way to many offices and jobs in San Francisco. At last under the great bridge we were heading for Market Street and our landing.

Barney, our bus driver, was rather nervous, but we helped him pick the right lane and found ourselves rushing with all the other vehicles. Here, coming down the long hills of San Francisco, a cable car would be turning around on a turn-table, the conductor and motor man pushing it by hand and a few good-natured passengers giving them some help. Having studied my road map carefully, I soon turned Barney sharply to the right past one of the turning cable cars. We ran up a few blocks of a rather steep hill, and then suddenly ahead of us our street was rearing back on its heels! "There? Straight ahead?" asked Barney, looking up the incredible street. "Straight up!" I answered. "Put her in low, Barney, and let's roll. Everybody else is driving it!" And we went straight up with the kids yelling, "Hold her, Barney! We'll make it yet!" And we were on top. But for just half a block! And then it pitched down just as steeply on the other side. And shifting our gears, we rode straight down the cable car tracks along with all the rest of the San Franciscans.

We rolled down through the older part of San Francisco and on to look at the Golden Gate Bridge. We looked at it incredulously, with the tide rushing out below it and a great tide of cars rushing over it, and I promised them we would ride over it in the next couple of days. We doubled back toward the entrance of the bay and eventually came to the famous Cliff House. There I let the kids get out and gaze at the glory of the Pacific Ocean stretching on beyond them towards China. Some of the kids just stood and watched the breaking of the waves and the seals, indifferent to all of that chaos of wild water about them. And some of the kids, whose middle name is Action, made their way down the steps and onto the beach. They scampered back and forth, shouting gleefully with the breaking and sinuous curling of the waves up the pure and indifferent sand. It was a great moment for all of them!

We rolled back through Golden Gate Park, first stopping to look at the "quite smallish" boat in which Amundsen made his famous discoveries near the pole. We didn't have time to visit the museums and galleries in the park, but we pointed them out to the youngsters and promised to come back when we had enough time. We found our way back to the bridge over the bay and were soon heading home.

We got back just in time to rest a bit, stretch out, and have our supper before the evening show. They were all professional enough by now that they used the time to advantage, ducking into their cottages, and many of them hitting their beds for a short rest before the evening show. We went to a nearby restaurant for a bite of supper. Then we loaded up again and were soon on our way to our first performance.

Our programs varied, but in general we followed more or less a rather strict idea. From over ten years of experience dancing all over the state of Colorado, we had learned to start our programs in early American costumes. In this first appearance we always made a great hit, for the youngsters were so beautifully dressed. The boys in old-fashioned coats with various lengths of old-fashioned tails, white collars standing erect with little old-fashioned flaps on the corners and with bow ties with rather long strings. Their shirt fronts were stiff and white, and there was no need in telling the audience that we bought these shirt fronts by the box and that they were only pressed white cardboard. They saved us the expense of washing. Even the brilliant vests weren't too perfect when examined closely. Some of the boys wore regular black dress-suit vests, but many of them had their mothers cover their vests with brightly-colored cloth so they were very conspicuous and dashing. Some of them wore white vests, and some of the colored vests reached quite a way up the shirt front, leaving only a small space of white shirt front showing. There was great variety and color and delight in their costuming, some of the boys even replacing the old-fashioned black covered buttons with bright brass buttons, which gave an air of great distinction.

Great distinction, yes! And there was no need at all of telling our audiences of how we had traveled up to Denver and visited all their second-hand shops and bought these coats and vests for one to five dollars each. They were just as "swell" as the fifty to one hundred dollars their owners had originally paid for them. They looked even more expensive when we got through adding the colorful vests and the brass buttons.

And the girls were truly as pretty as pictures. They had one-piece dresses with little puffed sleeves. But their chief glory lay in the skirts, which were built in flounce upon flounce, each larger than the one above it. The skirts spread out wide, and the bottom circumference would often be more than 20 feet, and they were held out from the body by a series of hoops, each much larger than the one above it. In an underskirt we arranged a series of three or four hoops and sewed them to special strips of material that held them out just so and made them easy to pack. Under these hoops were flounces and flounces of white underskirts, each profusely ruffled. Each girl had her mother make her dress so it would be easily distinguished from the others, with little bows, clusters of ribbons, and various colors. They were beautiful indeed.

And with it all I can still see the prideful cleanliness of each dancer. Their hair beautifully combed, just a touch of makeup to make their cheeks glow, their lips shine, and their eyes stand out more beautifully. I still recall how each girl carried a toothbrush in her bag and just before a performance would line up at an inadequate wash basin and brush her teeth. They were exquisite! They were just as clean and sweet as they looked! And each of them had her heart singing with the beauty and the harmony of what they were doing.

We usually entered with a fast waltz in Viennese tempo, with everyone doing a different routine of the many varieties of this fascinating and fast spinning waltz. Then we would form into two sets and do the Lancers Quadrille in five parts, the most formal of the quadrilles with each part showing a different aspect of stately dignity. This would usually fascinate our audience with its "presence" and its deep bows. Then we would usually do some of the old round dances such as the Redowa and the Mazurka. And for a break in our program, we would usually do a comedy variation of Life on the Ocean Wave. This old quadrille done in a very slow tempo of long ago and with exaggerated politeness, would usually leave our audience howling. Then we would follow it with grandmother's old and lovely polka, the heel and toe polka. Or perhaps we would move into a series of variations of the lovely Varsouvianna. Then we usually ended this section of the program by presenting the Singing Quadrille, in all five parts, shortening it by leaving out the repetitions. We presented it as being sort of intermediate between the old-time formal quadrille and the more recent "cowdrill" of the west. We always pleased everyone immensely with the precise exactness of the Singing Quadrille's different movements.

Given the limited number of seats on our bus and given the wonderful way that "Teach" Johnson played the piano, we had earlier decided to use only the piano (no fiddle or guitar) and use the two spaces gained on the bus to carry a ninth couple. Thus our show could go on with two full sets in spite of the sickness or indisposition of one individual. And we soon learned to let this ninth couple slip out while the rest were doing the Singing Quadrille and change their costumes. Then they would appear for a special interlude, leaving no break in the program. They would usually show the roots of things, presenting the first appearance of the waltz, a dance that has changed a great deal from the days when it was first introduced. Then they would lead into the Gallopade and work on to the first polka. Then they would finish off with a fast demonstration of the more complicated steps of the Viennese Waltz.

Next we would present the second section of our program, which we called "The Old Barn Dance." Each of the boys appeared in brightly colored overalls and the girls in sparkling clean pinafores. In this section their costuming was delicious. The boys wore striped clean bib overalls, as though they had just been invited to a party, and each of them had on a pink and white checked shirt, with the checks quite large and conspicuous. And each of them wore a perfectly engaging smile that had to be genuine, and it truly was. And the girls had the same pink and white checked material, made into knee-length dresses. They were sort of little girls' dresses, and over them they wore neatly pressed and highly flounced little white pinafores, standing out like something just lifted from a carefully wrapped box. And each wore full-length white stockings and little black Mary Jane shoes.

They would enter first doing the four-horse schottische or some equally jolly little dance. Then, if we had not given it in the previous part of the program, they would do the different varieties of the old Varsouvianna. Next we would give some examples of early American play-party "games." These weren't considered dances in churches where dancing was frowned upon, and the early inhabitants could get away with them at church parties. We did such things as Captain Jinks of the Horse Marines, Jolly Is the Miller, or perhaps Shoo Fly Don't Bother Me.

Shoo Fly, for instance, is a very simple dance, and our crowd of young dancers entered into it with a true theatrical spirit. Real actors on the stage often forget themselves in the spirit of the part they have to portray. True professionals, for the moment at least, become truly whatever they are acting. And so with my youngsters. They became hypnotized with the joy of the dance.

Shoo Fly would interest no one if handled in a superior, bored manner. But when they sang, they really sang, "Shoo, fly, don't bother me!" And they all surged into the center of the stage, holding hands, and then, "Shoo, fly, don't bother me!" and they all surged out again. "Shoo, fly, don't bother me, I belong to somebody!" and they all began to whirl in a contagious abandon of joy. And as they went on whirling and singing and joining with each other, they almost shouted, positively hypnotized with the simple beauty of the thing, "I do, I do, but I ain't goin' to tell you who. I belong to somebody, yes indeed, I do!"

It's the joy, the complete surrender to the charm of the old piece that is important! The dance is nothing, but the joy is as contagious as anything in this world. And with this joy, genuine joy, the dancers simply overflowed.

Then we would present a couple of old-time contra dances, still favorites in the New England states, such as Hull's Victory or Pop Goes the Weasel. Then we would do a few more old-time couple dances such as the Narcissus and the Trilby. Then we would do a very brief section of the famous old circle dances or progressive dances with couples gradually passing through couples in a large circle around the stage, such as Soldier's Joy, Sicilian Circle, or the old Spanish Circle. Then perhaps we would end with that old form of the square dance, the Kentucky Running Set, with the dancers in a big ring around the stage and half of the dancers advancing to the next couple after each repetition of the figure.

Each section would be given as quickly as possible, with very little repetition. However, by now the audience deserved a rest, and so we gave them an intermission. I do not mean to imply that this intermission was not just as welcome to my young dancers. They had spent themselves almost to the limit, and they deserved a rest.

But while my dancers and our audience are taking this deserved bit of rest, there is no reason why I should not tell you of the problem that we faced in making up our program. We had so many dances that we simply had to give in order to give a true picture of American dancing, and it made our programs much more interesting if we could change our costumes quite often. But

274

on the other hand, we traveled in a space-limited bus, and extra costuming was definitely limited. We simply didn't have room for all the costumes we would have liked to wear.

For example, we loved the overalls and pinafores of our Barn Dance section, but where were we to carry this set of extra costumes? The youngsters would pack their costumes in the large costume cases after each show, and as they piled them up in the open trunks, you couldn't help but wonder how they would ever be able to close the lids. But they learned to pack them very carefully, and then they would stand on the half-closed trunk lids and jump up and down to get the lids closed. But at last, after a couple of seasons of the back-breaking packing, we decided to leave the overalls and pinafores at home as being simply too much to carry with us. Yet I think we were still using these costumes when we danced at UC Berkeley.

Many of the dances of this Barn Dance section could be adapted to our story of the development of the Cowboy Dances and would be introduced in an early first section of Cowboy Dances. So it wasn't so much the choice of a dance as to what costume we should be able to wear. We finally had to divide the Cowboy section of our program into two parts, the first rather explanatory in nature, but with a lot of fun dances mixed in, and then we would do an interlude of Round Dances while our troupe caught their breath, and then we would come back for the final knock-out presentation of the best and most complicated of the Cowboy Dances.

But forgetting all about our costumes for the present, we knew our audience was now a little rested, and we called them back to their seats. My youngsters, who could always "come back" in a few short minutes of rest, were all costumed and ready for the second half of the program by now.

They came back in their Mexican costumes. When we decided to drop the Barn Dance costuming, we usually put this Mexican section in as the second part of the first half of our program and put in the two sections of Cowboy Dancing as the second half of our program. But these Mexican dances were too precious for us to drop. We had found them a few years before when we had danced with the famous Mexican Dancers at Padua Hills in California. In fact, they gave us a typical man's costume and woman's costume for us to use as our models. They were nearly worn out and would never be used again, but they served our purpose fine. The boys' "pantalones" were made of unbleached muslin and had the typical flap up the front and the tie-arounds for the waist that tucked in under this flap, with long tying cords. The shirt had full-length muslin sleeves, but the collar was a little straight thing with a little embroidery, and across the shoulders from side to side was a placket, often decorated with embroidery, below which the shirt was gathered in ample fullness. Then when each of our boys would get his costume on, I recall how they would tuck a long red sash into their belt, and, standing quite a distance away from the person holding the end of their sash, would turn and turn toward the person holding the end, until they had wrapped its long length up around them in a broad band, and they would then tuck in the end of the sash.

When they first entered, they would all wear Mexican sombreros of straw, brightly and variously colored. Beneath each sombrero was a long string looping under the chin. As they danced harder and harder, the sombrero would at last fall down their back and hang by this string. But by the end of the section, most of them had thrown their hats completely to the side.

The girls wore peasant dresses of the brightest colors. Their skirts were call "enaguas de percal," which, we were repeatedly told, means simply a "percale skirt," but it represented something special to our friends in Padua Hills. These were very brightly and variously colored. While the blouses that they wore were simply little short-sleeved full-bodied blouses, mostly only white, a few of them had simple patterns of embroidery on them.

The girls wore the simple Mary Jane slippers of the previous section, while the boys wore true Mexican "huaraches" for the most part. These were very simple little moccasin-like things which had a loose heel, so loose in fact that the huaraches make a peculiar little slapping sound along the floor as the boys dance in them. A few of the boys preferred going barefoot, which was also appropriate. These costumes added a note of authenticity to the Mexican part of the program, and they were very easy to pack, except for the sombreros, which we stacked one within another and tied in a little bundle on top of our trunks.

We would enter in this section with an old round dance such as La Camilla, a tricky little poquito schottische. Then we would do Jesusita, a circle dance that used to be done on the ranchos of early California in their Mexican days. Then we would do our favorite dance, Matlanchines, an ancient religious ceremonial dance of old Mexico. It was performed to the beat of a tom-tom. If anyone laughed while they were doing it, my youngsters were simply heart broken, for in it they danced their way up the path to the stars in this ancient ceremonial dance. Then perhaps we would do the Mexican form of the Varsouvianna, quite different, and showing many national modifications of this universal dance, or we would do La Raspa, a favorite dance of the gringo. We would usually end this part of our program by doing a Mexican quadrille in five parts, showing a distinctly different type of dance and one of unquestioned beauty.

Usually we would let the Mexican dancers clear the stage, and then a couple of our young dancers would enter and do a little group of old-time ballroom dances. They would do the Glow Word Gavotte, for example, and the Bolero. And becoming more modern, they would do such dances as the Skater's Waltz and the Merry Widow Waltz. They would do just a brief and charming section of these, or similar, dances. By this time the main troupe would have changed into their cowboy costumes and would appear with a whoop and a whirl while our couple of interlude dancers would hurry out and change into their cowboy costumes.

For these cowboy dances the boys blossomed out in colored shirts, some of them quite bright, but none of them overdone to the point of the modern drug store cowboy. They always wore special slender tight trousers, and they always wore cowboy boots. Some boys tucked their pants into the tops of these boots, and some of them did not, and some would have one pant leg tucked into the boot and the other flapping free, for they worked hard at their dancing, and tucked-in pants have a way of slipping. Some folks tried to tell us that with careful cowboys, the way your pants were tucked in indicated the number of cows that they owned, but we came to the conclusion that it showed only how well their pants and boots fit. The boys all wanted to wear cowboy hats at first, but I made a rule against this. Cowboys are gentlemen, perhaps rather meticulously gentlemanly, when they are indoors with real ladies, and never wear their hats indoors any more than any other gentleman does. Only a showoff wears a hat indoors when ladies are present, especially when he dances. (And some callers think that they have special permission to be "no gentleman" and wear their hats indoors and strut their obstreperous stuff.)

Our girls went in for the simple pioneer dresses of the eighties period. There were two lessons they had learned well by now. One of them was to have plenty of fullness under their sleeves, where an ordinary sleeve will often rip out with the strenuous action of the dance, and the other was to have their dresses be in one piece. We had had too many beautiful skirts come off in our early programs that we didn't need to stress this anymore. It can be embarrassing to lose your skirt in the middle of a fast dance. Variously colored, some quite striking, but none of them overdone, these dresses did not require many petticoats, for the dances were too strenuous to make wearing them very practical. While the old fashioned high heeled shoes of the period might have been more authentic, they had learned to wear their Mary Jane slippers as the neatest thing on their feet, which would at times have to move like blazes.

And I might mention that the girls had learned by now the absolute necessity of having adequate pantalettes on underneath. Otherwise certain eager-eyed young boys would place themselves right under the edge of the stage to ogle at the rising of the skirts in some of the fast dances. Knee-length pantalettes were long enough for the average costume, and they had several rows of lace running around them. In the Victorian costumes worn in the first part of the program, the girls needed longer pantalettes that reached down to the ankles, so they all fixed little extensions to their square dance pantalettes. It would take only a moment to slip them on, and they would give a coy effect to the full-skirted costumes of the Victorian period. Once in a while a girl would forget to take the extensions off, and she would show up in the next section of the program to the delight of everyone while the embarrassed girl would rush for the wings to strip them off.

We would enter for this last part of our program with a rush and a holler and bit of wild confusion. But we would soon find our places in a cowboy square dance and whirl to it with a will. Or sometimes we would enter with such a dance as the Mexican Mixer and then whirl into a cowboy square. Sometimes we would precede this or follow it with a bit of explanation and show them the structure and the idea of the square dance. Then we would whoop it up in our cowboy dance or "cowdrille." We would follow this with some old round dance to let the kids catch their breath again. And then perhaps we would do the Cowboy Weasel, which had become a western deterioration of a New England contra dance. Then perhaps we would demonstrate the graceful symmetry of the Texas Square and then put in a few rounds such as the Veleta Waltz. Then, having caught our breath, we'd finish with an exhibition of an all-out cowboy square, rushing off the platform at the finish of this last dance. We'd then call it an evening!

At first, while the youngsters were changing their clothes, I would drift out into the auditorium to receive the enthusiastic plaudits of the crowd. But one soon tires of this, and as we became more experienced, I would usually remain back stage and meet only those people who felt that they had to come back and say a word. I must admit that many of the most interesting people in the country would come back to meet me there. I enjoyed them immensely. We loved to dance, and the reactions of our audiences were usually very responsive. We made a lot of friends and we had a truly wonderful time.

On each of the following afternoons we would appear at the women's gymnasium. It was a beautiful building, a very gracious place, and we enjoyed our sessions very much. We would dance there for an hour and a half every afternoon with a crowd, mainly of adults who would come from all over the region. They were teachers and those especially interested in the dances. Usually I would set up a group of our youngsters to demonstrate a dance, one of the simpler ones at first, explaining each detail of its steps and formation. They would dance it a couple of times as an example to be followed. Then each of my dancers would take a partner from the group of people who had joined in the class, and the remaining people would take partners, and we would try to dance it. It would work rather well. Then we could take another dance, and I would take another group of my students on the floor to demonstrate and we would repeat the process. And so it went, gradually increasing the difficulty of the dances and the complexity of the movements until toward the end of the period they were all dancing pretty well. It was great fun!

My young people enjoyed it thoroughly! They were in much demand as partners and were treated like visiting royalty. And, being human, this was entirely agreeable to them! The class period would be over before we had fairly gotten into the swing of it, and Miss Czarnowski would have to insist upon our closing, for we were now part of a college curriculum, and other classes would follow us in that room.

Sometimes we would come back in the evening and put on a special teaching session for those who could not come in the afternoon. We had only four days of teaching, so we had to push our program hard to introduce people to enough dancing that they would be able to carry on by themselves after we were gone. We enjoyed every minute of it.

Out of this class and hundreds of others like it all over the country, I sometimes feel that the revival of the square dance movement came about in our particular era. Men and women would dance enthusiastically with us for a day or for several days. They would get the idea, which was the important thing, and then they would go home to their various communities, their distant towns, and start a group of their own. Having started, they could get out the old books and study them for additional material, and soon square dancing would be going again as a real activity for the joy of the people in some small spot. The spots grew in size and importance, until now it is spreading almost too fast.

[The program as described here is the one that was presented on the team's travels throughout the 1940s. It was only in the first few years of national performances that the program included European folk dances. Lloyd had an epiphany during the presentations at UC Berkeley. When his dancers performed some international folk dances, the response of the audience was not as enthusiastic as it was for the American program. He reasoned that the bay area was a major international port and that people there already knew about international folk dancing. From this time on he resolved to specialize in American dance, with the realization that there would be more material there than they could ever use.

Even when performances were not tied to clinics at educational institutions, Lloyd liked to involve his audiences. After the performance ended, they would be invited to come to a nearby gymnasium where Lloyd would get the crowd square dancing. His dancers helped by joining different squares and taking partners among the audience members. In this way many people were introduced to square dancing. They discovered that it was fun and that it wasn't difficult. From there they sought out square dance groups that they could join.in their community.]

SPIRIT AND LONGING: THE BUS TALKS (Lloyd)

So many former dancers refer to "your wonderful talks in the bus." I have tried to think just what I said to them. Of course, I remember absolutely nothing. But thinking and thinking about it, I have some ideas. The only great talks were when I completely forgot them as individuals and forgot myself just as completely as an individual and dared to move out on the path of dreams.

Often in our first trips, I was so happy at the new experience that I wanted to share it with them. And in spite of myself I would find that I was sitting on the arm of my seat at the front of the bus and just opening my heart out to them. I wanted to tell them of the wonderful things we were going to see on this trip, the wonderful experiences we were going to have. I let go of myself and floated out on the vista of pure dreams, wandered in the shady lanes of my eager search, carried them with me along the one beautiful road we would soon be sharing together. I led them on and on, sharing my tenderest dreams. It is only the subtle, the intangible, and words lost in the secret search that will live forever in their lives as "the moment," a moment of which they will remember not a thing. They can only remember that they had a moment when they felt something beyond this world touch them for a minute, something as transient as a dream. But they will never forget that moment.

There can be no rules. The search for rules, the search for methods, will only carry the whole attempt on to failure. To be sure, I had done a lot of debating and public speaking in my school and college days. I was in oratorical contests and declamation contests and gave a lot of thought to how I could express myself to others. But it is only forgetting them completely, forgetting even the personalities of your audience, and reaching on towards the dream that counts.

And you never know when you have reached someone's inner consciousness. They all sit and look at you with fixed eyes. What is going on in their souls you may never guess. I recall riding in the bus with a group of girls who were going camping, and my wife was touched by the beauty of the autumn colors along the roadside. Its singing beauty began to sing in her heart. In a little while she said to me, "Listen," and then she recited to me, half in a trance the words that had sung themselves to her. I was deeply moved. I stopped the bus and told the girls how beautiful the roadside was and what it had done to Mrs. Shaw. And then I asked her to read her poem. She sat on the arm of my seat and read the poem quietly, and they all perfunctorily accepted it. And we rode on. Some of girls dutifully asked her to write the poem down for them so they could copy it.

Some years later we had a letter from one of the girls who was in that bus, now a mother with little children of her own. She simply wrote to tell us what the poem had meant to her, how she had learned it and always treasured it since. And she quoted it back to us in her letter. It went:

> *Dust from the road has made the pine trees hoary;*
> *The rose runs little fires 'round all the stones;*
> *The spiry spruces keep in perfect silence*
> *Their heavy copper carillons of cones.*

> *The good oat hay is stacked against December*

284

And the mown hay holds the herd again.
Earth has forgotten grass, forgotten flowers,
But the gold trees—the little unquiet aspens—
Scurrying among the spruces whilst they sing,
Hoarding the suns of June, and the June rainbows,
The gold trees remember –everything.

It happened that Mrs. Shaw had caught that specific moment when her particular interior window was open to the beauty of the world, to the beauty of a Colorado autumn.

To be sure, some folks will wonder very sincerely just what it is that I am talking about. The dancers were always nice, always well behaved, according to them. And according to some standards, I expect they were. They would always speak nicely when spoken to. To an unobservant person, they may have seemed perfect.

Let us go even farther and admit that the average group of young people traveling together, crowded into a bus, meeting the exigencies of crazy travel time, having to start early, to ride for long and impossible hours, of course, would have their bitter moments. Thrown together in all sorts of places and under all sorts of circumstances, they of course developed fondness for some and dislike for others of the group.

And what would you do if you were managing such a group? Nothing! Absolutely nothing about their free time. That is their own business as long as they are decent enough not to be openly offensive. But in the show you would have to insist on their being perfect! Treating each other as though they were the best of friends! Fooling the public! Putting up a smooth professional front! You would insist on this! And this is what you would get! Smiles but often backed with bitter hatred. Smooth fronts, while the inner person often writhed in anguish. A slick show but really one based on heart break and misunderstandings.

285

And that is fine. If they are all excellent artists, they will put on a good show. That is natural to them. And there is no use in trying to get anything different with the average group of artists picked up under the average theatrical conditions. But with a small group of non-professionals, who are incapable of doing anything like a polished performance, you would have nothing at all. You simply have to get them to reach for something so high above them that they cannot quite comprehend it, but if they are reaching for it with all their might, they touch their audiences with something far more beautiful than the finest professional can touch them with. Even though some of them do not understand what you are reaching for, if they reach their very best, there will be enough of the blessed others who will carry them completely beyond the expectations of their audience. The sincerity of their reaching is the subtle measure of their mysterious and compelling appeal. And that sincerity must be lived for all the hours of every day and to the exquisite beauty of that particular day.

It seems that some of the best of these talks were given when I was under the heaviest strain. Let the youngsters on the trip go a little wild, let them forget what we were there for, and I would have to pull down their freedoms. I would have to impose on them to get in line again. And after a day or two of this, I would feel like talking to them and would, as I once did over the Palisades south of Los Angeles, begin telling them of what we were missing, what we probably had permanently lost. It was not an inspired or an uplifting speech, but it was a frank discussion of life as it eddied around us, and it bore down on the failures, the mistakes of humanity, with the sunset in a broken sky, out beyond the sea, always calling us on, though we had missed it so completely on this trip. People who were touched by that talk have written me about it since. I don't remember what I said, but I feel it as easily as I felt it then, facing the failure of a dream.

On that same trip as we left California and came up over the mountains on a little-traveled road, I was impelled again to talk

286

to them. For over an hour I talked while the sunset played its glorious colors around the desert mountains that we were approaching. My tone was frankly discussing our recent failure, but my dream was of the sunset sky, of that beauty that we had not reached but that was worth our trying for again and again. And many letters have recalled that little talk out of all of the rest.

Or we were starting on a trip, and I talked to them as we rolled down through Pueblo, of the simple rules that we would have to follow, and then, touched by the autumn colors making so glorious and beautiful the trees and bushes and the little weeds along the road, touched by the promise of another great experience, touched by the great seedbeds of garden flowers that had been planted there, all along the road, great patches of red or blue or yellow—until I couldn't help spilling over to what it all was that we were seeking. Another trip on the quest for beauty, as we found it in our wonderful country, as we found it in the lives of simple men and women that we should meet, and as we should find it wherever our seeking was earnest enough.

Or watching a lovely sunset over a great range of mountains out in our west as we rolled on towards California, I remember only how deeply moved I was by the size of it all, the simplicity of it all, the great flickering call to beauty beyond that distant range of mountains wreathed in their sunset clouds. I reached on and on, and I don't know how many of them followed me. I don't know how they felt, but I was on the quest of real beauty and I was very near my target that evening.

Or great cities in the East. How they would inspire us, as we approached their mystery or departed from their secrets. Great rivers and great lakes! Or the countryside in which the life of some great man seemed all intertwined. Or a little village that struck us somehow as containing more than the people within its walls, of being important somehow to the whole human race! Monuments and memorials! Famous battlefields, or the ample pass through which the early pioneers had pushed, or the simple

287

beauty of a quiet countryside that sank its beauty into the heart of some significant person. A factory that we had toured and its vital significance in the life of our people. A thousand changing facets of the wide expanses of our challenging country.

Or perhaps when the youngsters had been wrong about their attitude toward something or in their attitude toward life itself, and at last something would urge me onto my little pulpit in the aisle, and I would think out loud for them again. Perhaps they would have broken over and started to couple, a childish impulse, and at last, not being able to stand it any longer, I would scold them and separate them and fight with them for a day or two.* And then at long last when they would be in line again and would be their own sweet selves again, I would answer the impulse that pressed within me, and taking my seat on the arm of my chair, would talk to them earnestly about what it was that we are trying to get out of life. I would talk to them about the real values, the real joys that lay beyond these deceptive impulses. I would press on toward that beauty that lay beyond the real, the present, and the now.

Some of my dancers, I am sure, never caught what it was I was seeking, never caught even a glimpse of that distant beauty. They listened politely and thought I was just a little strange, but a rather nice fellow after all. But some of them came all the way on the quest with me. Over mountains! Beyond the sunset! Questing, questing for that subtle something that is life. They left the earth for a moment. They left the common things of life, and they dared seek into the great unknown for the beauty that is worth more than life itself.

*Despite Lloyd's efforts to discourage what he called "conspicuous coupling," some of his high school dancers did fall in love, became sweethearts, and went on to have long and happy marriages. Don Bymaster and Lorena Holmes married straight out of high school. Lloyd was initially miffed, thinking they needed to wait until they were older, but they ultimately convinced him that their love was genuine and their marriage solid. Indeed it was a long and happy one. Another such couple was Herb Egender and Erna Lovelady, who danced on some of the earliest national tours. They became sweethearts in the eighth grade and they too married after high school and later became national leaders in the square dance movement.

TRAGEDY VISITS THE TEAM (Enid)

The Cheyenne dancers were scheduled to perform in Los Angeles on their fall trip in November of 1948. During the team's travels in the 1940s there were occasional illnesses, once a broken axle, and once the toppling of the bus near Dodge City, Kansas, when it hit some mud, skidded into an embankment, and fell on its side, denting the top of the bus and shattering windows. But Lloyd and Dorothy had managed to bring their students home safely—until the fall trip in 1948.

In late October they headed south to Santa Fe where they performed. They then took a side trip to see Carlsbad Caverns in the southeastern corner of the state, crossed the border to visit Juarez, Mexico, and then headed west across Arizona, performing in Tucson and Phoenix. When they reached San Diego, they again crossed into Mexico to visit Tijuana before heading up the coast.

At La Jolla they stopped to take a look at the ocean. There had been a storm the night before, so the breakers, crested with foam, were unusually high. Three boys ran out to the end of a rocky breakwater to get a closer look. Suddenly a huge wave rolled in, and the boys began running back up the shore. One escaped the wave, but the other two, Tommy Collins and Bones Jones were swept into the ocean. As they floundered in the pounding white water, the next wave came along and tossed Bones to a handhold on the rocks but only swept Tommy farther into the middle of the deep water. Another team member, Donnie

Bymaster, risking his own life, leapt into the water and tried to get to Tommy, but Tommy was pulled out even farther, disappearing from sight, then bobbing up, then disappearing, not to be seen again. Miraculously Donnie was tossed to a place where he could get a handhold and came out of the water sobbing that his effort had been in vain. There were no ropes, no tanks, no life buoys, no life guards. The men found where this equipment was securely locked up and broke the door in, but by this time it was too late to save Tommy. The police and lifeguards arrived and looked fruitlessly for any sign of him, but they said they could not risk entering the rough sea. They would wait until the tide went out to recover his body. Lloyd went to a nearby house to call Tommy's parents with the heartbreaking news. Teach Johnson, the piano player for the team, took the two surviving boys to the house to change into dry clothes. There the boys were revived with coffee and Teach with brandy.

The stunned chaperones and students finally continued up the coast to the Mission of San Juan Capistrano. Dorothy, reporting only two days later to the families of the team members, wrote, "Then we went into the garden of the mission. It was full of the silent peace of flowers and the fluttering peace of white doves. As soon as we went into the garden, the doves came and lighted on our hands and shoulders and heads, cooing and whispering. They were like the Holy Spirit. We went into the little chapel where for two hundred years people have taken their troubles, and we knelt there and accepted our sorrow and began to let the full measure of it sink into us. Then we drove on to the beautiful, quiet Miramar Hotel where people were so gentle and kind. There was a wonderful telegram from Tommy's folks, asking us to go on with our performances for his sake."

People who saw the Cheyenne Dancers in their next performance say that their dancing was magical, that their feet hardly met the floor. They were dancing a prayer for Tommy.

PASSING IT ON (Enid)

Another venue for Cheyenne Mountain Dancer exhibitions was the little mining town of Central City, about 40 miles west of Denver. In its heyday, as in quite a few old mining towns in the west, its citizens erected an opera house. Visiting actors, musicians, orators would perform there, and of course there were operas. The opera house fell on hard times after the gold played out, but in the 1930s the building was restored and an opera festival re-established. By 1936 Lloyd had a team of dancers there, performing in Williams Stables, across the street from the opera house, before and after each opera performance. For the pre-performance show the dancers came down the road wearing their tuxes and hoop-skirted gowns and performed the traditional part of their program. After the opera they came running down the street in their square dance attire, whooping as they came, and performed an energetic exhibition of traditional cowboy dances. The very first summer, Lloyd took recently-graduated Cheyenne School students, but he found he didn't have the same degree of authority over them as he had over current students, so he took only current students in the following years. There was a war-time blackout beginning in 1942, but the exhibitions resumed in 1946. It was a challenge to assemble a dance team when so many Cheyenne students were committing to summer jobs. When the management at Central City insisted that the dance team should be there for all seven weeks of the opera performances, neither Lloyd nor the dancers could spare that much time, and they had to give it up.

Many of those Cheyenne Mountain School dance team graduates attended either the University of Colorado in Boulder or Colorado State University (then Colorado A&M) in Fort Collins. It was only natural that they formed square dance exhibition teams at both schools: Calico and Boots at CU and the Aggie Haylofters at CSU. Thanks to these descendants of the Cheyenne teams, square dance exhibitions in Central City continued throughout the remainder of the 20th century. Indeed Calico and Boots, consisting now of college alumni, continues to dance and offer exhibition performances in the 21st century.

When Lloyd first stumbled on the square dance in Colorado, he became determined to learn as much about this folk art as possible. It turned out that very little about these dances had been put into print. The one resource that met some of his needs was the book written by Henry Ford's dancing master, Benjamin Lovett. The book came out in 1926 and was titled *Good Morning*, "After a Sleep of Twenty-five Years, Old-fashioned Dancing Is Being Revived by Mr. and Mrs. Henry Ford." The book contains directions for traditional quadrilles, which were in the standard square formation but consisted of set figures to be memorized or called out by a dancing master. There were also some contra dances for six couples such as Opera Reel, Fisher's Hornpipe, and Hull's Victory. Instructions and illustrations explained how to do the waltz and other couple dances such as the polka, schottische, Rye Waltz, and Badger Gavotte. Photographs and drawings depict gentlemen in tuxedos and ladies in the shapeless shin-length shifts that were in style in the 20s. Decorum was carefully demonstrated with pictures of a gentleman asking a lady to dance. The standard ballroom dance position stipulated that the palm of the gentleman's right hand should not touch the lady's back; rather, he should hold an imaginary pen in his hand so only the back of his thumb and the side of his index finger would come into contact with his partner's back. (The Cheyenne Mountain Dancers came to Dearborn on their first eastern tour and danced an exhibition, reportedly scandalizing the Henry Ford dancers with their whoops and aerial figures.)

During the incredible busy-ness of the thirties, Lloyd taught classes, managed a growing K-12 public school, oversaw an extraordinary list of extracurricular activities, spoke frequently for civic and educational groups, and began taking his dancers on more trips around the state to perform. At the same time he was also conducting his own research on the western forms of square dancing that he found all around him. He traveled all over Colorado and beyond, seeking out square dances, interviewing fiddlers and callers and taking detailed notes on the dances they knew. Then during the summer months, when he was able to get away from school-year responsibilities by staying with his family at Coombe Corrie, he produced his first dance book, *Cowboy Dances,* which came out in 1939.

He wrote it partly in self-defense because he was receiving so many letters asking him questions about the dances he was exhibiting. He intended it as a manual that people everywhere in the country could use. As always, he delved into the roots of things, describing how the western square dance evolved from its origins in the eastern US and the Appalachians. He intended the book to serve not as a dance history, however, but as a manual that could guide people in learning the dances and sharing them with others in their community.

He took the reader, the would-be caller, through all the steps of teaching a first square dance beginning with the simplest of figures and slowly progressing through more involved dances. He also described some of the traditional couple (or round) dances, such as the Rye Waltz, the schottische, the varsouvianna, and the polka, which were a standard part of the square dances he had attended. He made sure that the reader was aware of the step, step, close pattern of the waltz with the help of diagrams of cowboy boots going through the steps. The book is generously illustrated with photographs of the various square dance figures as well as the couple dances. His daughter Doli drew diagrams for the book and is featured in the photographs depicting the schottische and the Varsouvianna, among others.

To make his book truly useful, he included the lead sheets for many common square dance tunes such as "Buffalo Gals" and "The Girl I Left behind Me," and also for couple dances such as the Schottische, the Varsouvianna, and the Rye Waltz. For later editions he was able to include information on procuring square dance records called by various callers including himself, Roy Rogers, a former Cheyenner Bud Udick, and other callers from around the country. He of course encouraged people to seek out musicians, but he also embraced the technology of recorded music as a way of enabling people to dance even if they had no musicians and were dancing in the basement of their home. *Cowboy Dances* would go through 13 printings.

A second book would follow in 1948, *The Round Dance Book*. For years he had a standing order with the owner of the Kamin Dance Bookshop and Gallery in New York City to send him every book on dance history that came into his possession. Combining all that he could glean from his growing library and from his travels around the country, Lloyd delved into the history of each dance form—the waltz, the mazurka and varsouvianna, the schottische, the two-step, the Viennese waltz, and circle mixers. He dedicated the book "To my daughter Doli who has danced many a happy mile with me from kitchen to parlor and back again." Colorado Poet Laureate, Thomas Hornsby Ferril wrote in the foreword, "Lloyd Shaw is an American genius. We in Colorado are proud to share him with our neighboring countries which have now caught up with what we have always known about him. The old square dances were never lost in America but, due to something temporarily lost in ourselves, got misplaced. Through Lloyd Shaw, more than any other man, we were able to restore our own dances to our own spirit. Now in this new book, he is giving us renewed access to our old round dances. It is an adventure to move up with him, through something like a century of round dances, to where we are now."

Another key event happened in 1939. When Lloyd and his dance team were performing and teaching at a convention of the American Association of Health, Physical Education, and Recreation in Chicago, he was approached by Henry Graef of the Chicago Recreation Department who asked him to offer a summer clinic to teach others how to teach and call square dancing. Thus began the summer classes. The first class that summer reportedly consisted of Henry Graef and 39 women from the Chicago Recreation Department. The next summer it grew to 45 participants from 15 states, most of them from universities and schools of education. The following summer there were over 100 people coming from 28 different states. With an interruption during the US involvement in World War II, the classes continued to grow until there were June, July, and August classes and waiting lists for each because Lloyd limited attendance to about 100, the number of people who could be accommodated in the Cheyenne School gymnasium. Despite the ratio of the first class he held, he did try to achieve a reasonable gender balance among the participants as attendance swelled.

Each morning began in the same way. Using his two canes, Lloyd made his way across the stage of the school auditorium to reach his perch on a tall stool. As he began to talk, he was invariably interrupted by Joe Beissen, the Cheyenne School custodian, who pinned a rose on his lapel and exited the stage. The topics of the morning talks were wide ranging. Lloyd of course talked about the dance, its origins, and the wonderful potential it had for bringing people together. For those who wanted to learn to call dances, he created the caller's tripod, consisting of clarity, command and rhythm. He urged dancers and teachers to reach for the ideal, which was a way of seeking for truth and beauty. "Keep it simple and beautiful and it will last," he said. He talked about the responsibilities of dance leaders. As the movement grew, especially after World War II ended, he became concerned about callers who went on ego trips because they would have a whole floor of dancers moving to their commands. Lloyd used the image of the flag bearer who led the parade, swelling with pride as he noted the cheering of the crowd as he passed. What was important, of course, was not the bearer but the symbol that he was carrying, and so it was with the dance. He stressed the tremendous potential that square dancing had for bringing people together. He liked to tell about the time that a bank president asked him to call a square dance for all his bank employees. When Lloyd asked him why he chose to have a square dance, the man replied that it was the only social occasion in which he felt he could ask the wife of his custodian to dance with him.

Some of the Cheyenne School dancers, often an entire square, would be available to demonstrate and also to partner the newer dancers, helping them learn the feel of the dance and the carriage of the body as well as the steps. Lloyd stressed the inherent beauty in the dances and the posture that made the dancers beautiful. Bob Osgood recalled that his first morning of dance instruction began with simple walking while Lloyd emphasized the erect carriage that characterized his Cheyenne dancers—and could be the goal of all dancers.

He also drilled participants in the correct way of waltzing. Lloyd was particularly passionate about the waltz, believing that when it was done right and with beautiful posture, it was capable of taking dancers to a higher plane of being. He taught participants to dance step, step, close; step, step, close. For some reason, it is easy for beginning dancers to fall into step, close, step; step, close, step—the pattern of the two-step. In Lloyd's dance library were a number of books by dancing masters who inveighed against the pernicious "two-step waltz," even calling it the "ignoramous waltz," perhaps in an effort to shame dancers into getting their

297

step, step, close in order. Bob Howell reminisced years later about his first attendance at the summer classes with his wife Phyllis. The participants were doing a turning waltz in a big circle. Suddenly Bob and Phyllis were singled out with an ear-shattering shout from Lloyd on his microphone, "Stop, you're two-stepping!" Phyllis was so upset that she burst into tears and announced that she wanted to go home. Fortunately Dorothy was nearby to comfort her. Dale and Florence Wagner from Milwaukee, another couple who also became nationally known and beloved dance leaders, told about how they avoided such a reprimand at one of the early summer classes. When the class was practicing a turning waltz in the school gym, Dale and Florence would dance down the side of the gym away from the stage, across the back, up the other side—and out the side door by the stage, passing behind the stage and out of Lloyd's sight— to re-emerge through the door on the other side of the stage. Despite such traumas, most who attended the summer classes emerged waltzing beautifully, prepared to share the special joy of the waltz with the people in their own communities.

Another quality about which veterans of the summer classes would reminisce was Lloyd's booming laughter. Bob Howell reported that in his first summer class, when it was his turn to call a square dance, he wore a cowboy hat, thinking that was the appropriate garb for a square dance caller. Lloyd took him aside afterward and told him that a gentleman never wears his hat indoors. Lloyd had also ridiculed the small terry cloth towels that some men had taken to looping over their belts so they could dab away the sweat from their brows. At a stunt night later in the week some of Bob's friends put a huge sombrero on his head, looped a beach towel through his belt, and shoved him toward the microphone to call a dance. To his relief he was met by "a roar of laughter from Pappy."

As usual Lloyd had to share the things that he loved, so an evening picnic at Coombe Corrie was a must, preferably at the beginning of the week. In the years after the War when there were huge classes and many applicants had to be turned away, the group was divided in two, and there were two evenings at the cabin, so as to accommodate everyone. (Fortunately Dorothy was able to have the food catered and to hire helpers to serve the food, macaroni and cheese or sloppy Joes, for the hundred or so people who would come to the cabin for the evening.) Participants took walks and played some of the same games that the Cheyenne students had played at the cabin. There was always singing, and there was always a talk by Lloyd, sitting by the fireplace.

The final evening of the week featured a picnic on Austin Bluff on the east side of Colorado Springs. From there people could look down on the spread of the city as the lights came on, and, most important, they could watch the sun set spectacularly behind Pikes Peak. Lloyd would often talk about Zebulon Pike and his quest to climb the peak, or he might ask Dorothy to recite her poem.

A Ballad of Zebulon Pike
By Dorothy Stott Shaw, 1936

> *Zebulon Pike was a red-haired lad;*
>   *(All along the Arkansas the dead leaves drifted)*
> *And a score of tired infantry was everything he had.*
>   *The wind swirled down from the north and sifted*
> *The leaves along the river with a sinister sound;*
>   *Twenty tired men trudged on and on—*
> *Up the muddy Arkansas and on to higher ground,*
>   *For the day's march ended when the light was gone.*
> *All along the river bed the buffalo had been;*
>   *You could see on the earth where their hooves had beaten;*
> *But three thin rabbits were all that they had seen,*
>   *And thirty-six hours since they had eaten.*

PASSING IT ON

But Zebulon Pike had a fire in his breast,
And a dream was in his eyes for a Mountain in the West;
The Mountain was a challenge and the Mountain was a
song
That called to twenty infantry all day long.

Zebulon Pike made a breastwork wide,
        Where the flat and muddy Arkansas joins the
Fountain;
Then he said to three who were stout and tried—
        "The world's a map from the top of a mountain.
Pack meat and blankets for one night's rest;
        Rifles and shells—but we'll travel light,
Taking this valley that turns northwest,
        And we'll camp at the great peak's foot tonight."
But night came hurrying across the cruel plain,
        And the wind came hurrying and mocked them
bitterly;
Their feet were clods of anguish and their fingers knives of
pain,
        And they slept in open country, beneath a cedar
tree.

But Zebulon Pike heard calling in his ear
The cruel and lovely mountain that withdrew as he came
near;
The mountain was a challenge—the mountain was a song
He dreamed its shining summit all night long.

The next day passed as the first had done—
        Twenty-two miles of stolid going.
They huddled in the valley when dark came on
        And woke with the dawn to find it was snowing.

300

The third day dragged like a frozen dream
Of bleeding feet and fingers and aching shoulders,
Following the trace of the little icy stream,
And sleeping in a cavern among the frosty boulders.
But the fourth day broke like a miracle
Of cold and sunny blueness above a clouded plain.
They stretched their aching muscles and dried their mittens
well.
And forced their tired bones to the trail again.

Zebulon Pike, waist-deep in snow,
On the highest hill where the wind cut keen,
Learned what the lovers of all mountains know,
Seeing the valleys that lay between.
Zebulon Pike was a red-haired lad,
But he turned his back on that holy place.
He would gather the handful of men he had,
He would follow again the Spanish trace,
He would seek once more the buffalo track,
And the river's source at the setting sun,
But his dream would always be turning back
To the soil untrod and the deed undone.
He knew that he would carry like a charm within his breast
The knowledge of that Mountain, like a challenge in
the west
And from every campfire builded on a high and open place,
He would see its summit floating over sunny miles
of space.

Zebulon Pike never lived to be old.
He lay beside a bastion with a flag across his face.
And along the far-off Arkansas the spring came cold,
And the buffalo, unheeded, stamped the sagebrush
for a space.

And another group of infantry who gravely stood apart—
Did they know he held a Mountain, like a grail
before his eyes,
Did they know he held a Mountain, like a balm within his
heart,
And knelt to kiss its summit at the gates of
Paradise?

For a man can do no better than to cherish in his breast
The cool and lofty presence of a Mountain in the west.
A Mountain is a challenge and a Mountain is a song,
And a man who's loved a mountain has already lived long!

THE EXPANSION OF THE FAMILY
(Enid)

1939 was indeed an eventful year, as it also brought an addition to the Shaw family in the person of Don Obee. He was completing a Ph.D. in biology at the University of Kansas and spending his summers as a ranger naturalist in Rocky Mountain National Park. Paul Nesbit, one of his fellow rangers, taught biology at Cheyenne School during the school year but had signed a contract to be superintendent of schools in Trinidad, Colorado for the fall of 1938. He urged Don to apply for the vacant position at Cheyenne School, saying it was an extraordinary school, but Don, planning to seek a university position when he finished his degree, was not interested. Paul pestered him so much about interviewing that finally Don arranged on one of his days off to drive to Colorado Springs to have an interview with Lloyd. He didn't get the job. Lloyd chose the other candidate who already had experience teaching at the secondary level. Don happily returned to Estes Park and in the fall to his studies at KU.

In December he got a call from Lloyd, offering him the biology position. It turned out that the man Lloyd had hired couldn't maintain discipline in the classroom, and Lloyd had fired him. Don said thanks but no thanks. He was still focused on finishing his Ph.D. The next day he received a two-page telegram from Lloyd explaining all the advantages of taking the position at Cheyenne school. Don consulted with his faculty advisors. Since it was still depression times and jobs were scarce, they advised him to take the job and return another summer to finish the degree.

Don had no difficulties in the classroom. His former students would reminisce about his method for maintaining discipline. If they got out of order, Don simply picked up his gradebook and deducted some points from their grade, looking meaningfully at the offender. Order reigned and biology was learned.

Shortly after Don began teaching at Cheyenne school, Lloyd met him in the hallway and congratulated him on his success in the classroom. Then he said, "I'm calling a dance at the American Legion hall tonight. Would you like to come?" Don replied that he "wouldn't know a docey do from a garden hoe," but Lloyd said that he had a daughter who would be willing to help him. Doli had completed her BA at Scripps College in Claremont, California in the spring of 1937 and had returned to Colorado Springs to live with her parents. After meeting at the dance she and Don dated, and they were engaged by the time school ended in the spring of 1939. They spent the summer in Estes Park where Don continued to work as a park ranger and Doli took a job as a wrangler at Cheley Summer Camp. They married at the end of the summer, a day before Hitler's Panzers rolled into Poland and World War II began. As they headed down the highway on their honeymoon, they wondered what sort of world awaited them.

Don continued to teach at Cheyenne School throughout the duration of the war. Some members of the local draft board were also members of the Cheyenne School Board. They assured Don that he was performing a vital function by teaching science—but if he took a teaching job elsewhere, he would find himself peeling potatoes on a battleship headed to Japan. Don continued to teach at Cheyenne. A son, Kent, was born in 1942, and a daughter, Enid, arrived in 1945. Don did return to KU one summer to complete his Ph.D., and in 1945 he took a job as Head of Life Sciences at what was then Boise Junior College and grew into

Boise State University. Don brought his calling and dancing skills to Boise and soon had the students and faculty of the college square dancing.

THE EXPANSION OF THE SQUARE DANCE MOVEMENT (Enid)

In the summer of 1945 Lloyd got a phone call from Darryl Zanuck, the producer at 20th Century Fox. He wanted Lloyd to come to Hollywood to direct the dancing in *Duel in the Sun,* a film he was making, but he provided few specifics. A few days later Zanuck called again to ask, "Why aren't you here?" At that point they discussed the assignment in detail, and Lloyd agreed to come. Once there, he worked with local square dancers in the area to choreograph a square dance scene at a party held at a ranch, and he also worked with the principals, Gregory Peck and Jennifer Jones, teaching them Varsouviana variations. The Jennifer Jones character was purportedly unfamiliar with the dance, but with the help of her partner, she picked it up with lightning speed. While Lloyd was there, he had the opportunity to record an album of square dance calls with the Duel in the Sun Orchestra. The album sold widely and gave posterity a rare recording of Lloyd's square dance calling.

While Lloyd was in southern California, he of course visited his oldest brother Ray, who had recently retired as vice principal of Venice High School. They attended an international folk dance where Lloyd met some other square dance callers. At that time the pattern had been established at the folk dances that there would be one square dance called in the evening. The callers were each hoping to be the one to get to call the square. Lloyd suggested, "Why don't you organize your own square dances where you can call all evening?" One of the callers in the group was Bob Osgood, who worked as a publicist for the Squirt soft drink company. As part of his job, he traveled around the country, writing articles about local bottlers and giving them suggestions for promoting their product. In his travels he sought out square dances and thus met callers and dancers around the country.

If Lloyd was a prophet, Bob was his most devoted disciple. Bob learned from Ray and other callers about Lloyd's summer classes and applied to attend in 1947. When he got back a reply that the class was full, Bob went to Ray and asked for his help in getting accepted to the class. The plea was successful. Bob and his wife Ginger attended the classes regularly for the next ten years, and he and Lloyd began an active correspondence. Bob reported to Lloyd in March, 1949 that in southern California alone there were 250 square dance clubs, 55 callers, and somewhere between 20,000 and 50,000 square dancers. In his travels around the country, Bob saw that there was no means for square dancers to communicate with one another. In consultation with Lloyd and many others, he eventually decided to resign from his job with Squirt and launch a square dance magazine, which he would call *Sets in Order*. The first issue came out in November, 1949, and was distributed for free at a performance of the Cheyenne Mountain Dancers in Hollywood. The cover featured four Cheyenne Mountain Dancers doing their aerial figure called eight hands over, and the lead article was about Lloyd Shaw and his dance team. Bob borrowed a description of Lloyd found in a 1941 *Saturday Evening Post* article: "an educator with the instincts of a showman and the zeal of a missionary . . . he loves square dancing for its color and its lustiness, but his crusading spirit is born of the conviction that it fosters the spread of democratic processes. For he is primarily an educator—a school superintendent and college trustee." Similarly, Bob would later reminisce that in his summer classes

Lloyd would put more stress on *why* people should dance than *how* they should dance.

Sets in Order, which originally sold for 25 cents, served as an essential source of information on local dances, callers, musicians, and new square and round dances. As the activity became more popular, the making of square dance apparel became a business itself, and its producers began to advertise in the magazine, as did the producers of recordings. Soon articles covered the national scene and helped connect teachers, callers, musicians, and dancers across the country. Dance festivals sprang up and were publicized in the magazine. By 1956 the magazine had 40,000 subscribers in all states of the US, all Canadian provinces, and in 36 other countries.

The back cover of each magazine featured a cartoon about square dancers and callers drawn by Frank Grundeen, a regular on the *Sets in Order* staff and a former cartoonist for Walt Disney. In 1957 the great Warner Brothers cartoonist Chuck Jones, an avid dancer and president of his square dance club, began writing a regular column, full of his special brand of zaniness. He was part of the team that created Buggs Bunny, and he is credited with creating Wile E. Coyote and the Road Runner as well as Pepe le Pew, the amorous skunk. With his love of wordplay, Chuck took to calling Lloyd "Pepe Shaw." A portrait of Pepe le Pew drawn by Chuck and given to the Shaws is dedicated to "Pepe Shaw et Dorothy avec amour from Pepe le Pew et Chuck le Jones."

Bob Osgood invited Lloyd to write annual editorials, and Lloyd often seized the opportunity to speak about the current situation of the square dance movement. In the January, 1951 issue Lloyd congratulated *Sets in Order* on its first year of publication and the thousands of dancers who had made the magazine so necessary. He likened the excitement about square dancing to the gold rush of '49, but in this case, "people have found the gold in their own backyards. They have found the pure joy of friendship and recreation that really recreates." He warned against commercial interests that "may try to jump our claims—but if we keep simple and sane, if we keep laughing joyously and keep our game clean, nobody can touch us, nobody in the world." He urged people to "keep it simple, keep it folk." He saw no need for uniformity across the country. Rather, he said, "The style and spirit of the dance in each area must come from the people of that area." In 1952 Lloyd wrote that people who were furiously trying to learn all the new rounds and square dance figures "are again finding the joys in the old dances that their grandfathers loved."

Some callers became full-time professionals, scheduling dance-calling tours around the country. Week-long institutes for dancers and dance leaders began to spring up. In June of 1951 Bob Osgood began his long series of dance institutes at the beautiful conference site of Asilomar on the Monterey Peninsula in California. He brought the leading square dance callers and round dance leaders from around the country to conduct sessions, and for many years he included Terry Golden to lead singing as well. Bob organized two summer sessions and in 1955 added a winter session.

Dance groups across the country began holding regional jamborees, festivals, round-ups, fiestas, fests, and hoedowns. Then in 1952 the first national square dance convention was organized by dancers in southern California and held in Riverside, CA with 6500 dancers in attendance. Subsequent conventions were held in the 1950s in Kansas City, Dallas, Oklahoma City, San Diego (which drew 12,254 dancers), St. Louis, Louisville, and Denver.

In 1949 Lloyd was honored by the American Academy of Physical Education with one of its rare citations "to the Lloyd Shaw Folk Dance Program, as a noteworthy contribution to physical education . . . Dr. Shaw has pioneered in the field of folk dancing, and his institutes and other promotions have done much to popularize this area of dance, especially for young people. His books have contributed significantly to a better understanding and appreciation for folk dancing and square dancing throughout the country."

Around the same time, Lloyd was approached by Fred Bergin to make recordings for his dances, especially the round dances. As Dorothy later wrote, "This gifted and experienced man turned up in Pueblo, having read *Cowboy Dances* and *The Round Dance Book* and having decided that the man who wrote them needed to make some records. If Fred had wanted to make doughnuts or bicycle tires it would still have been a great experience just to be working with him and sharing his sweetness of temper and his patience and versatility." Fred wrote in 1967: "My mother used to tell me that she met my father at a square dance back in Michigan, and I always had a very warm spot for square dancing. . . Henry Ford spent a million dollars trying to do something that Pappy did with no money. For those . . . that are not familiar, Henry Ford did spend that kind of money trying to popularize square dancing. The American people wouldn't buy it from that kind of source but did from Pappy."

Fred had played in some of the most famous dance bands of the thirties and forties and then set off on his own business venture, becoming the owner of roller rinks. With his extraordinary musical gifts he produced recordings of the current popular tunes and formed his own company, Rinx Records. Anyone who skated in a roller rink in the 1940s or '50s probably skated to Fred's music. He often overlaid his line of organ music with his piano playing. Whichever instrument or instruments were featured, Fred's music carried his genius for making a melody highly danceable—or skateable.

There were those who didn't think organ music was "authentic" for round dancing, but Lloyd countered, in a *Sets in Order* article, that in the latter half of the 1800s little foot-pump organs were common in dance halls and private homes, being more affordable and portable than pianos. He referred to the concertina and the accordion as the little sister and brother of the organ and pointed out that they were long-accepted instruments for folk dancing. "And now," he wrote, "with the refinements of the Hammond organ, beautiful music can be produced that carries the dancers along with it that almost impels them to dance. If the organ is brought up to full orchestration by the addition of a second organ, and then pointed up with a piano or some other instrument, it can give a solid body of tone that can be matched only by a symphony orchestra."

Living in Pueblo and then in Englewood, a suburb of Denver, Fred worked closely with Lloyd for years. Their little 45 rpm records might have two dances on them, or they might have the dance music on one side, and the same music with Lloyd's vocal cues to the dance on the other side. Their company flourished during the '50s and '60s. Fred, with his various business investments was financially comfortable and drove a Cadillac, while Lloyd preferred his Oldsmobile 98. At one of Lloyd's summer classes in the mid-1950s the two were commiserating about their recordings business, which had fallen off in recent months. Sherm Walker, a wonderful traditional caller from Oklahoma who was loved for the improvised verses that he slipped into his calls as the dancers were promenading home, overheard Lloyd and Fred talking. The next time Sherm called a square, he had his patter ready:

> *Poor old Fred and poor old Pappy,*
> *They sure are broke but they are happy*
> *In a Cadillac and an Olds 98*
> *They'll meet each other at the poor farm gate.*

Square dancing was popular nationwide in 1950 when Santa Monica staged its "largest square dance." In his open letter of invitation to the nation's square dancers, California Governor Earl Warren wrote, "Square dancing as a wholesome activity has grown to tremendous proportions in the state of California in the last few years. I am confident this will be well demonstrated by the turnout for this Diamond Jubilee Square Dance." In addition to the specially surfaced streets prepared for the dancers, grandstands for 6000 spectators were erected. Special lighting was arranged as were 40 speakers to carry the calls and music to all the dancers. Thirty large buses were booked to carry dancers coming from San Bernardino and Redlands, which lay to the east of Los Angeles.

Leading callers from around the country, but especially from Southern California, were scheduled to call one dance each. They included Ed Gilmore, Terry Golden, Jack Hoheisal, Bruce Johnson, Cal Golden, Ralph Maxheimer, Arnie Kronenberger, Doc Alumbaugh, Fenton (Jonesy) Jones, and Lloyd's brother Ray (who would die two years later while calling a square dance.) Most of the round dances on the program were those that Lloyd had popularized in *Cowboy Dances.* A newer round dance on the list was Lloyd's own choreography to the "Merry Widow Waltz."

The evening was a phenomenal success. The number of dancers was estimated at 15,200 and the crowd of spectators was thought to number 35,000. As the open limousine carrying Lloyd and Dorothy Shaw made its way through the crowd, dancers gathered around the car to extend their greetings and also their thanks to Lloyd for what he had given them, this joyous activity. Lloyd proceeded to the podium where he served with Bob Osgood as MC to introduce the dances and callers. Shortly thereafter the band struck up "California Here I Come" as Governor Warren's limousine moved through the crowd to the viewing stand. The Governor stayed to the last dance. The many police officers on hand at the dance found that there was little for them to do. They said it was one of the best-behaved crowds they had ever seen. Bob Osgood reported in the next issue of his magazine that a couple of teenagers leaned over the rail of the bandstand to ask when the band would play some tunes for "popular dancing." The band leader looked out over the huge crowd and replied, "You may not know it, kids, but this *is* popular dancing."

THE LAST YEARS (Enid)

After World War II ended, the population of Colorado Springs grew at a great rate. Many people who had been stationed at Fort Carson, the army base south of the city, chose to settle there, drawn by the beautiful setting and the fine climate. Housing sprang up, including apartment buildings, suddenly causing a dramatic increase in enrollment at Cheyenne School. Not only were there more students, but of course the new ones had not grown up with the Cheyenne traditions and did not know Lloyd as did those who had met him when they entered kindergarten. Pressure was growing in the school district to create a separate grade school, junior high, and high school.

By this time Lloyd had settled on a pattern for the Cheyenne Mountain Dancers' tours. In the fall they would go to the west coast but in a three-year rotation so that no student would go to the same places twice (unless they made the team as freshmen.) They would go to the Pacific Northwest one fall, the Bay Area the next, and Southern California the next. In the spring they went east, dividing it into the northeast, the mid-Atlantic states, and the southeast. Thus students who were motivated to do the work to make the team could see most of the country during their high school years.

Most of the engagements came from requests to Lloyd to put on clinics around the country. He would reply that he could come if arrangements were made for the Cheyenne Mountain

Dancers to perform. He had learned early on that a well-organized schedule of performances paid for the trips in full and even provided funds for other school projects.

In these post-war years the school sponsored a very good ice hockey team. This sport was made possible by the generosity of the Broadmoor Hotel, which lay only a few blocks south of the school and had made its ice rink available to the students. There weren't many other schools that could field an ice hockey team, and the Cheyenne School team beat all the opponents they encountered. Lloyd noticed that the hockey team members were so full of themselves and their skating prowess that they had little use for square dancing. Indeed they called it an activity for sissies, but they were nonetheless attracted by the possibility of the cross-country trips.

Given that possibility, they worked hard enough to make the team. But on the fall trip to the west coast in 1950, Lloyd found them to be impossible. He reported, "They broke rules, sneaked smokes, and looked down on me with tolerant pity. Finally at Monterey one of them made himself so disagreeable with the troupe that he broke up the whole show and had Mrs. Shaw and the other women and most of the girls in tears before he was through. When I met him at the hotel, he was ready for me with three of his henchmen and told me where things stood. When I had heard him out, I took out my wallet and counted out some bills. I told the four of them to go to bed and get some sleep. They were to take an early train back to Colorado. They were to go directly home and enter school the minute they got there. Any irregularity or fooling around and they would be expelled.

"They were startled and immediately lost their swagger and begged to be allowed to finish the trip. I foolishly relented and let them stay. They behaved from then on. Our last two shows were perfect in detail, but the spirit was gone. When we got to Glenwood Springs, our last night out on the way home, I called the whole bunch together in the hotel and told them that this would be the last Cheyenne dance trip. I was through. The following June I left the school forever."

Now Lloyd was free to devote himself full time to the activity he had introduced to the nation. He continued to offer his summer classes, still in the Cheyenne School gymnasium, a new one, considerably larger than the old one, having been built in 1950 to serve the growing student body.) He was in demand across the country to serve as guest of honor or MC at dance festivals or to give dance workshops. He and Dorothy traveled often and widely during the early 50s. There was, however, a break in their travels and the summer classes in the summer of 1952 when Lloyd had a stroke. His convalescence took several months, but he was soon back at his schedule of speaking and teaching engagements. In the summer of 1953 he admitted 160 dancers to his July class. In addition to Lloyd's classes and Bob Osgood's institutes at Asilomar, 27 sessions for aspiring callers were offered that year by others, including Herb Greggerson and Al Brundage.

In 1953 Lloyd built a dance hall on his own property, across the circular drive from the house. He named it "La Semilla," *the seed* in Spanish. It was 18 by 40 feet, with benches built in along the walls. In his yearly letter, always headed "Annual Belated Christmas Greetings," which he sent to friends, relatives, and summer class attendees, he wrote, "And we don't care at all whether one set comes to dance with us, or four sets crowd into the same space. The number is entirely a matter of indifference to us. The spirit of the dance is all. And the spirit so far has been beautiful. We are delighted with it. It keeps friends coming who really want to come, with whom we can work out new dances or take joy in the old or sing old songs or make live again those things that are really worthwhile." And in return hundreds of Christmas cards came from across the country, many of the writers reporting that they were starting new square dance groups in their own communities. Over the years a nucleus of some of the finest callers and choreographers in the country continued to come each summer and to share their dances and teaching techniques. In the summer of 1955 Lloyd began holding much-reduced summer classes in La Semilla instead of the new Cheyenne School gym, which was twice the size of the gym it replaced and which he described as "very much too large and rather cold and inhospitable."

While Lloyd did much to make square dancing a national pastime, he could not control the movement, try as he might. His mantra became "Keep it simple, keep it folk." However, he was never a purist and he never advocated dancing only the figures compiled in *Cowboy Dances.* After all, he and his Cheyenne Dancers had created figures to spice up their exhibition performances. He felt that such invention was part of the folk process.

However, he was becoming concerned about the rapid proliferation of new calls. On one of his last trips to Boise, Idaho around 1957 to visit Doli and her family, callers from around the region came to talk with Lloyd. The topic could be summed up as "what are they doing to our dance?" With all the new dance figures, it was becoming increasingly difficult for new dancers to be absorbed into square dance clubs. It is impossible to know how Lloyd would have felt about the creation of Callerlab in the 1970s, which sought to establish different levels of square dancing, so that dancers would know which figures would be included at a dance they attended. Certainly there were differing opinions among the callers who attended the Fellowship after the founding of Callerlab.

Not surprisingly, people were also inspired by The Cheyenne Mountain Dancers to form exhibition teams of young people. Lloyd was certainly appreciative of some groups such as Red Henderson's Silver Spurs. But after the Louisville convention in 1958, Lloyd wrote in his notes, "All TV Exhibition groups should be completely banned from the program. They are not at all typical of square dancing with their spins and whirls and somersaults and speed, and only do legitimate square dancing a disservice. . . it would be well, according to me to refuse all groups of youngsters from exhibiting. The Louisville convention had over half of its groups teenage or younger—down to five-year-olds. They can do only their routines and are helpless on a general dance floor and give a wrong picture of square dancing."

JULY 1958

Dorothy was at Lloyd's side at his summer classes and during all his travels. She was an eager traveler herself, but she was also watching over him especially in the wake of the stroke. She had taken to writing him a poem for his birthday in their later years together. Her finest is the one she wrote in 1957 for Lloyd's 67th birthday.

MICHAELMAS BIRTHDAY – 1957
This day has been forever;
It has existed always, at the heart of God.

Certainly I know that it is the feast
of Saint Michael and all the Angels,
and incidentally, the Holy Sabbath,
and, most important of all, your birthday!
These are but bright devices
with which to pin this span of shining hours,
like a pressed gold leaf,
against a blank square on the calendar,
thus acknowledging our obligation
to a man-made thing called Time,
cruelest of all inventions!

But, if you try to tell me:

THE LAST YEARS

Next week it will all have passed!
All this clotted gold of aspen trees
tufting the tawny hills
with great designs and patches of a light
we never found elsewhere.
All these thick sluggish rivers of cottonwoods
running rich ocher down cliffed and vigorous valleys
and through umbered meadows stacked with bronzing hay.
All these crimson hedges of rose and currant
and woodbine seaming the roadside . . .
If you try to tell me that a great wind will have arisen
and stripped the aspens and the cottonwoods
to frenetic silver ghosts, and that it will be
       gone, past, existing no longer,
you will be mistaken!

What I have learned today . . .
(This is your birthday and this is my gift to you)
is that only the fleeting is eternal.

This day has been forever
and will be always, in the heart of God.
It is simply that we finally reached it, you and I:
stepped over the threshold into it,
aware of the presence of angels!

Nothing is more durable
than the bedizened wings of a late September butterfly,
unless it might be an unfallen aspen leaf,
gold, new-minted . . .
unless it might be a man and a woman
stepping, hand in hand, across a glistening threshold
into the presence of angels!

God, I think
works with the eternal fleeting,
the everlasting ephemeral:
like gold leaves not yet fallen
and men and women in love with each other,
and the presence of angels.

Dorothy was prescient. It was to be Lloyd's last birthday. Those dear friends, happily looking forward to the 1958 August class, were stunned to learn the news when Lloyd died suddenly of a stroke on July 18, a few months short of his 68th birthday. Only eight days later Dorothy wrote a letter to their long list of class members and friends. It was an extraordinary letter, so extraordinary that some of those friends, decades later, when they were downsizing or moving into retirement homes, couldn't bear to throw their copy away. A number of them chose to send their copy on to me, Lloyd and Dorothy's granddaughter. It is understandable that they had to find a home for it. Here is what Dorothy wrote:

Dear Friends and Gentle People:

The little slender soul sits swiftly down and takes the oars.

So many times in the past month Lloyd has stopped me and himself suddenly short with an excited, shining, bewildered look, to tell me again about eternity. Right in the middle of a walk around the lake, where we have been noting the blossoming and the fading of the lindens and the incredible knowingness of the baby ducks, he would stop and say, "You know, I have to keep talking about it because, for some reason, it has just hit me—this business of infinity and eternity. Here is our cozy little solar system, lost in its galaxy, and that galaxy set in a universe of

319

galaxies, and beyond that—well, nothing. 'Nothing is what the mind says because it seems to be easier to understand nothing than something. But there *is* something, really, all the way—on and on and on. It makes me dizzy. And I seem to *have* to keep thinking about it. I have to understand it, and I can't. Or, take time. We say 'today' and 'tomorrow' and 'forever and ever.' And beyond that, nothing. But that's not true either! Beyond forever is forever, and beyond forever is forever. And I have to try to understand it!

"On Friday morning, July 18th, he said, 'I woke up with it today. I can't get it out of my mind—infinity, eternity. I'm going to have to tell you all about it again!' At the breakfast table we decided that perhaps you could say that *Something* was a complete absence of negation, an eternal 'Yes!'

"He worked all morning at the typewriter on the instructions to go with the beautiful tape he had made for the album 'Learning to Waltz.' When I called him to lunch out in the arbor, he came a little slowly. He ate automatically, not speaking. Deeply and immediately I knew that something was wrong. But when I questioned him, he smiled and said, quietly but very firmly, 'I feel perfectly fine.' His skin was boy-clear; his eyes were clear and shining; there was a kind of radiance about him. I left him sitting quietly there, staring raptly off among the trees, tapping his fingers on the table a little, while I went to the telephone to try to summon the help that I knew I was going to need. Finally he got up docilely and let me put him to bed. It was as if he were walking down a long green trail, slowly and serenely, until he got so far away that he could no longer hear me. Just at the point where I think he lost me entirely, he turned his head to look out of the window, and the strangest little triumphant smile played for a few moments across his mouth. After we got to the hospital there was a brief, terrible battle while the courageous body fought it out, but I think Lloyd was not there. The slender soul had already sat down and was eagerly checking the oarlocks, heading out onto that sea where the answer was waiting. Lindsay Patton, our rector and beloved friend, was with me, and George Bancroft, old schoolmate and great surgeon, and a fine, strong, anonymous doctor. To all of them my inexpressible gratitude wells up.

"People will tell you that it is exactly like being cut in two, and they will be right. But they do not always take note of where the other half is, or of how vividly *alive* it is. It is difficult for me at first to be half in Heaven. The atmosphere is extraordinary. I shall have to learn how to breathe.

"But, oh, what splendor! People—dozens of people—were coming to me, all shining. Surely no one could have missed the glory. There were even a few people who had the wisdom and the courage to say to me, "My dear, this is very wonderful!" My sister and her good husband were here within the hour. Our staunch daughter and her children flew in ('and Dad was leaning over my shoulder all the way.') Kirby came soon, and Dena and Elwyn, and Muriel. Bob flew in from Los Angeles in time to give us his strong shoulder to lean on. Fred and Doris were with us, of course, and Lloyd's brother Glen—how fine to have his quiet acceptance of the whole of life right here beside us instead of halfway across the world. The loving thoughts of Doli's Don enveloped us. All of you who were too far way or too lost in time for us to find you quickly were represented by these dear ones.

"And then my *children* began coming in. I felt like the old woman who lived in the shoe! Except that I knew quite well what to do with them—they took me in their arms and loved me, and I loved them. Men who were once our little boys in Cheyenne School, trooping up the steps—a little worn, perhaps, a little bald, a little paunchy, but shining like little boys, telling me how grateful they were to Pappy. Women, bringing children of their own, laughing and weeping. 'Do you remember,' said Millie, 'when I knew my little Pam was coming, the first person I told was Pappy. I wrote him a letter!' (We have it still.) 'Isn't that crazy? Writing your school superintendent a letter to tell him you are going to have a baby!' And her laughter filled the room with light. Dear people who taught alongside us all those years standing up to this new assignment, bless them. People who had danced with us holding out their hands in a new kind of grand right and left, moving at the level of the tree tops.

"Monday was a beautiful day. Cool and soft, with broken sunshine making clean shadows. The noble arches of Grace Church soar upward. The world is filled with flowers. The mighty organ is singing a song of triumph. Then it slips into 'Jesu, Joy of Man's Desiring,' and then into 'Fair are the woodlands, fairer still the meadows.' Embroidered in gold on the silvery pall is one word: 'Alleluia!'

'—and though this body be destroyed, yet shall I see God: whom I shall see for myself and my eyes shall behold, and not as a stranger . . . therefore will we not fear, though the earth be moved and though the hills be carried into the midst of the sea . . . I will lift up mine eyes unto the hills . . . for I am persuaded that neither death nor life nor angels nor principalities nor powers nor things present nor things to come nor height nor depth nor any other creature shall be able to separate us from the love of God.'

"Now we are standing, and the choir is singing the one song we always sang in every joy and every need and every sorrow, 'In Dulci Jubilo.' All over the congregation behind us the voices of our children, our generations of school children, rise and break—and rise again—

> *'In dulci jubilo! Let us our homage show!*
> . . .
> *Alpha es et O! Alphas es et O!*
> . . .
> *There are angels singing Nova cantica;*
> *There the bells are ringing, in Regis curia,*
> *O, that we were there, O that we were there!'*

322

It is Christmas again at Cheyenne Mountain School. It is October night above the sparkling pattern of San Francisco. It is a sung prayer that we may dance well, as we ride in the bus to an important engagement. It is the wild coast of California where we lost Tommy in the surf. It is Pappy going home.

"We went out of the church with trumpets, and, just as we rode away, down from the tower came the song again on the bells, 'In Dulci jubilo . . . O, that we were there!' Under the great tree at the cemetery our friends were waiting in speckled sunshine—our hundreds of grown-up children, old school and college classmates, our dear dancers, my precious poets, the good fine people of the town, and the dear many who drove a long way into the heart-achingly beautiful mountains. Dear, dear hands carried him—Fred Bergin's, Kirby Todd's, Frank Evans' (for the teachers of Cheyenne School), Howie Jones' (for the children), Bob Osgood's (for the dancers of America), and Gernot Heinrichsdorff's (for our little group of local dancers.) On the clean steel casket quivered a great bunch of mariposa lilies, gathered among the aspens at Coombe Corrie by the grandchildren and Howard Jones' dear two.

'I have fought a good fight. I have finished the course. I have kept the faith.'

"Why am I writing you this strange long letter? Because I think you might want and need to know how things were. Because some of you have already written, 'Could you find the time to write us a letter?' Or perhaps because I have something to tell you.

"Lindsay said afterward something like this, 'Dorothy, the most wonderful thing happened after you left the cemetery. I have never seen anything like it. Those people *didn't go away!* They just stayed there, greeting each other, loving each other, recalling to each other all the wonderful memories.' Like those astonishing early Christians, after they discovered that the Kingdom of God was within them.

"Dear people, don't go away! Pick up your spark from the relinquished torch and light a big brand! Let us close ranks into a tighter phalanx against those enemies that Lloyd and all good men have battled—the cheap, the selfish, the vain, the unlovely, the unloving. There is still so much to do. Lloyd has left in my hands (and yours) things that must go on. He has not left me for one moment. But suddenly he has acquired, I think, a strange new way of being in several places at once. He has been with some of you too. As he moves straight on from where he left off, with vastly expanded capacities and with complete freedom, he comes close to us, and we remember that we must be more careful about loving each other and about being joyous. "For a long time I have been his willing feet, rejoicing to do a hundred little errands every day. Suddenly he has become *my* wings. And it seems altogether possible that I might learn to fly! But the tasks are unfamiliar to my hands and heart, and I am not strong enough, I know, to do them all alone. Most of all is the beautiful book that Lloyd has been working on—somehow I shall have to assemble the many sections of finished manuscript that, like a jig-saw puzzle, are all going together to make a lovely story of teaching, and dancing, and living. But I do not know *how* to put this book together, and it will take me a long time. God is very near, but you also stand beside me. Stand 'round me in a ring of tenderness. *Dance* 'round me to the singing of the stars.

"Beautiful things have happened in the past months—each like a pearl rounded: a perfectly miraculous visit with the family early in May; a reunion of our college class that was a joyous rededication; the lovely ride across the green country to Louisville with Dena as a good companion; the sweet friendliness there. So much savor to everything, so much awareness of the terrible beauty of God's world. People dropping in whom we hadn't seen in years—all in a silvery pattern.

"And now the pattern weaves on. The little group of old-timers who were coming to the Fellowship in August are telling me quite flatly, 'We are still coming!' How welcome they will be! How the presence that fills this house will rejoice to go lightly onto

324

the floor with them and *dance* again—no canes, (suddenly it comes to me how often he has said to people lately, 'I am going to throw these away pretty soon'), no crippled heart that must be used so cautiously, no inexorably mounting weariness of mind and body—free.

"Lindsey prayed that new opportunities of service might be granted him. I too am praying that they may, not only in Heaven, but here also, through you and me.

"God bless you.

Dorothy"

Colorado Springs
July 26, 1958

EPILOGUE (Enid)

The August class, the Fellowship, did come, and they had a magical week. Dorothy stepped easily into the leadership of the event. After the week was over, she wrote up the dance material that had been presented in what came to be called the Syllabus. There was no question that the Fellowship would continue.

Dorothy's next challenge was the Eighth National Square Dance Convention, which was scheduled to take place in Denver in May of 1959. It was hardly surprising that Lloyd and Dorothy and Fred Bergin and his wife Doris had been chosen to serve as official hosts of the event. Following Lloyd's death, Dorothy was featured as "our Official Honorary Hostess. " But there was nothing merely "honorary" about the work she did before and at the convention. She was Honorary Chair of Hospitality and Reception and the moderator for a panel on the future of square dancing, but her biggest assignment was to take Lloyd's place and work with Chuck Jones to organize and MC a historical pageant of American folk dance. She delved into Lloyd's dance library and, working with Chuck, generated a history of the American square dance, beginning with its ancestors in Europe. In the process she and Chuck bonded. Both were guided by his mantra, "only the love must show."

The pageant they organized was comprehensive. After the grand march with the entire cast, the program began with two English country dances in square formation, followed by early

Kentucky pioneer dances and Appalachian big circle dances. Next came a forerunner of the round dance, a minuet choreographed by Dena Fresh and danced in colonial dress by Dena and her husband Elwyn. The program then moved on to the New England contra dances and then the Spanish dances of old colonial California, followed by dances of the Mormon migration, complete with pushcarts and a camp fire.

Next came the Lancers Quadrille, which Dorothy had researched. She went to Fort Collins to meet with the Aggie Hayloffters and their student leader Cal Campbell to invite them to perform the Lancers as a "royal" quadrille, which consists of a square of eight couples, two on each side. The group had done squares in that formation before but not a Lancers. Dorothy created the scene for them in a ballroom right after the Civil War when many men would still be wearing their uniforms. The dancing master would call for the quadrille, and each man would consult his dancing card and seek out the woman who had agreed to do this dance with him. Cal would report later that meeting Dorothy and performing the Lancers at the convention was a life-changing experience. Rather than establish a private veterinary practice, he chose a different avenue in his field that would permit him the time to stay involved with dancing.

The waltz was introduced by folk dancers, performing the landler and then the Viennese Waltz under the direction of nationally known folk dance leader Vyts Beliajus. (The convention program featured folk dance workshops and exhibitions every day, so many folk dancers were in attendance.) The great quadrille period included the Mazurka Quadrille, performed by Kansas dancers under the direction of Dena and Elwyn Fresh. More dances from south of the border included a schottische, a waltz, and a varsouvianna. The late 19th century featured an Oklahoma "play party"-- dances done to singing in areas where people believed that dancing was evil and that the fiddle was "the instrument of the devil"-- but still felt the need to socialize and move to music. Next came dancers representing "Three Important Groups that Sparked the Current Revival:" the Henry Ford Dancers (1925-1959), Herb Greggerson's Texas Blue Bonnet Set (1937-1947), and finally the Cheyenne Mountain Dancers (1934-1951). The latter were represented by students from Calico and Boots at the University of Colorado with Bob Cook, a former Cheyenner, as their caller. Bill Litchman, who danced with that team, reported that Dorothy drove to Boulder to see them dance to ensure that they would represent the Cheyenne Mountain Dancers appropriately. She gave them her approval but commented that they were "too smooth," apparently lacking the impression of spontaneity that the Cheyenners had mastered. For the finale, all of the dancers in the pageant came out on the floor and danced the Alabama Jubilee to the calling of Joe Lewis.

Dorothy and Chuck bonded over the task of organizing the pageant and carried on a lively correspondence. For the college groups, the experience of meeting Dorothy and performing before the huge crowds at the convention helped create the next generation of dance leaders. Students from the Aggie Haylofters and Calico and Boots subsequently arranged with Dorothy to have a "one-day fellowship" each spring at La Semilla. The students would literally sit at her feet to hear her talk, and then she would observe as they called and taught their dances. In addition, some, like Cal Campbell, would make the two-hour trip down to Colorado Springs to call at the little Monday night dance that Dorothy hosted each month in La Semilla.

Leading the August class only a month after Lloyd died and then carrying out his commitments to the Denver Square Dance Convention helped establish Dorothy's leadership. She was also assisted and inspired by the extraordinary talents in the Fellowship, which included some of the outstanding dance leaders and choreographers in the country. It was not at all a closed group, for newcomers were welcomed each year to join the nucleus of repeat attendees. The two remarkable round dance choreographers were

Dena McMillan Fresh from Wichita, Kansas and Carlotta Hegemann from San Antonio, Texas. Dena grew up attending Cheyenne Mountain School and is featured in the earlier chapter on discipline at Cheyenne. Her father was the chauffeur for Spencer Penrose, owner of the Broadmoore Hotel. (One night when Penrose was hosting the prize fighter Jack Dempsey, the two men decided on a lark to attend a local carnival. They also decided that they needed some children, so Penrose called down to the chauffeur's home and asked if Dena and her brother Shelly were available. They were, and Dena spent the evening riding on Jack Dempsey's shoulders.) During her years at Cheyenne Dena participated in the international folk dancing that was taking place at that time, and later she attended the nationally known Perry Mansfield Summer Dance Institute in Steamboat Springs. Her most famous round dance, which has achieved the status of a "folk dance," is her choreography to the tune of "Edelweiss."

Carlotta Hegemann grew up in southern California where she studied as a girl at the famous Denishawn School of Dance, led by Ruth St. Denis and her partner Ted Shawn. In addition to embracing folk dancing, Carolotta was an expert in the dances of Asia and the Pacific. Her arms and hands appeared to be fluid when she danced a hula. She and her husband Otto settled in San Antonio, where she absorbed the flavors of the Southwest. Her waltz quadrille "Serenata" creates the scene in a Mexican community where the young people stroll around and around the plaza in the evening to see and be seen.

A number of the best callers in the country came to the summer classes on the Shaw property. Bob Osgood, fulltime dance leader and editor of the square dance magazine he founded, came whenever his schedule permitted. Sherm Walker, a traditional caller from Oklahoma, came for many years, as did Bob Howell, the junior high school administrator from Cleveland. Bob became a nationally known and beloved dance leader for "keeping it simple." He could handle a crowd of hundreds by following this mantra. A different sort of leader was Don Armstrong, whose keen intelligence made him a superb caller, choreographer, teacher, and dance researcher. He and his wife Marie operated a public square dance venue and also a radio station in Florida. The two of them were a double threat as Marie had extraordinary talent whether it was leading singing, calling a dance, or organizing whatever needed organizing. It was Marie who brought to the Fellowship its theme song in 1957, a round sung in Latin: "Pauper sum ego, Nihil habeo, Cor meum dabo" (I am poor, I have nothing, I will give my heart.) Much correspondence among Fellowship members carried the closure, "Cor meum."

Mary Jo Bradford, a caller and school teacher from Oklahoma, had attended one of Lloyd's big summer classes and gotten permission to bring her teen-aged children Mary Josie and John to participate the following year in 1946. Lloyd, thinking John needed something to give his teen-aged years more status, dubbed him "Uncle John," a name that has stayed with him ever since. John danced with exhibition teams in Central City and still carries on the repertoire and styling that he learned from Lloyd Shaw. Others who would be influential dance leaders were Ken Kernen and Gib Gilbert who danced with the Calico and Boots exhibition team at the University of Colorado, and Cal Campbell who danced with the Aggie Haylofters at Colorado State University. Later they would be joined by Bill Litchman, also a Calico and Boots alum and an exceptional caller and dance historian. A dear friend of Lloyd and Dorothy, indeed the extended Shaw family, was Kirby Todd, who taught public school music in Illinois. He became so inspired about promoting American folk dance that he took a position teaching recreational dance at Illinois State University in 1964. Kirby would bring a new generation of young dancers to future summer classes, and those dancers would in turn become dance leaders and teachers.

After Dorothy successfully led the gathering in the summer of 1958, there was no question that "the Fellowship," as it had come to be named, would continue. Many in this original group came year after year. Others heard of the event, asked if they might come, and were welcomed. Each morning began with singing led by Kirby Todd, Marie Armstrong, and others. Then Dorothy took her place before the group to give the morning talk, interrupted at the beginning by a designated person who pinned a corsage on her. Dorothy's style was quieter than Lloyd's, but it was easily as effective. She too was an experienced public speaker, with the eloquence of a poet as well. People responded to her leadership as they had with Lloyd's—they were inspired to be better, kinder human beings and even more beautiful dancers in her presence.

The week's program consisted largely of leaders sharing their dances and teaching techniques. There were sessions on square dances and quadrilles, round dances, contra dances, dance styling, dance music, and teaching techniques. Fred Bergin would share his vast knowledge about dance music, and one evening he would sit at the piano playing requests. The Sunday supper at the cabin and the final evening picnic on Austin Bluffs were fast traditions. On Thursday evening it was stunt night with a sharing of talents and Bob Howell leading the group in his wonderful and often ridiculous party games.

One aspect of the Fellowship changed, however. Lloyd had dedicated Wednesday evening to having the group go to a public square dance, sometimes in Acacia Park and sometimes on the terrace of the Broadmoor Hotel, where Fellowship members would share the microphone with local square dance callers, some of them Cheyenne School alumni. In 1961 the group decided to have their own dance at a rented hall to which they could invite local friends and Cheyenne alumni. Then, two years later, Don Armstrong suggested that the Fellowship stage a cotillion ball, still including local guests. A dance hall was reserved, and a theme chosen. The first one was the Columbine Cotillion. Some Fellowship members began planning favors and designing dance cards. Dena Fresh would bring dresses and hoopskirts from her exhibition groups in Kansas so that some of the ladies could experience that elegant and novel form of attire. Each cotillion was a beautiful and memorable event.

The week worked its magic on Dorothy too. She would later write about it in her annual year-end letter, which was never belated, arriving always before Christmas: "In August came the Fellowship. There are no words for this communion of bright spirits. They dance like beings from a better planet, they sing like junior-grade angels, and they are filled with grace. Such love— such gladness. . .There is something so special and so precious about the Lloyd Shaw Dance Fellowship that the thought of it brings a little choke to the throat. It is so little and so valiant, so gentle and so wise. We blossom from it, like orchids on a mossy tree."

In the following years Dorothy, working closely with Fred Bergin and dance choreographers, carried on the work of Lloyd Shaw Recordings, using the efficient little mailings office in the cellar of her house to fill orders. Don Armstrong contributed to the inventory by assembling a band of musicians to record tunes for the contra dances that he was teaching and promoting. Dorothy, like Lloyd before her, carried on a constant correspondence with Bob Osgood, placing ads in his magazine and contributing articles. The Fellowship week became a laboratory for the research and resurrection of some traditional dances such as the Blonde Lancers and the Five-part Singing Quadrille, which were then recorded and made available through Lloyd Shaw Recordings.

By 1964 Fellowship members were brimming with ideas. Some were researching old dances, some were concerned about the quality of dance instruction, some wanted to create a clearing house for communication among dance leaders and groups, some were interested in developing an archive of dance material, some wanted to make music more readily available to dance leaders, and some had ideas for books, pamphlets, and teaching aids. By Friday these ideas had coalesced into the realization that they were talking about a foundation. Don Haney, a Cheyenne School alumnus and local attorney, was called to write up articles of incorporation with the objectives and purposes given: "To perpetuate the memory and work of Dr. Lloyd Shaw, the Foundation shall endeavor to preserve, encourage and extend the arts of American folk and square dancing, music, songs, and associated dances and arts, in recreational and educational fields.

Toward this end The Foundation is to be created to:

    a. Conduct research for itself and/or for others

    b. Publish books, articles, pamphlets, teaching aids, etc.

    c. Produce recordings, music, transcriptions, tape and films, as may be needed by all means now known or developed in the future.

    d. Conduct and promote educational institutes, conferences, as well as festivals for the promotion of the Foundation activities, or fund raising in connection therewith.

    e. Provide a clearing house for information related to the Foundation activities and purposes, and to maintain a relationship of reciprocity with similar or affiliated groups in other areas who wish to share in ideas and recreational materials such as games, songs, music, folk dances, books, tapes, and records.

    f. Establish a library consisting of material already assembled or to be acquired in the future.

    g. Obtain land or construct buildings or whatever physical properties as may now be needed, or may become necessary in the future, for the purpose of carrying on the activities of the Foundation.

    h. Solicit and raise funds by donation, bequest, and any and all available means to provide for operating the Foundation and sustaining its operation in the future, including the establishment of trust funds to assure income for future requirements.

i. Operate as a "non-profit foundation," authorized to disburse funds necessary for the operation of the Foundation and the purposes above.

Don Armstrong was chosen to be the first president of the Lloyd Shaw Foundation (LSF), but a year later, feeling that he could be more effective as the enactor of projects, he remained on the Board of Directors but ceded the presidency to Dorothy's son-in-law Don Obee. Other Board members were Fred Bergin, Kirby Todd, John Bradford, Don Obee, Lewis Chase (a dance leader from Alabama), Bob Cook (a former Cheyenne student and traditional caller), Elwyn Fresh, Otto Hegemann, Red Henderson (whose teenaged dance team the Silver Spurs in Spokane, Washington was modeled after the Cheyenne Mountain Dancers), Bob Howell, Sherm Walker, and Mary D Walsh.

Mary D. and her husband Howard were Texas philanthropists who summered in Colorado Springs and happened to hear about and then join Lloyd's summer classes simply because they heard that attendees were having so much fun. They would take on the task of staging *The Littlest Wiseman* in Fort Worth in the same tradition that the tickets were free—as long as they lasted. They would also create the Dorothy Shaw Bell Choir to enhance the production of the play. The bell choir traveled to Colorado Springs occasionally where they played for Dorothy, and in the tradition of the Cheyenne Mountain Dancers, they would travel to other states and even other countries to perform. In 1972 the Walshes brought a film crew to the Fellowship and financed the making of a film about Lloyd and Dorothy Shaw and the Foundation called *A Visible Anthem*. The Walshes would also extend the Fellowship week at each end by inviting attendees to dinner at their Colorado Springs home on the Saturday before the week began and then to dinner at the elegant Penrose Room in the Broadmoore Hotel on the Saturday after the Fellowship ended.

The new officers and members of the Lloyd Shaw Foundation shared an urgent sense of the need for improving the quality of dance instruction, in the hope that children would be exposed to this precious folk activity and would love it—if they were effectively taught. To that end an educational kit was created to make available the music and the instructions for a curriculum of dances for adults and secondary students. Contacts were made with faculty members at Colorado State University to arrange for summer workshops to be held for school teachers. The first such workshop was held just a year later in 1965 with Dorothy giving morning lectures and the dance instruction conducted by John Bradford, Muriel Smith, and Kirby Todd. Other expert teachers, all Fellowship attendees such as Dena Fresh and Gib Gilbert, would supplement in their areas of specialization. The secondary level class was offered again the following summer, and in the adjoining room a staff consisting of Bob Howell, Mary Jo Bradford, and Enid Obee workshopped materials for a pilot elementary kit. Groups of first and second graders, third and fourth graders, and fifth and sixth graders came each day to be taught dances in order for the staff to determine at which grade level each dance would be most appropriate. From this workshop came the elementary kit. At first the kits, which consisted of a manual and accompanying 45 RPM records, drew on records from different labels. The inevitable frustration of finding some records from some distributors out of stock would eventually prompt Don Armstrong to secure recording rights from American and European producers so that the LSF could have control over its inventory. Over the ensuing years the kits would change with technology and would feature CDs as well as a DVD that depicted the various dances being performed. The Sales Division would be operated by various individuals until in 1988 Don Armstrong ultimately found Audioloft, a recording studio in Missouri that would take the LSF inventory and manage its sales (see appendix 3.) By the time

EPILOGUE

Audioloft finally closed down, the LSF's music could be sold digitally over the internet.

With the nucleus of teachers at the Fellowship, supplemented by the students that Kirby Todd was bringing from Illinois State University, teams of teachers went to colleges and universities around the country to conduct workshops for classroom, physical education, and dance teachers. (See Appendix 2 for a partial list of workshop venues.)

The archival function of the Foundation would lie dormant until Bill Litchman and his wife Kris began coming to the Fellowship in 1969. While trained and holding a faculty position at the University of New Mexico as a chemist, Bill was also an outstanding caller and a born researcher. He soon took on the archival task of the Foundation, which began formally in 1972 with a monetary donation from Howard and Mary D. Walsh and one artefact: a film of Red Henderson's teenage exhibition team, the Silver Spurs of Spokane. Over the ensuing years Bill amassed a library of dance materials. He first housed the collection in his home in Albuquerque and then in a small adobe building that had become available. Then in 1986 the veteran folk dancer and LSF friend Rus Acton came forward with an offer: he would donate the money to purchase a suitable building to house the archives. Bill began looking and found—a dance studio! It had a large wooden floor and two other rooms that would hold the books, magazines, recordings, and films of the archives. In 1986 the archives would be designated by the Library of Congress to be the "central clearing house for folk dance archives." Eventually, the archival function outgrew the resources of the Foundation, and in 2003 the entire collection was donated to the Carson Bryerly Dance Library at the University of Denver where it currently resides and where cataloguing and research continue. The dance building in Albuquerque continues as the Lloyd Shaw Dance Center, under the management of Donna Bauer. Dancing of every sort (Irish,

Scandinavian, tango, waltz, square dancing, contras, etc.) takes place there every week.

Don Armstrong was an innovator in the Lloyd Shaw Foundation, foreseeing future needs and implementing solutions to meet those needs. Noting that more and more people wished to attend the Fellowship, which had definite space constraints, he proposed that in addition to the Fellowship there be an open dance week where all comers could be accommodated. This suggestion came at a time when Dorothy's superb mind was beginning to fail her, and the burden for organizing the Fellowship week was falling more and more on her daughter Doli, who lived 900 miles away in Boise and did not feel equipped to step into her mother's shoes.* Nobody could. But Doli shared her father's decisiveness and called a halt to the Fellowship. The last gathering would be in 1978, but in the same summer the new public dance week called the Rocky Mountain Dance Roundup was held at a lodge in Steamboat Springs. Drawing scores of participants and featuring dance leaders from the US and Europe as well, it would continue for thirty years, meeting at venues in Colorado, New Mexico, and Wyoming. Don Armstrong brought national and international dance leaders to these events: Bernie Chalk from England, and Philippe Callens, Luc Blanck and Frieda van Vlanderen from Belgium. Don and Marie Armstrong also founded an eastern camp that took place for a number of years at Copecrest, a dance facility in northern Georgia.

*Dorothy would spend her last few years in a nursing home in Boise, Idaho, near Doli and Don and would pass away on March 12, 1985 at the age of 93. She is buried in Evergreen Cemetery in Colorado Springs next to Lloyd and David.

A new generation of Foundation members would eventually help found two spectacular family dance camps: a summer camp, Cumberland Dance Week, which at this writing is held in Kentucky in July, and a year-end camp, Terpsichore's Holiday, which is held in West Virginia. A new generation of dancers has now grown up attending these camps. A display of their talents is breathtaking. They are beginning to take leadership positions and are further strengthening these camps and ensuring their future. As one young college student said to her mother, "When I marry and have children, I want to bring them to Terpsichore's Holiday."

And so the dance goes on.

APPENDICES

Appendix 1

Here is a partial list of the places where the Cheyenne Mountain Dancers performed

Spring 1937
Alumni trip to Claremont Colleges with performances also in Padua Hills and Los Angeles

Fall 1938
Alumni trip to Santa Fe for the Fiesta de Los Conquistadores

Spring 1939
First trip with current CMS students: Washington, D.C., National Folk Festival
Bennington School of Dance, Swarthmore College

Fall 1939
Trip to perform and teach at the University of California at Berkeley

Fall 1940
Denton, Texas: performance at Texas State College for Women
Exhibitions and teaching sessions at University of California at Los Angeles

Spring 1940
Chicago Recreation Department
Detroit: City College of Wayne University
Bowling Green, OH: Bowling Green College

Spring 1941
St. Louis, Missouri: the St. Louis Physical Education Club,
Massachusetts: YWCA in Northampton

Northampton, MA: Smith College
Philadelphia, Pennsylvania: Pennsylvania State Teachers College
and University of Pennsylvania
New York City: the Rainbow Room at the Plaza Hotel for Lowell
Thomas
Atlantic City, New Jersey: National Convention of American
Association for Health, Physical Education, & Recreation (AAHPER)
Washington, DC: National Folk Festival followed by the
Madeira School and the Washington Dance Association
Chicago, Illinois: University of Chicago, Chicago Parks and Recreation
Dept.

Fall, 1941
Dodge City, Kansas: Physical Education Teachers,
Wichita Falls, Texas: Annual Meeting of Physical Education Teachers
Shreveport, Louisiana: Civic square dance group
New Orleans, Louisiana: Exhibitions and teaching sessions for two days
for the American Association for Health, Physical Education, &
Recreation. The third day the team took a showboat outing on the
Mississippi where they conducted exhibitions on the deck.
Kelly Field, Texas: exhibition and teaching session (tour of Carlsbad
Caverns)
Denton, Texas: Texas State College for Women
Stillwater, Oklahoma: Oklahoma Agricultural & Mechanical College,
(now OSU)

The cross-country dance trips were suspended during the US
involvement in World War II, but Cheyenne students performed for
soldiers at Phipps Hospital in Denver, for Mexican beet pickers in
Lyons, Colorado, and at Camp Hale in west-central Colorado where
soldiers trained for winter and mountain warfare.

Fall, 1945
Trinidad, CO and Santa Fe, NM with a tour of the pueblos and cemetery
of Taos

LLOYD SHAW AND THE CHEYENNE MOUNTAIN DANCERS

Spring, 1946
Wichita Falls, Texas: High School Auditorium
Norman, Oklahoma: University of Oklahoma
Tulsa, Oklahoma: Will Rogers HS
Dallas, Texas: Southern Methodist University
(Sightseeing in San Antonio)
Houston, Texas: YWCA Music Hall
Galveston, Texas: Million Dollar Pier Ballroom for the Lumberman's
Association

Fall, 1946
Milwaukee, Wisconsin: Wisconsin State Teachers Association
Chicago, Illinois: University of Chicago and Chicago Recreation Dept.
La Grange, Illinois: Lyons Township HS
Sheboygan, Wisconsin: Municipal Armory and Auditorium for the
Catholic Youth Organization
La Crosse, Wisconsin: Wisconsin State Teachers College
St. Cloud, Minnesota: State Teachers College
Milwaukee, Wisconsin: State Teachers College
Minneapolis, Minnesota: University of Minnesota
Lincoln, Nebraska: University of Nebraska
Denver, Colorado

Spring, 1947
Fort Collins, Colorado: Colorado Agricultural College (later CSU)
Ogden, Utah: Ogden Recreation Department
Boise, Idaho: Boise Junior College (later Boise State University)
Seattle, Washington: University of Washington
Vancouver, B.C, Canada: British Columbia Teachers Association
Spokane, Washington: Inland Empire Meeting
Pullman, Washington: Pullman State College, (later WSU)

Fall, 1947
Provo, Utah: Brigham Young University
Palo Alto, California: Stanford University, followed by three days of
teaching sessions (12 & ½ hours scheduled) for 250 members of the
Folk Dance Federation of America

Reno: University of Nevada
Spring, 1948
Dodge City, KS: Senior High School
St. Louis, Missouri1: Normandy High School
Camden, New Jersey: YMCA
New York City: various locations hosted by Michael Herman and Ed
Durlacher
Pittsburgh, Pennsylvania: YMCA and YWCA
Philadelphia, Pennsylvania
Washington, D.C.

Fall, 1948
Santa Fe, New Mexico
El Paso, Texas
Phoenix, Arizona
Los Angeles, California
Hollywood and Pasadena
Albuquerque, New Mexico

Spring 1949
Great Lakes: Chicago Dept. of Recreation
Milwaukee

Fall, 1949
Atlanta, Georgia
St. Augustine, Florida: University of Florida
New Orleans, Louisiana: Tulane University

Spring, 1950
The Mid-Atlantic States

Fall, 1950
Idaho Falls, Idaho: Bell Junior HS Auditorium
Reno: University of Nevada
Colusa, CA: Colusa HS
Merced, CA: Merced Union HS
San Francisco, CA: San Mateo HS

342

LLOYD SHAW AND THE CHEYENNE MOUNTAIN DANCERS

Redwood City, CA: Sequoia HS
Carmel, CA: Sunset Auditorium
San Luis Obispo, CA: California Polytechnic College
Ogden, UT: Ogden HS
Salt Lake City, UT: Lake City Coliseum

Appendix 2

Lloyd Shaw Foundation workshops have been held at the following institutions.

Colorado State University, Fort Collins, CO
University of New Mexico, Albuquerque, NM
University of Missouri at Kansas City, MO
Central Michigan University, Beaver Island campus, MI
Kansas State University, Manhattan, KS
Kearney State University, Kearney, NE
University of Nebraska at Omaha
University of Wisconsin at Oshkosh
Jefferson County Public Schools, Denver, CO
Orff Schulwerk National Conference, Denver, CO
Callers Workshops in Canyon City, CO
Colorado HPERD Convention, Denver, CO
Carleton College, Northfield, MN
Teikyo Loretto Heights University, Denver, CO
Texas Boys Choir, Fort Worth, TX
St. Joseph's College, Albuquerque, NM
Colorado College, Colorado Springs, CO
Purdue University, West Lafayette, IN
California State University at Sacramento

Appendix 3 LSF quarterly publications

Under Dorothy Shaw's administration the new Lloyd Shaw Foundation put out an occasional newsletter called "The Long Shadow" (It takes a tall man to cast a long shadow.)

With the reorganization of the Foundation when Dorothy Shaw left the scene, Foundation members settled on a quarterly magazine that they called *The American Dance Circle,* a name that was inspired by the circle of dancers that Linda Bradford designed. Editors would be:

Cal and Judy Campbell, 1979-1981, with the assistance of Bill and Kris Litchman
Linda Bradford and Linda Plaut, 1982-1987
John Forbes, 1987-1990
Diane Ortner, 1990-2001
Enid Cocke, 2001-the present (2014)

Appendix 4 The LSF Sales Office

After the creation of the LSF, John and Linda Bradford helped Dorothy with the mailing function. They ultimately took the inventory into their basement in Denver and handled the mailings for the Foundation. They were succeeded by Don Trummel, then George and Onie Senyk, who would move the inventory first to their home, a millhouse in the Catskills of New York, and later to Florida. They were followed by Libba Grey in Canon City, CO, who was followed by Kris Litchman and Sharon Kernen in Albuquerque. Finally in 1988 Don Armstrong found the long-term solution of Audioloft Studios in Macks Creek, MO. By the time Audioloft closed down in 2010, all the tunes in the Lloyd Shaw collection could be sold electronically.

For more information about the Lloyd Shaw Foundation's current activities, services, and products, go to www.lloydshaw.org.

ACKNOWLEDGEMENTS

Heartfelt thanks go…

To Bill Litchman, creator of the Lloyd Shaw Archives, who preserved and organized much of the material used in this narrative. It was Bill who copied and bound all of Lloyd's articles that were published in the *Colorado Springs Free Press* as "Half a Century of Memories." Without Bill's stewardship, some priceless narratives might have been lost forever.

To Ken Kernen, who supplied me with other essential resources. He gave me the tape recordings that he made during the Fellowship gatherings, helping me retrieve some stories that would otherwise have been lost. Thanks to Ken as well for giving his discerning editorial eye to the manuscript.

To Cal Campbell who also shared stories and resources. His work in locating all past issues of the LSF publication, *The American Dance Circle*, and getting them digitized made my task easier.

To John Bradford, who generously shared essential private correspondence from Dorothy Shaw and provided information I could find nowhere else. Thanks too for his thorough review of the manuscript.

To Lorena Holmes Bymaster for generously sharing her time, her photographs, and her letters from her years as a Cheyenne dancer.

To my wise and well-published daughter Erica Johnson for her counsel.

To my husband and favorite dance partner Lew for his love and support, both emotional and technical.

To my astonishingly gifted and generous grandparents, Lloyd and Dorothy Shaw, for living this story.

****

Parts of several of the chapters written by Lloyd Shaw were originally published in 1957as "Half a Century of Memories" in the *Colorado Springs Free Press* (later acquired by the *Colorado Springs Gazette*). They appear here with the permission of the *Colorado Springs Gazette*.

Cover photographs:
Front page: Photograph of Lloyd Shaw (photographer unknown).
Back page: Photograph of Cheyenne Mountain Dancers taken by Sgt. Edward A. Lane, published in the *Saturday Evening Post* Aug. 2, 1941.

I am grateful to Carmen T. Bontz for permission to use photos taken at the Lloyd Shaw Fellowship by her father, Myron J. Smith.

PHOTOGRAPHS

Lloyd Shaw at his desk at Cheyenne Mountain School
(ca 1920).

Lloyd Shaw at the Cheyenne Mountain School rodeo

Coombe Corrie

The extended family. From left: Don Obee, Doli Shaw Obee, Enid Obee, Kent Obee, Lloyd Shaw, Dorothy Shaw. (ca 1949).

Dorothy and Lloyd Shaw ca 1955. (Portrait photo by Knutson
Bowers, Colorado Springs).

Lloyd Shaw the Square Dance Caller (ca 1950).

Dorothy Shaw and Fred Bergen at the 1964 Fellowship
(Photograph by Myron J.Smith).

Fellowship 1964. With instruments, from left: Marie Armstrong, Kirby Todd, Enid Obee, Linda Bradford, John Bradford. Seated in background from left: Bob and Phyllis Howell, Gib Gilbert (photograph by Myron J. Smith).

Dorothy Shaw and Dena Fresh at the 1964 Fellowship Cotillion (photograph by Myron J. Smith)

(For pictures of the Cheyenne Mountain Dancers, see *The Round Dance Book.*)

www.ingramcontent.com/pod-product-compliance
Lightning Source LLC
Chambersburg PA
CBHW051813090426
42736CB00011B/1459